W9-AON-269

BASEBALL AND BILLIONS

BASEBALL

AND

BILLIONS

A Probing Look
Inside the Big Business of
Our National Pastime

ANDREW ZIMBALIST

BasicBooks
A Division of HarperCollins*Publishers*

Library of Congress Cataloging-in-Publication Data
Zimbalist, Andrew S.
    Baseball and billions: a probing look inside the big business of our national
pastime / by Andrew Zimbalist.
        p.   cm.
    Includes bibliographical references and index.
    ISBN 0-465-00614-0
    1. Baseball—United States—Finance.   2. Baseball—Economic
aspects—United States.   3. Baseball—United States—Organization
and administration.   I. Title.
GV880.Z56   1992
338.4'7796357—dc20   91–59016
                                                                          CIP

Copyright © 1992 by BasicBooks, A Division of HarperCollins Publishers, Inc.

All rights reserved. Printed in the United States of America. No part of this book
may be reproduced in any manner whatsoever without written permission except in
the case of brief quotations embodied in critical articles and reviews. For information, address BasicBooks, 10 East 53rd Street, New York, NY 10022-5299.

Designed by Ellen Levine

92 93 94 95 **CC/HC** 9 8 7 6 5 4 3 2 1

*To Jeffrey, Michael,
Sam, Manuel, and Olivia*

Contents

CONTENTS

Preface

While Lou Piniella was still managing the Yankees, after a loss one night his wife commented: "I'm forty-three years old and I'm married to a five-year-old."[1] It sounded like something my wife might have said, and I never managed the Yankees . . . except in my fantasies.

Just how far Major League Baseball had penetrated my home life became strikingly evident during the 1990 thirty-two-day lockout. One night during the lockout I was putting my eleven-year-old son, Jeffrey, to bed, looking at his walls, which were covered ceiling-to-floor with baseball cards. All of a sudden Jeffrey, who had been scheming all winter about how his Little League team would win next year's championship, said pensively: "Dad, I don't think I want to play in Little League this year." He might as well have told me that he didn't want to eat for three weeks. After many moments I thoughtfully replied: "Why?" He responded: "Because I don't have any role models anymore." (My wife is a psychotherapist.) Pursuing his feelings, I discovered it wasn't that he was blaming the players for the shutdown of spring training. He was simply frustrated. So was I, and judging by the letters to the editor in the newspapers, a variety of polls, the columns of sportswriters, among others, so were millions of other Americans.

Perhaps most frustrated were the merchants and fans in Florida and Arizona. In each of the previous two years attendance at spring training games had soared to over 1.8 million a year. In 1990, 362 out of the scheduled 410 games were never played. The St. Petersburg Times (March 4, 1991) ran a special section of human interest stories on the impact of the lockout. Some of the impact is obvious: the tens of thousands of fans who took their annual vacation treks to follow their favorite teams and players up-close in Florida and Arizona, the tourist hotels and restaurants, the airlines, the car rental businesses, and the souvenir vendors—they all suffered. Less apparent victims were the Dunedin, Florida, Little League (where the Blue Jays have their training camp), which finances itself on sales of seat cushions and programs at the Blue Jays exhibition games, or the Clearwater High School Band, which supports itself on selling parking at the Phillies games. Overall, eighteen teams bring into the Florida economy over $300 million every spring and eight teams bring into the Arizona economy over $145 million, and with indirect effects the overall economic impact is likely to be double or triple these figures.[2]

But baseball fans are like good lovers: They are willing to forgive and forget. There have been five work stoppages in baseball since 1972. Each time the fans go nuts. Most of us fans are thinking to ourselves: Why doesn't someone do something to stop this? A Taft-Hartley injunction perhaps? Why should the owners with skyrocketing franchise values lock out the players? Why should players making millions of dollars go on strike? What would Samuel Gompers or John L. Lewis say? Then the work stoppage ends, and each time we fans return to the ballparks in record numbers. There is at least one good thing about labor relations in baseball: The Basic Agreements each have lasted for three to five years.

But good lovers also try to figure out what is wrong and what can be done about it. That's where this book comes in.

My training is not in the economics of the entertainment industry; it is in development economics and comparative economic systems (though I have dabbled in labor economics). But before Jeffrey went to sleep that night, he got around to asking me what the lockout was all about. I had only perfunctory responses. Jeffrey, knowing I had just completed a manuscript on the Panamanian economy, had one final provocative thought before falling asleep. "Dad," he said, "why don't you write a book about the economics of baseball?"

Customarily, prefaces end with a list of acknowledgments and a disclaimer that the mistakes in the book are the author's fault. My acknowledgments follow, but any inaccuracies are not all my doing. Anyone who has tried to inquire into the business of baseball knows that the industry is run like covert operations at the CIA, or perhaps as the CIA would like them to be run. Almost all the franchises are privately held and do not publicly issue income statements or other financial reports. One must dig, scrape, and beg for information. It shouldn't be this way, but it is. I am confident that I have assembled sufficient evidence to discern and analyze the industry's trends and problems, but if there is an occasional inaccuracy, take your complaint to Fay Vincent.

One important exception to this generalization is that the Players' Association was very open and helpful to me. They provided me with whatever information I requested, except the teams' summary income statements, which they have been receiving since 1985 but are not allowed to share. Donald Fehr, the association's executive director since 1984, was willing to meet whenever I pleased. Marvin Miller, the previous director, was also generous with his time.

On the owners' side, after much persistence, I did have some success. The former head of the owners' Player Relations Committee, Chuck O'Connor, conceded me a short audience. His law firm colleague, Rob Manfred, provided me with information sporadically and clarified some technicalities. Baseball's director of broadcasting, David Alworth, granted me a lengthy interview, and Frank Simeo of Major League Baseball Properties answered a few questions for me on the telephone. Several present or former owners and executives were also willing to speak with me: Jerry Hoffberger, Eli Jacobs, Bernie Mullens, Eddie Einhorn, Bill Giles, Mike Ryan, Frank Heffron, Mark Driscoll, and Pete Bavasi. Bavasi was extremely helpful. Deep thanks as well to several individuals involved in Major League Baseball who asked not to be mentioned.

Many others involved in the minor leagues, other professional sports, law firms, player representation, salary arbitration, television and cable companies, Congress, sports journalism, as well as some former and current players helped me along the way: Jerry Mileur, Charlie Eshbach, Bob Sparks, Dick Moss, George Pfister, Glenn Wong, Abe Pollin, Richard Sandomir, Mike Dodd, Jim Wetzler, Ira Berkow, Jim Kaplan, Connie Prater, Joni Balter, Terry McDermott, Phil Mushnik, John Mansell, Stephen Ross, Ken Gordon, Tom Newell, Joe Durso, Sue Liemer, Monroe Price, John Kelly, Steve Campbell, Christine Dolche, Phil Hochberg, Cy Block, Mike Pagliarulo, Whitey Ford, Fran Healy, Brian Blaise, Pete Lambert, Tom Francis, Holt Hackney, Paul White, Ted Zeegers, Mike Connelly, Branch B. Rickey, Chris Harvey, Gary Betman, Art Wolf, Lisa Gursky, and Frank Coonley.

Several academic colleagues guided me at the outset, filled me with suggestions, and read drafts of the manuscript: Peter Dorman, David Salant, Rodney Fort, Kevin Ryan, Gerry Scully, Paul Teplitz, Mark Lindenberg, Roger Noll, Jim Quirk, Phil Porter, Bill Gormley, John Kirk, Roger Kaufman, Phil Green, Ron Story, Charles Staelin, Mary Ann

Coughlin, Maria Toyofuku, Betty Nanartonis, Deborah Haas-Wilson, Don Baumer, Liz Savoca, Paul Sommers, Bob Buchele, Donald Coffin, Robert Baade, Larry Kahn, Gary Roberts, Bob Averitt, and Robert McIntyre. Yan Zhang and Jackie Lavoie were the best research assistants I could have hoped for, and Holly Jones kept me on my toes.

Steve Fraser, my editor at Basic Books, is a gem. His support, substantive advice, and stylistic suggestions were invaluable. Clerical assistance from Agnes Shannon and Barbara Day, as always, was professional and congenial. Friends and neighbors, some who only yawned at my previous research projects, came to my aid: Kenny Coplon, Joel Zoss, Clay Cox, Bart Gordon, Paul Surgen, Leo Campbell, Bill Newman, Fred Itterly, Robert Meeropol, Grant Moore, and Jim Freedman. John Bowman's detailed comments on drafts of each chapter were indispensable. The wonderful folks at the Baseball Library in Cooperstown, New York, could not have been more helpful.

My nephews, Sam and Manuel Rosaldo, provided enough enthusiasm and baseball trivia to nourish me for five books. My sons, Jeffrey and Michael, were not only a thorough clipping service out of *Sports Illustrated* and the local papers, but their active involvement in playing the game in its various incarnations (wiffle ball, pickup, home run derbies, Little League) kept me in touch with the real subject of this book. To my wife, Lydia, go my gratitude and love for living with a five-year-old all these years.

Introduction

Baseball's commissioner, Fay Vincent, recently stated: "Baseball is poised for a catastrophe and it might not be far off."[1] Most casual and even many close observers of the game might wonder to what he was referring.

Attendance at major league games had risen from 38.7 million in 1977 to 56.9 million in 1991 and had set a record in six of the last seven years. Local and national television revenues were soaring, with the promise of pay-per-view on the horizon. Income from the licensing of baseball products had grown by leaps and bounds to over $100 million in 1990. And, according to baseball's own figures, total industry revenues practically had doubled, from $718 million in 1985 to nearly $1.4 billion in 1990, while operating profits went from a negative $7.1 million in 1985 to a positive $214.5 million in 1989.[2]

Many in the industry had feared that the coming of free agency in 1976 would undermine team profitability and upset competitive balance on the playing field. But profits have been healthy, franchise values have gone through the roof, and, judging by the outcome, there has been more competitive balance on the field than ever before in baseball history. In the first fifteen years of free agency, only three teams failed to win their divisional title, sixteen different teams won the pennant in their respective leagues, and twelve different teams won the World Series.

So, Mr. Vincent, what catastrophe?

It has been politically fashionable since 1980 to blame the problems of U.S. industry on a meddlesome government. Is this what has the commissioner concerned? Not likely. Consider the three branches of government.

Judicial.   The Supreme Court in 1922 declared that baseball was not involved in interstate commerce and, hence, was not subject to the country's antitrust laws. The high court reaffirmed this decision in 1953 and again in 1972. Baseball stands alone among professional sports in its exemption. Baseball is a legal monopoly, euphemistically known as the "baseball anomaly."

Legislative.   Both in 1953 and in 1972 the Supreme Court stated that if baseball's exemption is to be lifted, it should be done by Congress. The closest Congress has come to doing this was back in 1977—and it was not very close. In April 1976 the U.S. House of Representatives passed a resolution establishing a Select Committee on Professional Sports (a.k.a. the Sisk Committee) to investigate the stability of the country's major sports industries. The Sisk Committee issued its report on January 3, 1977, concluding: "Based upon the information available to it, the Committee has concluded that *adequate justification does not exist for baseball's special exemption from the antitrust laws and that its exemption should be removed in the context of an overall sports antitrust reform.*"[3] To accomplish such a reform, the Sisk Committee recommended the establishment of a successor committee to undertake a broad study and then propose a specific legislative course of action. The successor committee was never created.

No bill to lift baseball's exemption has ever made it out of committee in either the House or the Senate. Thus Congress has shown itself to be content with baseball's legal monopoly. In other cases where the government has deemed it desirable to sanction a monopoly, such as with public utilities, the government has also sought to assure through regulatory controls that the monopoly did not abuse its privileges. Not so with baseball; it is a self-governing, unregulated monopoly.

Executive.   Ronald Reagan was a baseball announcer. George Bush was a first baseman at Yale and is the father of the principal owner of the Texas Rangers. There is no threat here.

It turns out that baseball's problems are of its own making. If one did not know better, could it be imagined that labor strife would beset an industry with salaries growing at 20.6 percent annually over the last fifteen years, average salaries at $1,086,988 in 1992, and growing employment? Since 1970, each time a baseball labor contract has expired there has been a work stoppage. And neither the commissioner nor the baseball Players' Association expects the turmoil to dissipate.

The players' rapid salary growth has been largely underwritten by baseball's increasingly bountiful media contracts. But the ratings for baseball on national television have been low and falling during each of the first two years of the contracts with CBS and ESPN. Industry sources estimate that CBS lost $100 million and ESPN $40 million on their baseball contracts in 1990. Expectations are that the next contracts, commencing in 1994, will not be as lucrative to baseball teams. Pay-per-view television has worked for boxing championships, but there are only a few of these "jewels" a year. In baseball, as of 1993 there will be twenty-eight teams, each playing 162 games; few of these are jewels. Besides, will the fans accept having to pay $10 to watch each game on television? Perhaps even Congress would object. On the positive side, local cable contracts have increased handsomely in recent years and give every indication of continuing on this trend. Overall, however, growth in media revenues into the mid-1990s is likely either to moderate or to stop.

Here, then, seems to lie one of baseball's dilemmas. What to do about the players' expectations for high and rising salaries in the face of stagnation or slower growth in media revenues? And if these tendencies do clash, what will happen to baseball's already stormy labor relations? Do star baseball players really deserve $6 million a year, and how do their long-term contracts affect their performance on the field?

Like U.S. society, Major League Baseball franchises have an upper class and a lower class. The Yankees, thanks to the large media market and baseball tradition in New York City, earn over $50 million a year in local media rights. The Seattle Mariners, with neither a large market nor much of a tradition, earn under $5 million.[4] Yet both teams must compete in the same free agent market and carry player payrolls of over $20 million. How can the Mariners survive? How can they compete on the field with the Yankees (assuming competent management)? And if there are problems today, what will happen in 1994 when central revenues from national television rights might diminish? Should baseball engage in extensive revenue sharing among the clubs as in football, or should it institute a salary cap as in basketball? Will baseball's organizational structure and labor relations allow it to make the most desirable reforms?

Major League Baseball (MLB) must put its internal house in order, but it must also tend to its backyard and its neighborhood. Consider the following.

Item.   Although 650 major leaguers gained the rights of citizenship with the introduction of free agency after 1976, the 3,200-plus minor league ballplayers have no union, can be held under reserve for as long as twelve years, earn borderline-poverty wages, and have practically no benefits. MLB dismisses these issues because, it says, the minor leaguers are apprentices, most are young without families, and one day they might make the big show. Major league teams say it costs them over a million dollars in player development expenses to produce each major league player. They do not want to spend more, and, indeed, in 1991 MLB and the National Association (the organization of minor league clubs) almost filed for divorce, threatening to disrupt or to end minor league baseball in 150-odd communities across the country. What would happen to the plight of minor leaguers if they were not reserved by one club or if, before signing a professional baseball contract, they received competing bids from teams in different leagues or if they received a college education while playing apprentice baseball?

Item.   In the past five years citizens in San Francisco, San Jose, Chicago, Detroit, Cleveland, Denver, Baltimore, Milwaukee, and Dallas–Fort Worth have been asked to go to the polls to approve issuance of a municipal bond and/or new taxes for the construction of new baseball stadiums. In each case there was the threat that if the bond and/or taxes were rejected, the city's baseball team would flee to greener pastures. The citizens of other cities hopeful of attracting an expansion or migratory team have also voted to finance the building of new ballparks via new bonds and/or new taxes. Tampa–St. Petersburg, first hoping to lure the White Sox out of Chicago, then hoping for a National League (NL) expansion team, and now coveting the Mariners, actually built a new domed stadium at a cost of $140 million.

In 1991 eighteen prospective ownership groups in ten cities competed for the two NL franchises that were auctioned off at $95 million apiece. Demand for major league teams exceeds supply. Supply is restricted by a self-regulating monopoly. The inevitable result is that some worthy cities do not get teams and that the fortunate cities with teams are held hostage to threats of moving. This leads to the construction of new public stadiums filled with luxury boxes and elaborate electronic scoreboards, city guarantees on ticket sales, and heavily subsidized rent.

Fay Vincent has said that after the two new NL teams are added in 1993, there will be no more expansion in this century. Why not? Are we to believe what former Commissioner Bowie Kuhn told Congress on several occasions: that the talent is not there for expansion? By what criteria? Even if there is no expansion, should owners be allowed to move teams virtually at will as if city subsidies and cultures had no claim to them? Why is there no municipal ownership of MLB teams? Why did MLB in 1990 prohibit Padres' owner Joan Kroc from giving her team to the city of San Diego or in 1991 prohibit the city of Montreal from taking an equity stake in the Expos?

Item.   For a ten-month period during 1989–90, many sports fans in New York City could not see the Yankees, the basketball Knicks, or the hockey Rangers on cable television, and over-the-air broadcasts were either eliminated due to exclusive contracts or drastically cut back. Cable coverage became unavailable because the Madison Square Garden (MSG) cable network, which is owned by Paramount and is part of the Prime Network group,[5] outbid SportsChannel, which is owned by NBC/Cablevision, for exclusive rights to carry Yankee games. Cablevision owned the majority of cable delivery systems servicing the New York City area. After its affiliate lost the Yankee contract, Cablevision refused to carry MSG on its systems.

Congress decided back in 1984 to deregulate cable companies. These companies are granted local monopolies and then set their programming and pricing policies without meaningful oversight. Over the years the industry has grown increasingly integrated so that programmers and delivery systems are owned by single entities. This integration has meant programming restrictions and higher prices to viewers. As more baseball teams have signed up with pay television networks, higher subscription prices, the absence of cable in some areas, and manipulation of programming have curtailed fans' access to view games.

Baseball compounds these problems with its own restrictive media practices. For instance, it assigns geographical territories to each team. Thus almost all of New England is Red Sox territory. This means that cable networks carrying the Yankees, Mets, Phillies, or any other team are not able to enter contracts with cable delivery systems in New England. A New England fan can pay a premium on her monthly cable bill to buy New England Sports Network (NESN) and watch the Red Sox (NESN is partly owned by the Red Sox), but she cannot buy a subscription at any price to MSG or SportsChannel-NY to watch the Yankees or Mets. Some marketplace! Thanks to baseball's antitrust exemption, these practices are not illegal. But given the tendency toward siphoning from over-the-air to cable telecasting, should public policymakers continue to be indifferent?

The economics of baseball encompasses all of these questions. The health and stability of the game requires that they all be answered. This book suggests how to go about looking for the answers. Chapter 1 discusses the evolution of baseball's legal institutions and labor practices to provide a context for understanding its present predicament. Chapter 2 first considers the baseball owners and the structures they have created to run the game. Chapter 3 attempts to uncover and disentangle the facts about the game's financial condition—profits, franchise values, attendance and ticket pricing, tax write-offs, and so on. Chapter 4 analyzes player salaries and their relationship to performance as well as to competitive balance among the teams. Chapter 5 describes the changing role and organization of minor league baseball. Chapter 6 presents the dilemmas of baseball's relationship to the cities and policies of expansion. Chapter 7 is about the changing world of baseball and the media. Chapter 8 attempts to bring the disparate elements of the economics of baseball together and to consider internal organizational as well as public policy options for overcoming, to use Commissioner Vincent's word, the coming "catastrophe."

Yet, as we shall see, if catastrophe does befall the sport, Major League Baseball has no one to blame but itself. Society's support for the game, from ballpark attendance, to myriad municipal subventions, to media infatuation, is robust and rising. Commercialism, greed, and poor management do threaten the game, but solutions are within easy grasp of the long-dormant public policy toward our national pastime.

Monte Ward to Marvin Miller

Evolution of Legal and Labor Relations

I always regarded baseball as our National Game that belongs to 150 million men, women and children, not to sixteen special people who happen to own big league teams.
—Commissioner Happy Chandler, before leaving office in 1952

Although baseball's origins as a sport will always remain shrouded, its origins as a business are clearly traceable to the 1860s.[1] The National Association of Baseball Players (NABP) was established in 1858 as an amateur organization that prohibited remuneration for the players. As the Civil War drew to a close and the game's popularity spread, however, opportunities for exploiting the sport's financial potential became too good to ignore. Some teams began to enclose their ballparks and charge 10 to 25 cents admission to their games.[2]

Then, as today, gate revenue grew with a team's success on the field, and the incentive to attract the best players induced teams to break the NABP's rules. Some teams divided the gate receipts among the players. Some passed the hat.[3] Other teams procured phantom jobs for the star players, so they were paid for their alleged work rather than playing baseball. Others obtained real jobs for their players with the understanding that the player would be released for all practices and games. Albert

Spalding, for instance, accepted an offer to play for the Chicago Excelsiors in return for a $40-a-week job as a clerk in a wholesale grocery. Other teams made illegal side payments and offered perquisites to their stars.[4] In 1866 a resentful member of the Philadelphia Athletics charged that his club was paying three players $20 a week for their services.[5] The financial reward for the best players was substantial enough to lead them to play a few games with one club and then move on to another. This practice, called revolving, was sufficiently widespread that the NABP soon passed regulations to curtail it.[6]

Money, then, was already a significant part of the game when the first professional baseball team, the Cincinnati Red Stockings, was formed in 1869.[7] The team's captain, Harry Wright, was paid a salary of $1,400; the other salaries varied between $600 and $1,200. The team traveled the country winning exhibition games wherever they went. Their enormous success on the field and at the box office (averaging $1,000 in ticket receipts per game)[8] amply demonstrated the feasibility of professional baseball. The next year nine additional professional teams were started, and in 1871 the National Association of Professional Baseball Players (NAPBP) was born.

The NAPBP was loosely organized. The membership fee per club was only $10, and there were no firm schedule and no stable roster of teams.[9] Lacking a clear distinction between players and owners, the NABPP continued to allow revolving. The Boston Red Stockings won four of the five championships during the NAPBP's life, and club profits rose to $3,261 in 1875.[10] Gambling on the NAPBP games was widespread, with pools running as high as $20,000 on individual games.[11] Team salaries ran from $15,000 to $20,000, or just over $1,000 per player, approximately four times the average salary in the country. Players in the 1870s had $30 deducted from their salaries to pay for their uniforms and received 50 cents a day for road expenses.

Baseball was still a fledgling business at that time, groping for its appropriate institutional forms. Although professional baseball's institutions began to take clearer shape after 1876 and more solid form after 1903, the business of baseball really has been in steady flux since its inception. The pursuit of new commercial opportunities and profit has motivated owners over time, inter alia, to fight competitive leagues; sabotage free labor markets; enter into radio, television, and cable contracts; and redefine the game's playing rules. Political and social conflicts have ensued, the ramifications of which Major League Baseball is still struggling with today.

THE NATIONAL LEAGUE

The owner of the Chicago White Stockings, William Hulbert, perceived the organizational deficiencies of the NAPBP and in 1876 launched a plan for a new baseball league based on territorial monopolies and a restricted number of financially solid franchises. Among other things, Hulbert reasoned, the reduction in the number of teams would limit the demand for players, reduce salaries, and enhance profits. Hulbert's strategy was first to convert his White Stockings into baseball's strongest franchise and then to lead a rebellion against the NAPBP. To accomplish this, Hulbert depended on Albert (A. G.) Spalding, a leading pitcher in the era of underhand pitching (overhand was not allowed until 1884). Hulbert induced Spalding to jump his contract with the Boston Red Stockings and then to help persuade three other Boston stars to jump with him.[12]

Hulbert's National League of Professional Baseball Clubs (NL) came into existence with the signing of its constitution on February 2, 1876. Eight charter franchises paid $100 each as annual dues. Until then baseball leagues were player associations; with the National League, baseball became a business with distinct, separate roles for players and owners.

Also in 1876 Albert Spalding and his brother opened a sporting goods store with an initial investment of $800. Repaying Spalding for his collaboration, Hulbert awarded the Spalding company an exclusive contract for provisions to the NL. Spalding also began his self-declared "Official Baseball Guide" in 1876. He quit active play in 1877 to concentrate on the management and business of baseball.

Within the Chicago organization, Spalding rose from captain to manager to president to principal owner of the White Stockings. He succeeded in building the White Stockings into baseball's most successful franchise in the 1880s, although his tactics were not always commendable. After his team lost in the championship series to the St. Louis Browns of the American Association in 1886, according to one newspaper account, Spalding was so disgusted that in a Schottian fit he refused to pay his team's train fare home from St. Louis.[13] With Steinbrenneresque flair, Spalding on at least one occasion showed up in the locker room after a game to berate Cap Anson, who had twice popped out with the bases loaded in a loss to the Giants.[14] In 1883 Spalding had built a new Chicago ballpark in which he ordered a telephone line run from the clubhouse into his luxury box "to enable him to conduct the details of the game without leaving his seat."[15]

In the early years of the NL, however, probably only the Chicago club earned a profit. The finances of some franchises were so dismal that their teams began to forfeit road games, and two clubs were booted out of the league. In 1877 estimated team losses ran from $1,500 in Boston to $8,000 in St. Louis.[16] The franchises from St. Louis, Hartford, and Louisville all dropped out of the league before the 1878 season.

THE RESERVE CLAUSE

Necessity being the mother of invention, the stage was set for another business innovation. Now the NL followed the lead of the avaricious owner of the Boston club, Arthur Soden. Soden, who drew notoriety for using his players as turnstile attendants before games and obligating players' wives to pay their way into the ballpark, proposed baseball's first reserve clause. His proposal secretly to reserve five players per team was adopted by the owners at a meeting in Buffalo, New York, on September 30, 1879.[17] The number of reserved players was enlarged to eleven in 1883, twelve in 1885, fourteen in 1887; by the early 1890s the reserve clause had been extended to cover the contracts of all players.[18]

While the player reserve system succeeded in stunting salary growth and augmenting profits, it also invited the formation of competing leagues that offered the players free contracting. The Cincinnati Red Stockings, having been expelled from the NL in 1879 for playing on Sundays and allowing liquor to be consumed in the stands, became a major organizing force behind the American Association (AA), launched in 1882.

Besides abolishing the reserve clause, the AA distinguished itself by allowing the sale of beer and liquor in the stands. Little wonder that most of the teams were owned by breweries. The AA charged 25 cents admission, half the price charged by the NL, and attracted the working class to games, for which it was roundly criticized by Hulbert. The AA also introduced the concept of hiring a salaried corps of umpires to bring order to the game, a practice the NL soon emulated. But Hulbert found it in his interest to compromise, and in 1883 a pact between the two leagues was signed calling for an eleven-man reserve per team, protection of clubs' territories, blacklisting of players working outside the system, and a championship series.[19]

The 1883 pact made the reserve system universal again and opened the way for yet another competitor. In 1884, with the backing of railroad millionaire Henry Lucas, the thirteen-team Union Association was founded. After the 1884 season, Lucas accepted an offer to enter his St. Louis Maroons into the NL and the Union Association folded.

Without the pressure of a new league to bring free contracting or otherwise boost salaries, the players began to organize. Under the inspired leadership of John Montgomery (Monte) Ward, the Brotherhood of Professional Base Ball Players was founded in 1885. Ward was a star pitcher and shortstop for the New York Giants, the only player in Major League Baseball history to record both 100 wins as a pitcher (Babe Ruth had 94) and 2,000 hits as a batter and one of fifteen pitchers ever to have pitched a perfect game.[20] Writing in *Lippincott's Magazine* in 1886, Ward decried what was happening to the game:

> Ten years ago baseball was looked upon merely as a pastime. Individuals of means and leisure organized clubs for pleasure, and were perfectly satisfied if at the close of the season the nine had won a fair majority of the games and receipts balanced expenditures. . . . Three institutions—the National League, the reserve rule, and the national agreement—have changed entirely the nature of the game. What was formerly a pastime has now become a business, capital is invested from business motives, and the officers and stockholders of the different clubs include men of social standing and established business capacity.[21]

Ward's Brotherhood had a long list of demands: an end to the reserve system; an end to salary caps (set at $2,500 for the vast majority of players in the 1880s); an end to extra duties for players, such as collecting admissions tickets or sweeping up around the ballpark after games; and an end to player sales wherein one owner paid another and the player received nothing.[22]

The reserve clause, which was touted by the owners through 1976 as being necessary to preserve the game's competitive balance, was perfectly compatible with player mobility. In the 1880s, just as in the 1950s and 1960s, poor clubs sold players to rich clubs, which helped the poor clubs to survive financially. Free agency was not necessary for rich clubs to accumulate talent disproportionately. The Boston club, for instance, in 1889 reported having bought fifteen players from other teams for a total of $73,000.[23]

During the 1889 season Ward began discussions with a number of financial backers regarding his idea of starting a players' league. The establishment of the Players' League (PL) was announced on November 6, 1889. The league was to be operated on a cooperative basis with both backers and players on the boards of directors. To lend some stability to the clubs, in lieu of a reserve clause players were signed to three-year contracts. Gate receipts were split evenly among clubs, so there was no financial disadvantage for clubs from smaller cities. The backers were to keep the first $10,000 in profits per club, the rest going back to the league and eventually to be shared with the players. Tim Keefe, the secretary of the Brotherhood, made plans to open a sports equipment company to provide for the new league, depriving Spalding's company of its monopoly in baseball. As preparations for the new league advanced, the NL owners professed no concern but nonetheless decided to lift the salary cap of $2,500 they had imposed at the beginning of the 1889 season.

Most stars went to the new league for the 1890 season. Seven of the eight PL franchises played in existing NL cities. The NL initiated a salary war to win players back, along with an intense public relations effort including giving tickets away to win the attendance battle. The final attendance figures for the two leagues in 1890 are not reliable, as each league employed various chicaneries to inflate its success, but by one often-cited estimate the PL drew 913,000 and the NL drew 853,000; most observers seem to agree that the PL outdrew the NL.[24] The turnstile victory was a small consolation for the PL backers whose clubs suffered substantial losses. The NL, whose profits totaled $750,000 between 1885 and 1889, experienced even deeper losses.[25]

During the bidding war over players, several NL clubs sought court injunctions to prevent players from moving to the PL. Courts found that the contracts lacked mutuality. That is, players could be dismissed by the clubs with ten days' notice but were obligated to play for the club for life. As they lacked mutuality, the contracts were not enforceable.[26] In the 1890 decision in New York Giants versus Monte Ward, the New York Supreme Court wrote that granting an injunction "would permit the ball club to reserve the player in perpetuity while it also reserved the right to terminate the player's contract on ten days' notice. Such a concentration of power in one party could lead to its complete control over the terms of any future contract."[27] These were empty court victories for the players involved because by the time legal dust had settled, there was no PL to play for.[28]

After the 1890 season, under the aggressive leadership of A. G. Spalding, the NL turned up its destruction campaign with bribes and purchase offers to the backers of the PL clubs. The PL backers, after all, were investors, not idealists, and found Spalding's offer of incorporation into an expanded NL too good to refuse. The PL, thus, never having established an independent financial footing, met its demise after only one year.[29] The competition from the PL and NL also brought the American Association to its knees. The AA dissolved after the 1891 season with four of its teams added to the NL. Thus the NL emerged from the PL challenge with its reserve system intact and having recovered its monopoly status.

Unregulated monopoly, however, leads to abuses, and the 1890s in Major League Baseball was no exception. Dissatisfied with falling salaries (they fell an average of 40 percent in 1893),[30] rising profits, and no competition from an external major league, irrationally the NL owners also sought to ensure that intraleague competition on the playing field would not be a problem. Owners began to buy into each others' clubs.[31] They would then transfer most of their best players to one club. The result was that three clubs (Baltimore, Brooklyn, and Boston) won all the pennant races between 1890 and 1899. Fans gradually lost interest and profits began to fall.[32]

Meanwhile, the enforcement of baseball's reserve clause and the consolidation of the NL's monopoly after the collapse of the PL and AA opened an opportunity for the creation of the Western League under Ban Johnson in 1892. After the 1899 season Johnson renamed it the American League (AL). Before the 1900 season began, the AL had bid more than one hundred players away from the NL, and prior to the 1901 season Ban Johnson proclaimed the AL to be a major league.

Napoleon Lajoie, the second baseman for the NL Philadelphia team, was receiving the league-imposed maximum salary of $2,400 and was lured across town by the new AL Philadelphia club. The NL franchise sought to prevent Lajoie's move with an injunction and lost, again on grounds of lack of mutuality in the contract.[33] The case, however, was appealed to the Pennsylvania Supreme Court, which found that mutuality was established by Lajoie's $2,400 salary and enjoined Lajoie, who played the 1901 season in the AL and set an all-time AL batting record of .422, to return to the NL club for 1902. Haggling over Lajoie resulted in his being traded to the Cleveland AL club, where his only handicap was being banned from playing in Pennsylvania. This restriction was also lifted with the 1903 agreement reached between the American and National leagues.[34]

THE 1903 AGREEMENT

In 1902 the AL drew 2.2 million fans to its games, the NL drew 1.7 million, and the bidding war between the leagues grew fiercer. Both leagues now saw it in their interest to compromise. A truce was signed in January 1903. Under its terms, the organization of modern Major League Baseball, basically as we know it today, was established.

With its monopoly and the reserve clause intact, MLB was again feeling its oats, and Albert Spalding believed one victory deserved another. In 1905 he established a commission to prove that baseball was purely American in origin. After nearly three years of "investigation" and without a shred of credible evidence, the commission dutifully concluded the game was invented in Cooperstown, New York, in 1839.[35]

By 1910 attendance boomed to 7.25 million, but salaries languished. The average player salary was still below $2,500 in 1911.[36] Ty Cobb and Christie Mathewson each received $9,000, and the World Series share for the winners was $3,000 a head.

Baseball's first players' strike, if you can call it that, occurred on May 16, 1912. The members of the Detroit Tigers struck over the suspension of Ty Cobb for fighting with a fan who had taunted him from the stands. The owner of the Tigers hired players off the street as scabs to play before 20,000 fans. The next day a *New York Times* editorial proclaimed: "The sole underlying cause of [the strike] is the growing resentment of all authority and discipline throughout the world. . . . If the president of the AL expels the entire Detroit team for breach of contract he will do right."[37] AL president Ban Johnson ordered the players back to work on Monday, and each player was fined $50. Cobb was allowed to return after ten days.

It would be wrong to suppose that Cobb's bellicosity was not also grounded in the material realities of the ballplayers' working conditions at the time. Locker rooms had one shower and no hot water; uniforms were all put in a common bin where they lay in a "natural sweat-soaked state" and were worn many times before being washed.[38]

Cobb's troubles with baseball's authorities, however, were not over. At the outset of the 1913 season, Cobb, who had been paid $9,000 three consecutive years despite batting averages of .385, .420, and .410, undertook a salary holdout. The soon-to-be-ignominious National Commission (baseball's governing body until 1920) promptly slapped a $50 fine on him and commended the Tigers for its firm stand. His salary travails notwithstanding, Cobb was one of dozens of players to defend the reserve clause before the U.S. Congress hearings on organized baseball in 1951.

THE FEDERAL LEAGUE AND THE ANTITRUST EXEMPTION

In 1913 the owners' avarice was again challenged by the formation of a new competitive league. The Federal League (FL) was founded as a minor league, but in August it announced that it would seek major league stars and expand to play in eastern cities. The FL eschewed the reserve clause and pursued long-term contracts in its stead. Only eighteen major leaguers jumped during 1913, and their salaries nearly doubled. According to one account, as many as 221 players defected to the FL during 1914–15.[39]

In the celebrated 1914 case of Hal Chase, who defected to the FL Buffalo club, the New York State Supreme Court ruled that Major League Baseball was not subject to antitrust laws because "[though] as complete a monopoly . . . as any monopoly can be made . . . baseball is an amusement, a sport, a game . . . not a commodity or an article of merchandise."[40] Nonetheless, the court reversed the mutuality precedent set in the Lajoie case, ruling that the contract lacked mutuality, and refused to enjoin Chase to return to the AL Chicago club.

As in the past, the advent of a new league with free player contracting put strong upward pressure on major league players' salaries. Average salaries jumped from $1,200 in 1914 to $2,800 in 1915. As already stated, Ty Cobb's salary was $9,000 in both 1911 and 1912, despite batting .420 and slugging .621 in 1911. His batting average then trailed off steadily to .369 by 1915, but the competitive pressure from the FL lifted his 1915 salary to $20,000.[41]

The salary wars of 1914–15 undermined the profitability of both leagues. By one estimate, the two leagues together lost a total of approximately $10 million.[42]

In January 1915 the FL brought suit against MLB for denying access to the players' market.[43] In the Illinois U.S. District Court, Judge Kenesaw Mountain Landis declared: "As a result of thirty years of observation, I am shocked because you call playing baseball 'labor' ";[44] and then took the case under advisement to encourage settlement. After almost a year of waiting for Landis's decision, MLB and the FL reached an agreement in November 1915, ending the FL after only two seasons of play. Eventual compensation to the FL owners totaled some $600,000. Several FL owners became MLB owners, including Phil Wrigley, whose Wrigley Field was built originally for the Chicago FL franchise.

The Baltimore Terrapins of the FL, however, were virtually excluded from the benefits of the settlement. MLB owners then imprudently added insult to injury. Charles Comiskey, owner of the Chicago White Sox, ridiculed the city of Baltimore by saying "Baltimore is a minor league city and not a hell of a good one at that." Charles Ebbets, owner of the Brooklyn Dodgers, echoed affirmation, adding it was a minor league city, "will never be anything else," and that it was one of the worst minor league cities because "you have too many colored population to start with."[45] The Terrapins' owners rejected the paltry $50,000 settlement offered for their franchise and instead filed an antitrust suit in 1916. In April 1919 Terrapin owners won their suit for triple damages of $240,000 in the Indiana State Supreme Court. This decision, however, was reversed in the District of Columbia Court of Appeals in April 1921, which found "the players . . . travel from place to place in interstate commerce, but they are not the game . . . [which] is local in its beginning and in its end . . . The fact that the [owners] produce baseball games as a source of profit, large or small, cannot change the character of the games. They are still sport, not trade."[46] This ruling was upheld on May 29, 1922, by the U.S. Supreme Court in a decision written by Justice Oliver Wendell Holmes, a former amateur baseball player, for a court headed by former President William Howard Taft, himself an erstwhile third baseman at Yale University (and the first president to throw out a baseball to open the season).[47]

THE ROARING TWENTIES THROUGH WORLD WAR II

As MLB was absorbing the FL and having its monopoly sanctioned by the Supreme Court, professional gamblers were increasingly penetrating the game of baseball. With the closing of the racetracks during World War I, professional gamblers flocked to MLB. Neither the National Commission nor the owners did much to curtail them.

These problems culminated in the alleged fixing of the 1919 World Series. Chicago White Sox owner Charles Comiskey had primed his players to be receptive to attractive financial overtures. Comiskey paid the lowest salaries in the league.[48] Shoeless Joe Jackson, purchased from Cleveland for $65,000, was paid less than $6,000 in 1918 and 1919 after batting .408, .395, and .372 during the three previous seasons.[49] Pitcher Eddie Cicotte in 1919 had been promised a $10,000 bonus for thirty wins but was benched after he gained his twenty-ninth victory with three weeks of the season left.[50]

In part to clean house and to present a better image, MLB replaced the ineffectual, three-man National Commission with an authoritarian commissioner. Judge Kenesaw Mountain Landis filled the post, earning $50,000 a year over the course of a seven-year contract. Landis suspended eight Sox players for life, and baseball declared victory.

To many baseball fans, a more heinous practice in the business of baseball still went unchecked. Opportunistic owners were engaging in shameless barn sales of extraordinary player talent. Most egregious were Connie Mack's wholesaling of the Phillies in 1913 and again during 1929 to 1931, Clark Griffith's evisceration of the Senators in 1933, and Harry Frazee's decimation of the Red Sox between 1919 and 1922. Frazee, the owner of the Boston Red Sox and a producer of Broadway plays, sold Colonel Jacob Ruppert's Yankees Babe Ruth, Dutch Leonard, Joe Dugan, Carl Mays, Herb Pennock, Waite Hoyt, and Everett Scott, among others. Ruth was sold for $100,000 plus a $350,000 loan (with Fenway Park as collateral), which Frazee needed to finance his Broadway production of *No, No, Nanette*, with his new girlfriend in the lead role.[51] Although they had won the World Series in 1915, 1916, and 1918, after selling Ruth the Red Sox have never again won the national title. It was Frazee himself who put a curse on the Red Sox, but his transgression has become known in baseball circles as the "Curse of the Bambino."

The industry of baseball flourished during the 1920s. According to leading baseball historian Harold Seymour, both leagues made a profit every year from 1920 to 1930, with the Yankees making the biggest profit—$3.5 million over the decade. Seymour adds that this figure is probably too small, "accounting legerdemain being what it is."[52]

Ty Cobb, while earning $50,000 in 1925 (second only to Ruth's $52,000), ruminated on the problems that affluence had brought to baseball:

> The great trouble with baseball today is that most of the players are in the game for the money that's in it—not for the love of it, the excitement . . . and the glorious thrill of it all. . . . [But] I cannot, if I look at the thing from a cold-blooded, commercial viewpoint . . . blame the players of today for not taking too many chances, or for not burning out their energy too soon, and for saving themselves. That's good business for them . . . so they will earn big league money for a long time.[53]

Ruth's salary continued to rise, reaching $70,000 in 1927 when the median salary on the highest-paid Yankees was only $7,000. When Ruth's pay hit $80,000 in 1930, he was reminded that his compensation exceeded that of President Hoover (which stood at $75,000). Ruth retorted: "What the hell has Hoover got to do with it? Besides, I had a better year than he did."[54] The Yankees certainly thought Ruth was worth it; they had taken out a $300,000 insurance policy on the slugger.[55] Under the direction of his press agent, Christy Walsh, Ruth was carefully choreographed through barnstorming tours, endorsements, hospital visits, and movie roles to become baseball's first national celebrity. Walsh and Ruth thus not only foreshadowed the days of Jim Palmer and

Bo Jackson, but also elevated the national pastime to a new level of player worship and commercialism.[56]

While reflecting the vicissitudes of the economy during the 1930s, baseball proved to be rather resilient. Attendance had fallen from 10 million in 1930 to 8 million in 1936, but with falling player salaries[57] the industry remained profitable in every year except 1932 and 1933.[58] Attendance was off again during World War II, but only in 1943 did MLB report a combined operating loss. Even then, twelve of baseball's sixteen teams earned a profit, and the combined loss totaled just $240,000.[59]

MURPHY, GARDELLA, AND CELLER

With the end of World War II, hundreds of ballplayers came home from the battlefield. The Veterans Act assured them the right to return to their previous jobs for at least one year. In several cases players were not taken back by their previous team. MLB claimed that baseball was not covered by the act, but the courts generally upheld the players.

Meanwhile, a new league in Mexico also bid for the services of the returning players. This competition, albeit remote and fleeting, wreaked considerable havoc on the baseball establishment. First, according to the testimony of Pee Wee Reese (Brooklyn Dodgers Hall of Fame shortstop during the 1940s and 1950s) before the U.S. congressional hearings on organized baseball in 1951,[60] the opportunity for the players to jump to the Mexican League spurred the organization of the Players' Guild in 1946 and the subsequent agreement on player benefits. The guild was organized by Robert Murphy, a lawyer and former examiner of the National Labor Relations Board. Although Murphy was unsuccessful in galvanizing the guild into a collective bargaining entity for the players, his efforts almost bore fruit in Pittsburgh, and the owners took heed of the potential threat. A joint committee was formed to discuss player contracts, and in 1947 a variety of reforms emerged: Baseball's first pension fund with owner and player contributions was set up;[61] a minimum salary was established at $5,500 along with a maximum salary cut of 25 percent in the option year;[62] spring training expense money for the players was introduced at $25 a week; the ten-day severance clause in the players' contract was increased to thirty days; the owners allowed two player representatives to attend meetings of their executive council, although the players had no vote and could attend only when matters of player welfare were being discussed explicitly.

Second, a spate of legal battles ensued after Commissioner Happy

Chandler announced in June 1946 a five-year ban on all U.S. players who jumped to the Mexican League. The most significant case was that of Danny Gardella, a twenty-seven-year-old outfielder who in 1946 had been offered $5,000 to play for the New York Giants and $8,000 plus a signing bonus of $5,000 to play in the Mexican League.[63] Gardella chose to play in Mexico, but like the other U.S. ballplayers who made this choice, he found the playing conditions there intolerable and tried to return to MLB. Gardella found himself blacklisted under the Chandler ruling and sued for $300,000.[64] After losing the first ruling in July 1948, Gardella appealed. The Second Circuit Court of Appeals found in Gardella's favor, ruling that the advent of radio and television had clearly involved baseball in interstate commerce, and, hence, the sport was covered by the Sherman Act. The court's decision stated that the reserve clause is "shockingly repugnant to moral principles that . . . have been basic in America . . . [since] the Thirteenth Amendment . . . condemning 'involuntary servitude' . . . for the 'reserve clause' . . . results in something resembling peonage of the baseball player."[65] Damages of $300,000 were awarded to Gardella, and the Holmes decision of 1922 was, in effect, reversed.[66]

Fearing the end of its exemption and the end of the reserve clause, baseball was sent into a tizzy. Pittsburgh Pirate general manager (GM) Branch Rickey, feeding off the rising political hysteria in the country, declared in April 1949 "that the reserve clause was opposed by people with avowed Communist tendencies."[67] Rickey left no doubt as to the usefulness of the reserve clause to owners in the following year when he told slugger Ralph Kiner that he would not raise his salary more because the Pirates "finished last with you and could have finished last without you."[68]

MLB appealed the Gardella case. With a new trial set for November 1949, Chandler pronounced an amnesty for Mexican League jumpers in June 1949. Then, in October, Gardella settled out of court for $60,000, which he shared with his lawyer.

The Gardella scare and the uncertainty over whether the Court of Appeals ruling or the 1922 Supreme Court ruling would be in effect in the future led MLB to seek the congressional stamp of exemption. Protracted hearings before the Subcommittee on the Study of Monopoly Power of the House of Representatives took place during 1951, chaired by New York Congressman Emmanuel Celler. When the hearings opened in July, no less than eight antitrust cases were pending against MLB as well as three bills that would have legislated antitrust exemption to baseball and other sports. At the hearings Ty Cobb and dozens of other ballplayers and sportswriters, innocently echoing the owners' repeated refrain, testified that the reserve clause was necessary to preserve competitive balance in the game. Longtime baseball executive and owner Bill Veeck was the only dissident voice in the baseball establishment.

In his testimony, National League president and soon to be commissioner Ford Frick likened the reserve clause to Milton Berle's thirty-year movie studio contract. Frick, of course, overlooked two crucial facts: When Berle signed his contract he was able to choose among competing offers, and Berle had long-term job stability.

More generally, it is remarkable that, given the prevalence of player sales throughout the years, the reserve clause/competitive balance myth was so tenacious. Economist Simon Rottenberg was the first to point out in 1956 that as long as player sales were allowed, baseball talent would be distributed according to the various teams' ability and willingness to pay, with or without a reserve clause. As we shall see in succeeding chapters, competitive balance has been enhanced since the coming of free agency in 1976.

In any case, the Celler hearings concluded without adopting any legislation. According to one legal specialist, the Celler Committee believed the 1948 Court of Appeals ruling in the Gardella case had superseded the 1922 Holmes decision and that by not adopting legislation to grant baseball an exemption, the sport would be subject to the nation's antitrust statutes.[69]

As Paul Porter[70] has documented, the Celler inquiry hardly exhausted congressional interest in the legal status of baseball during the 1950s. Between 1951 and 1961 there were six separate congressional hearings (three before Celler's House Subcommittee and three before Senator Estes Kefauver's) into organized baseball and thirty-seven bills dealing with its immunity. Perhaps in baseball's favor, the 1950s were generally lean economic years for the game. Despite a doubling of radio and television revenue, total revenue for organized baseball fell from $65 million in 1950 to $60 million in 1956.[71] Between 1951 and 1956 the average net income (profit) per club was only $29,154.[72]

None of the bills in the 1950s challenging baseball's unique self-regulating, monopoly status ever made it out of committee in either chamber. Indeed, the same can be said for all subsequent bills to this day, with one insignificant exception.[73] The owners have held the day in Congress for one enduring reason, explained by Representative Celler himself: "I want to say . . . that I have never known, in my 35 years of experience, of as great a lobby that descended upon the House than the organized baseball lobby. . . . They came upon Washington like locusts."[74] Bill Veeck offered a similar view: "To keep the Justice Department from being overworked, baseball has enlivened the halls of Congress with its own lawyers to keep the 'friends of baseball' supplied with whatever encouragement . . . was necessary to protect and preserve the privileges of the Grand Old Game."[75]

In light of congressional inaction, the judgments on baseball's status were left to the courts. In 1953 the case of Toolson versus the New York Yankees came before the U.S. Supreme Court. George Toolson had been a minor leaguer playing for the Yankees' Newark club. After the Yankees reassigned him, he refused to report. While organized baseball's lawyers had assumed that the Holmes decision was no longer good law, the Supreme Court fooled them, reaffirming in a 7-to-2 vote the 1922 Holmes' decision *(Federal Baseball)*. The one-paragraph opinion ran as follows.

> In *Federal Baseball* . . . this Court held that . . . professional baseball . . . was not within the scope of the federal antitrust laws. Congress had the ruling under consideration but has not seen fit to bring such business under these laws by legislation. . . . We think that if there are evils in this field which now warrant application to it of the antitrust laws it should be by legislation. Without reexamination of the underlying issues, the judgments below are affirmed on the authority of *Federal Baseball*.[76]

It appears that the Congress and the Supreme Court were playing a game of cat and mouse. Congress did not enact legislation because it believed the 1948 Court of Appeals decision removing baseball's exemption was good law, not the Holmes decision. The Supreme Court putatively did not reverse the precedent of the Holmes decision because it interpreted congressional inaction in 1951 as an endorsement of baseball's exemption. Whether this view of good intentions and confusion on the part of the Congress and the high court is accurate for the early 1950s, it seems to be of little relevance since neither body has done anything about baseball's status since.

Baseball's exemption from antitrust statutes, based on the notion that it was not involved in interstate commerce, erroneous back in 1922 and more so in the 1950s, became even more anomalous in 1957, when the Supreme Court declared football to be subject to antitrust statutes and stated that baseball's exemption was "unreasonable, illogical and inconsistent."[77]

NOW YOU SEE IT, NOW YOU DON'T

Despite its legal victories, MLB took its lumps during the 1950s. Attendance had peaked at over 20 million in 1948 and 1949; it fell to a low of 14.4 million in 1953 and did not surpass 20 million again until 1960. The relative attendance difficulties of the early 1950s along with new opportunities from the growth of television disrupted the geographical stability of the game. From the time of the 1903 agreement until 1953, each of baseball's sixteen major league franchises remained in the same city. This stability was punctured in 1953 when the Boston Braves moved to Milwaukee, ushering in an era of frequent franchise relocation and expansion.

The most controversial moves of the 1950s were those of the Brooklyn Dodgers and New York Giants to California following the 1957 season. The circumstances of these moves are discussed in detail in chapter 6; for now, it suffices to note that indignant New York City Mayor Robert Wagner set up a committee to investigate the possibility of inducing another NL team to move to New York. When this effort failed, Wagner prevailed on prominent lawyer William Shea to organize a third major league.[78] Shea hired seventy-seven-year-old Branch Rickey in the winter of 1958–59 to lead the project. Rickey lined up wealthy backers along with experienced baseball people and launched a plan to form the Continental League (CL). The idea was to integrate the new league with the existing major leagues, including cross-scheduling, media revenue sharing, and common player pools.

Amid calls in Congress to legislate the creation of a third league, MLB met in Columbus, Ohio, on May 21, 1959, and issued a statement indicating that a third league would be welcomed.[79] Among other things, this cooperative pledge induced Shea and Rickey to urge Senator Kefauver and Representative Celler not to pursue hearings or new bills challenging the game's antitrust exemption during 1959. Following this stated support, however, baseball engaged in stalling tactics and put forward what one historian termed "extortionate demands"[80] regarding high compensation levels for territorial rights sought by the owners of the minor league franchises in the cities where the CL wanted to put teams (Minneapolis, Houston, Denver, Toronto, New York, Buffalo, Dallas, and Atlanta).[81]

In May 1960 Senator Kefauver called hearings around the issue of the establishment of the CL and his related bill to limit the number of minor leaguers that could be controlled by the existing major league teams. MLB did extensive lobbying, and the bill was defeated by the close margin of 45 to 41, although it was sent back to committee for reconsideration by an overwhelming majority—meaning the legislators wanted another crack at it, depending on what MLB did.[82] Further, when the CL tried to create a new minor league in March 1960 to help stock its teams with talent, Commissioner Frick refused to sanction it.[83] Rickey then took the offensive, threatening that if MLB did not begin to cooperate, the CL would raid its players.

The CL was finally co-opted on July 18, 1960, when the NL voted to expand to ten teams and to form a committee including representatives from the CL to study how expansion should proceed. Shortly thereafter, the AL decided to expand as well. At an August 2 meeting, MLB promised the four new franchises to CL syndicates.[84] Thus, the Continental League jarred MLB out of its fifty-seven-year-old complacency and provoked a long-overdue expansion. Then it went the way of the Players' League and the Federal League before it.

MARVIN MILLER AND THE BASEBALL PLAYERS' ASSOCIATION

Unhappy over the progress in bargaining for an improved pension plan, in the spring of 1954 the players formed the Major League Baseball Players' Association (MLBPA), with Bob Feller elected as the first president. Although not a bargaining unit at the time, the MLBPA did articulate a series of demands that the executive committee presented to the owners. The resulting deal stipulated that 60 percent of television revenues from the All-Star Game and World Series would go to finance the players' pension fund and that the minimum salary would be raised to $6,000. (The players had asked for $7,200.)

The Players' Association was not an active force until after 1966. Indeed, their legal counsel was Judge Robert Cannon, a man who aspired to be baseball's next commissioner; he supported the reserve clause and praised the players' pension plan as the finest in the world. On the players' economic status, Cannon told Congress in 1964 "we have it so good we don't know what to ask for next."[85] Historian James Edward Miller reports that when Cannon was selected to serve as the MLBPA's first executive director at $50,000 a year in 1966, the owners were so pleased that they voted to put aside 35 percent of profits from the All-Star Game to pay for a New York office for him. But Cannon turned down the offer, and Marvin Miller, a longtime negotiator for the United States Steel Workers, was chosen in his stead.

Before Marvin Miller had a chance to work his magic, Dodgers Don Drysdale and Sandy Koufax double-handedly set out to make baseball economic history. Dissatisfied with their 1965 salaries, before the 1966 season they formed a two-person negotiating team and hired a lawyer to represent their salary interests. They were asking for a combined $1 million over three years. Dodger president Walter O'Malley was outraged, vowing that he would never bargain with an agent. After a short joint holdout, the players received substantial increases: Koufax's salary nearly doubled to $125,000 and Drysdale got $115,000.[86] Later that year the MLBPA and the owners signed their first agreement altering the pension financing system. They scrapped the old formula taking a percentage of All-Star Game and World Series proceeds in favor of a flat $4.2 million owner contribution per year.

The first comprehensive bargaining agreement between the MLBPA and the owners was signed in February 1968. The agreement established a formal grievance procedure, with the restriction that the owner-appointed commissioner was designated as the final arbiter. It raised the minimum salary from $6,000 to $10,000 a year and set up a joint study group on the reserve clause. When new baseball commissioner General William Eckert, in office only since November 1965, ruled in favor of a player, the owners fired him and replaced him with Bowie Kuhn, who served from February 1969 until September 1984.

THE DISMANTLING OF THE
RESERVE CLAUSE

Curt Flood was a slick fielding outfielder who batted over .300 six times in his major league career. After the 1969 season, at the age of thirty-two, Flood received notice that he had been traded from the Cardinals (for whom he had played since 1958) to the Phillies for Richie Allen. Flood had friends and business interests in St. Louis, had bad feelings about racial politics in Philadelphia during the days of Mayor Frank Rizzo, and did not want to move at the end of his career. On Christmas Eve 1969, perhaps hoping for a miraculous gift, Flood wrote a letter to Commissioner Kuhn asking him to nullify the trade. The letter read in part as follows: "After twelve years of being in the major leagues, I do not feel I am a piece of property to be bought and sold irrespective of my wishes."[87]

No miracle was forthcoming. In January 1970 Flood filed suit against MLB for $3 million, triple damages, and free agency. Flood lost round one in federal district court. He appealed in January 1971 but lost again in the second circuit court of appeals. The appeals court decision read: "If baseball is to be damaged by statutory regulation, let the congressman face his constituents the next November and also face the consequences of his baseball voting record."[88] This judicial decision, like the ones before it, conveniently overlooked the fact that the courts, not Congress, were the source of baseball's exemption. Flood appealed again.

On June 18, 1972, the Supreme Court voted 5 to 3 with one abstention[89] to uphold the Holmes decision. Though terming the decision "an aberration," the majority argued on the basis of *stare decisis* (let the old decision stand), maintaining that too many long-term commitments had been made relying on the 1922 decision for the courts to lift the exemption. One of the dissenters, William Douglas, went on record as having erred in voting with the majority in the 1953 Toolson case. Douglas's dissenting opinion stated: "This is not a romantic history baseball enjoys as a business. It is a sordid history."[90]

After the final Flood decision, a June 23, 1972, *New York Times* editorial opined: "The only basis for the judge-made monopoly status of baseball is that the Supreme Court made a mistake the first time it considered the subject 50 years ago and now feels obliged to keep on making the same mistake because Congress does not act to repeal the exemption it never ordered."

Flood's personal setback, however, shook the foundations of the reserve system. The Players' Association's sights were now clearly fixed as it set out to win in collective bargaining what it could not win in the courts.

A first step was taken with the second Basic Agreement signed in 1970. Not only did the players succeed in raising the minimum salary to $15,000 by 1972 and reducing the maximum salary cut to 20 percent, but, more important, they gained the right to have impartial arbitration of grievances outside the commissioner's office.

The first industrywide players' strike occurred during early April 1972 over funding for the players' pension plan. The players struck for thirteen days (nine during the regular season) and ended up losing more in forgone wages ($600,000) than they gained from the strike ($500,000). The owners, on the other hand, took a worse beating: They saved $600,000 in unpaid salaries but lost the settlement of $500,000 and lost $5.2 million in forgone revenue from eighty-six missed games.[91] The players wanted to be able to use the surplus that had accumulated in the pension fund to augment their pensions. The owners, apparently unaware of the surplus, refused to increase their contributions. Leonard Koppett wrote a summary of the 1972 strike in the *New York Times:*

PLAYERS: We want higher pensions.
OWNERS: We won't give you one damn cent for that.
PLAYERS: You don't have to—the money is already there. Just let us use
           it.
OWNERS: It would be imprudent.
PLAYERS: We did it before, and anyhow, we won't play unless we can
           have some of it.
OWNERS: Okay.[92]

The first great strike in baseball history, then, was something of a dud.
It seemed to adumbrate the conflicts that lay ahead and to have more to
do with each side staking out some turf than it did with the manifest
issues at hand.

Negotiations over the third Basic Agreement commenced in November 1972. The Flood case had put free agency at the top of the players'
agenda. The owners offered to end the reserve clause for players with five
years of major league service if their team offered them less than a
$30,000 salary and for players with eight years of service if their team
offered less than $40,000.[93] This kind of bargaining made for long strikes.
Yet the start of spring training was delayed only briefly; the Players'
Association opted to accept the owners' offer for player salary arbitration
and to hold the reserve clause for the next round. Salary arbitration was
to take effect following the 1973 season. It enabled all players with two
years plus one day of major league service to go before an impartial
arbitrator to resolve salary disputes with the owner. Today all observers
recognize salary arbitration as a powerful weapon in the players' arsenal,
and the owners have been trying to vitiate the arbitration system for
several years (see discussion in chapter 4). The players also exacted
another concession from the owners, the so-called 10-and-5 Rule (a.k.a.
the Flood Rule). The rule states that any player who had ten years of

TABLE 1.1
Industrywide Work Stoppages

Year	Nature	Length
1972	Strike	13 days
1976	Lockout	24 days
1981	Strike	50 days
1985	Strike	2 days
1990	Lockout	32 days

service, the last five with the same team (as had Curt Flood), will have the right to veto any trade. With this rule, some players were granted control over where they played for the first time since 1879.

In 1974 Catfish Hunter signed a two-year contract with Charlie Finley of the Oakland A's. One provision called for half of Hunter's salary to be paid into an insurance company fund during the season for the purchase of an annuity. During 1974 Finley made no payments into the fund, and Hunter filed a grievance against him after the season. The three-person arbitration panel, headed by Peter Seitz, ruled in December 1974 that Finley had violated the contract and Hunter was no longer bound by it—that is, he was a free agent. Hunter went on to sign a lucrative multiyear contract with the Yankees in 1975, becoming the only MLB player to have a multiyear contract.[94]

Dave McNally of the Montreal Expos and Andy Messersmith of the Los Angeles Dodgers were each dissatisfied with the 1975 contracts offered by their clubs, and each refused to sign a new one. The clubs exercised their rights under the standard contract's renewal clause, which permits them to renew any contract for one additional option year without a player's signature. After McNally and Messersmith played out the 1975 season, they claimed they had played out their option year and were no longer bound to their clubs. In this they were assaying an unprecedented challenge to the reserve clause in baseball based on a literal interpretation of the renewal provision.[95] Again the case went before a grievance panel headed by Seitz. This time the ramifications of the ruling were infinite and the implications profound. Seitz urged the owners and the players to resolve the matter at the bargaining table, outside of arbitration. Four weeks went by before Seitz issued his sixty-one-page decision on December 21, 1975. Seitz ruled that players were free to bargain with other clubs once their contracts expired. He again urged that a suitable procedure for free agency be established in the new Basic Agreement. The owners immediately fired Seitz and then appealed his decision at federal district court and the federal circuit court of appeals. Each court rejected the appeals with the latest court ruling in March 1976.

The owners then took out their frustration on the players and the fans by locking the players out of spring training. In one of his more enlightened moves, Kuhn persuaded the owners to reopen the camps on March 17. The baseball season proceeded without a new Basic Agreement. Negotiations continued and an accord was reached in July. Free agency was granted to players with six years of major league experience.[96] For the 1977 season, 281 players signed multiyear contracts.[97] The average salary almost tripled between 1976 and 1980.

By 1979 the owners had regrouped and were ready to do battle. Three preparatory steps were taken. First, in 1979, each team contributed 2 percent of its home gate receipts to a strike war chest.[98] Eventually, the owners took out a $50-million strike insurance policy with Lloyds of London and accumulated a $15-million strike fund.[99] Second, at their November 1979 meeting, the owners decided military discipline was imperative and imposed a gag rule, prohibiting them from discussing labor relations issues with the media. Violators were to be fined $50,000. The rule was more than hortatory. The Brewers' Harry Dalton was hit with the full fine during the negotiations when he commented that he expected the players to compromise and hoped the owners would do the same. Third, the owners hired a new chief negotiator, Ray Grebey, to head their Player Relations Committee (PRC). Grebey previously had earned a reputation as a tough negotiator working for the General Electric Company. His appointment was a clear signal that the baseball owners were going to take a hard-line position.

The 1976 Basic Agreement would expire on December 31, 1979, but serious negotiation did not begin until February 1980. The players wanted to reduce the free agency eligibility from six to four years of service and to eliminate the five-year waiting period before a player could become a free agent for a second time. The owners were determined to reverse the rapid salary growth since 1976 and were not about to make further concessions strengthening free agency. On the contrary, their strategy was to weaken it by introducing a plan to compensate teams that lost free agents by penalizing teams that signed them.

Under the 1976 Basic Agreement the only compensation for loss of a player to free agency was an amateur draft choice. Primarily because college baseball was much less developed than college football or basketball, this compensation was much less significant in baseball than in the other sports. The owners wanted to add a major league player to the compensation package. With the negotiations stalled, the players voted to authorize a strike beginning on May 29. A strike was averted when the two sides agreed on a deal including everything but free agent compensation and followed Marvin Miller's suggestion to set up a joint study committee to look into the compensation issue. The committee was to report its plan by January 1, 1981. If that plan did not lead to a compromise, the owners would be able to impose their compensation scheme. But the players would be able to strike. This is precisely what happened.

Baseball fans remember 1981 as the split season, with division winners in each half and a one-game playoff at the end. The strike began on June 12, 1981, and lasted until August 1, seven days before the owners' insurance policy was to run out of funds.[100] Fifty days and 713 games were lost. Owners' losses from the strike were estimated to be over $72 million, while players' losses from forgone salary totaled around $34 million.[101] The economic costs to the affected cities and the psychic costs to the fans were incalculably larger.

The final compromise did little to alter the cost of signing a free agent. Indeed, Miller claims the compensation formula agreed upon was basically the one he had proposed before spring training.[102] The new plan maintained the amateur draft pick and added compensation from a major league player pool. Each team signing a Type A free agent (a player ranked in the top 20 percent according to various performance criteria at his position) would have to put all but twenty-four protected players into this pool. Teams losing a Type A free agent could select any player from the pool, not necessarily one from the team that signed the free agent. Clubs that did not sign a Type A free agent could protect twenty-six players, and up to five clubs could become exempt from the compensation pool by agreeing not to sign Type A free agents for three years.

The 1980–81 Basic Agreement expired on December 31, 1984. Negotiations began mid-November of that year with hopes of reaching an accord prior to spring training. Peter Ueberroth had replaced Bowie Kuhn as commissioner on October 1, 1984, and he made his influence felt immediately. Three issues stood out. First, baseball's new national television package with NBC and ABC quadrupled the annual value of its previous contract, and the MLBPA, now directed by Donald Fehr, sought a commensurate increase in the owners' pension contributions, from $15.5 million to $62 million. Second, the MLBPA wanted to eliminate the free agent compensation pool. Third, the owners wanted to weaken salary arbitration.

In February a snag arose in the discussions, when the owners requested a recess in order to review a "serious financial situation."[103] The owners pleaded financial distress. In the past, when the MLBPA had requested it, the owners refused to open their books. Since they were now invoking economic hardship as a relevant factor in the negotiations, by National Labor Relations Board (NLRB) precedent the owners were required to show the MLBPA their books. Ueberroth successfully prevailed upon the reluctant owners to do so.

The "opened" books showed a $42 million combined loss in 1984, with twenty-two of twenty-six teams losing money. Moreover, MLB's accounting firm of Ernst & Whinney was projecting losses of $58 million in 1985, $94 million in 1986, $113 million in 1987, and $155 million in 1988.[104] (Of course, reality evolved quite differently, as detailed in chapters 3 and 7, since media contracts continued to grow handsomely and the licensing of major league products became a $100-million-plus annual business.) The MLBPA hired economist Roger Noll to decode the books and concluded the industry really had an operating profit of $9 million in 1984.

With matters once again approaching a stalemate, Ueberroth indicated that in order to head off a work stoppage, he might invoke Rule 12A, which allowed the commissioner to make any decision deemed to be in the game's best interest. A strike ensued nonetheless, but after two days the sides reached a five-year agreement. Players got a $32.7 million annual contribution for their pension fund,[105] and the owners got the service requirement for arbitration eligibility lifted from two to three years beginning in 1987. Minimum salaries were raised from $40,000 to $60,000, with cost-of-living increases for future years.

The owners agreed to open up the free agent market by eliminating both the free agent reentry draft and the professional player compensation for Type A free agents.[106] All that remained was amateur draft pick compensation. Type A free agent losses would be compensated by a first-round draft pick from the signing club.[107] Type B free agents (ranked between the 20th and 30th percentiles in performance by position) would be compensated by a "sandwich" pick between the first and second rounds.

Thus Ueberroth's heavy hand contributed to a relatively efficient negotiating process and quick compromise. Yet what his heavy hand accomplished over the bargaining table, it took away under the table. He was preparing the owners not to bid on free agents.

Ueberroth began sowing the seeds of collusion as soon as he took office. At an owners' meeting in October 1985 during the World Series in St. Louis, he reportedly scolded them for overspending on mediocre free agents. Lee MacPhail, director of the owners' Player Relations Committee, argued that players with contracts of three years and more spent nearly 50 percent more time on the disabled list than those with one-year contracts and that the average player with a three-year or more contract experienced a nearly twenty-point decline in batting average after signing the contract.[108] At owners' meetings later in October and mid-November came more reprimands and admonitions from Ueberroth, as he called long-term contracts "dumb" and said "he would want to know the economics of clubs that signed free agents."[109] Soon Ueberroth would turn the owners' meetings into criticism/self-criticism sessions with owners volunteering *mea culpas.*

Teams began announcing policies of no contracts longer than three years for hitters and two years for pitchers. Star players such as Kirk Gibson found that teams were not bidding for his services. Of the thirty-three free agents between the 1985 and 1986 seasons, twenty-nine went back to their former teams without receiving bids from any other teams. The four who did move were marginal players whose teams did not want them anymore. Free agent salaries grew by only 5 percent in 1986; two-thirds of the free agents received just one-year contracts. In February 1986 the MLBPA filed its first grievance (Collusion I).

The next year, following the 1986 season, free agents again encountered a barren market. Star players such as Jack Morris, Andre Dawson, Bob Horner, Bob Boone, Tim Raines, and Lance Parrish were attracting little or no owner interest. Something had to be amiss. Every year between 1984 and 1987 new attendance records were set. According to its own figures, in 1986 MLB had its first pretax operating profit in eight years, and in 1987, with average salaries down 2 percent and revenues up 15 percent, operating profits grew to $103 million.

Andre Dawson's agent, Dick Moss, decided to test the owners' resolve. He left a blank check in the Cubs' general offices with the message to fill it out as they saw fit. Then he told the press what he had done. After screaming expletives at Moss, the Cubs' management filled it out, lowering Dawson's base salary by 60 percent from his 1986 salary. The average salary of free agents in 1986–87 declined 16 percent, and approximately three-quarters of them got only one-year contracts. On February 18, 1987, the MLBPA filed its second grievance (Collusion II).

In September 1987 arbitrator Thomas Roberts ruled, in Collusion I, that club owners were guilty as charged. This led the clubs to soften their approach to the 1988 crop of free agents. The owners' new plan was to create an information bank where they reported their bids on players to each other. On January 19, 1988, the MLBPA filed its third grievance (Collusion III).

In July 1988 arbitrator George Nicolau found the owners guilty in Collusion II. And in July 1990 he found them guilty in Collusion III as well, reasoning: "[The information bank] converted the free-agency process into a secret buyers' auction, to which the sellers of services—the players—had not agreed and the existence of which they were not even aware . . ." and ". . . it is evident that many clubs used the bank to report offers to free agents and to track just how far they would have to go with particular players."[110]

Damages from collusion were fixed in stages. First, Roberts, based on the average of three statistical methodologies, found the salary shortfall in 1986 due to collusion to be $10.5 million. Then Nicolau, in September 1990, found, also on the basis of statistical studies, the salary shortfall to be $38 million in 1987 and $64.5 million in 1988. To these salary shortfalls were added lingering salary effects from multiyear contracts, losses due to shorter contracts, fewer guaranteed contracts, fewer option buyouts, fewer and smaller performance and award bonuses, fewer and smaller signing bonuses, and fewer no-trade clauses.[111]

A settlement for total collusion damages of $280 million was reached by the MLBPA and MLB on December 21, 1990. Owners paid the MLBPA $120 million on January 2, 1991, and were scheduled to pay the balance in four equal installments of $40 million each on July 15, 1991; September 15, 1991; November 15, 1991; and April 15, 1992.

True to form, the next Basic Agreement negotiations brought yet another work stoppage. This time, without the imposing leadership of Peter Ueberroth, the stoppage was prolonged—a thirty-two-day lockout by the owners during the 1990 spring training. The regular season was delayed, but with some contortions it was played in full. The most contentious issue was eligibility for salary arbitration—the players wanting to revert to the old, two years of service eligibility requirement, the owners proposing to do away with salary arbitration altogether and replace it with a complex pay-for-performance formula for players with between two and five years of service. The owners also proposed to introduce a salary cap, as in professional basketball, at 48 percent of pooled income from ticket sales and broadcast rights.[112] The rationale given was that such a cap would preserve competitive balance in the game.[113]

Eventually, the owners backed off from the salary cap and pay-for-performance plans, but they insisted on not lowering the eligibility requirement for arbitration below three years of service. The ultimate settlement involved a small concession from them: 17 percent of the players with more than two but less than three years of service (amounting to 13 players in 1991) would be eligible for salary arbitration.

Other parts of the new Basic Agreement included an increase in the minimum salary from $68,000 to $100,000 in 1990, with a cost-of-living increase (to $109,000) in 1992; an increase in the yearly pension fund contribution from $34.2 million to $55 million; and triple damages for any owner collusion in the future regarding the signing of free agents. The agreement lasts until December 31, 1993, but can be reopened by either side after the 1992 season.

Since the early 1970s, while there have been no important judicial or legislative challenges to baseball's antitrust exemption, labor relations in baseball have been turbulent. The Congressional Task Force on baseball expansion, formed in November 1987, derived most of its energy from Senators Tim Wirth of Colorado and Connie Mack of Florida.[114] Since their states received franchises in the latest NL expansion (and Florida may receive another from relocation), it is doubtful that significant congressional challenges to baseball's unique legal status will be forthcoming in the near future. Nonetheless, the issues raised by free agency and salary arbitration have not become any more tractable over the last two decades. Commissioner Fay Vincent told *Baseball America* in June 1990: "I think it would be romantic and somewhat silly to assure you or the American public that there isn't going to be confrontation the next time around. The history tells you that there will be."[115] Indeed, Donald Fehr of the Players' Association seems to resonate to these words. The MLBPA is already building a strike fund for the next negotiations, setting aside one-third on its $50-plus million in annual licensing fees. And the merry-go-round continues.

Baseball's Barons

When the Supreme Court says baseball isn't run like a business, everybody jumps up and down with joy. When I say the same thing, everybody throws pointy objects at me.
— Bill Veeck, former owner of the Indians and White Sox

It's hard to imagine any group of people less sensible and less practical than the people who run baseball.
— Whitey Herzog, former player and manager of the Rangers, Royals, and Cardinals; now general manager of the Angels

Either baseball owners and general managers are the greatest optimists since Pollyanna, or they are the greatest dopes since Goofy.
— Ira Berkow, sports columnist, *New York Times*

To me, one of the most exciting things in the world is being poor. Survival is such an exciting challenge.
— Tom Monaghan, owner of the Detroit Tigers and Domino's Pizza chain, which earned $10.5 million in profits during 1990–91

I'm a write-off.
— Mike Pagliarulo, third baseman for the Minnesota Twins, on the economics of baseball

Whether or not Commissioner Vincent's premonitions of catastrophe are realized, there are real tensions and potential problems in baseball's economic future. Big-city teams maintain an appreciable financial advantage over small-city teams. Television ratings for nationally broadcast games on ESPN and CBS are down. Owners are increasingly expressing their disparate parochial interests. Labor relations remain unsettled.

Whether baseball's governing structure will find the wisdom or the harmony to confront these challenges successfully is questionable. As long as baseball remains a self-regulating industry, its solutions must be found internally, and the people who must forge them are the captains of industry, baseballs' owners, and their hired gun, the commissioner. It is fitting, then, to begin our inquiry with a sketch of ownership and its evolution: who are the barons of baseball, what are their goals, what are the structural pressures and constraints that encircle them?[1]

We will find that with few exceptions, franchise owners have always been out to maximize their profits, and they have changed baseball accordingly. Though the circumstances and institutions of ownership have changed over the years, there is certainly no more reason today than there was fifty or a hundred years ago to entrust the well-being of our national pastime to the self-interested machinations of sixteen or twenty-eight owners.

PATTERNS OF OWNERSHIP

With today's high salaries, long-term contracts, and corporate penetration of the ownership ranks, it is commonplace to hear commentators rue baseball's growing commercialization, claiming it is undermining the aesthetics and competitive spirit of the game. In fact, baseball's growing commercialism has been a constant since the 1860s. The last chapter quoted star players Monte Ward in the 1880s and Ty Cobb in the 1920s expressing their concern with the sport's creeping contamination by business interests.

Yet today the notion of the good ol' days prevails: the supposed times when players did not care so much about money and the owners were "sportsmen," connoisseurs of the game without an eye to the bottom line. In his otherwise excellent three-volume history *American Baseball*, David Voigt falls into this stereotype of owners in identifying the end of the sportsmen-owner era with the passing of Connie Mack and eight other owners during the 1950s. Following them, he contends, came a new breed of owners with outside business interests and appreciable wealth. The operating criterion for Voigt is whether baseball was the owners' principal source of income, and he notes that by 1969 at least eleven of the twenty owners had a more important income activity than baseball.

While it is certainly true that, as baseball franchises grew more expensive, new owners needed more wealth to enter the game, the development of this trend toward wealthier owners has been particularly uneven. In 1950 already, for example, ten of the sixteen owners had principal business interests outside of baseball, a higher proportion than Voigt cites for 1969 after the supposed transformation of ownership.[2] It is also true that the early years of the century witnessed many well-off owners whose wealth emanated from outside the sport—for example, Jacob Ruppert, Harry Sinclair, Emil Fuchs, Frank Farrell, Harry Frazee, William Wrigley, Charles Stoneham, Tom Yawkey, Walter Briggs, and Alva Bradley.

In his *Sports in America*, James Michener expresses another typically schematic approach to the evolution of baseball ownership:

> In the early years of every professional sport, the owners were men of great dedication and expertise. . . . Their type was soon superseded, however, by the business tycoon who made his fortune in trade, then dabbled in sports ownership both as a means of advertising his product and finding community approval. The beer barons—Jacob Ruppert with his New York Yankees and Augie Busch with his St. Louis Cardinals—were prototypes; they became famous across America and the sales of their beer did not suffer in the process. It is interesting that when William Wrigley, the Chicago tycoon, wanted to buy into the National League, he was strongly opposed by Colonel Ruppert, who feared that such ownership might be used to commercialize chewing gum.
>
> Then came the third echelon of ownership, the corporate manager who bought a club not only to publicize his business enterprises but also to take advantage of a curious development in federal tax laws.[3]

There is both truth and falsehood here. Michener's stage 1, to be sure, did include men of great dedication, but it also included the tycoon (for example, Hulbert, Spalding, Soden, Chris Von der Ahe, the latter the owner of the St. Louis Browns) without whom professional baseball would not have thrived. His stage 2 is more complex than he makes it out to be. Ruppert, for instance, became a Yankee owner in 1913, and although he was a beer baron, he did not mix baseball and beer promotion as did Gussie Busch.[4] It was not, after all, until the 1920s that radio came to carry baseball games and the late 1940s that television first broadcast major league action. The promotional synergy that motivated Busch, Jerry Hoffberger, Ted Turner, John Fetzer, Gene Autry, and others did not become a dominant ownership motive until the 1950s. By the same token, sales synergy was there from the beginning for some owners, such as Spalding's sporting goods company and baseball guide or Von der Ahe's tavern business. Michener's stage 3 does capture a trend toward the corporate manager, but it hardly depicts the majority situation in baseball today because most teams are still privately held partnerships. In short, the historical progression of ownership is less linear than Michener and Voigt suggest.[5]

While acknowledging the unevenness, it is possible to discern a trend toward owners with deeper pockets, owners with outside business interests who stand to gain by association with baseball, and, finally, toward larger partnership groups and corporate ownership. Pushing along this evolution were the advance of new communications technology after 1920, the uncovering of an appreciable tax shelter by Bill Veeck in 1959, and the explosion of franchise values after 1976.

THE PROMOTIONAL FACTOR

Gussie Busch, grandson of Adolphus Busch, the founder of Anheuser-Busch Breweries, is usually credited with being the first to actively exploit joint product promotion opportunities in baseball. When Cardinals' owner and real estate tycoon Fred Saigh was found guilty of income tax fraud in 1953, Commissioner Ford Frick ordered him to sell the team. Anheuser-Busch bought it for $3.75 million, and Gussie Busch immediately proclaimed: "I am going at this from the sports angle and not as a sales weapon for Budweiser Beer."[6] This was utter folderol. At a previous board of directors meeting, Busch had justified the purchase of the team on the grounds of its promotional potential. Indeed, he set right to work in using radio, television, and the ballpark to advertise his Budweiser. According to a biography on the Busch family, "The Cardinals were quickly transformed into a traveling billboard for the brewery."[7] Gussie Busch even wanted to rename the team's stadium Budweiser Park but was persuaded to settle for Busch Stadium when it was pointed out to him that the Cubs' home grounds was called Wrigley Field, not Wrigley's Chewing Gum Field. Busch apparently succeeded in gaining a monopoly for beer sales in a number of ballparks. He boasted in 1978 that Budweiser sales grew from 6 million barrels in 1953 to 35 million in 1978. By 1988 sales were over 70 million barrels.[8] To be sure, not all of this growth is attributable to Anheuser-Busch's ownership of the Cardinals, but it certainly helped.

In any event, Busch's lead was soon followed by Jerry Hoffberger, who wanted his National Breweries to gain sponsorship rights over the Orioles,[9] and others, including Labatt's Breweries' purchase of 40 percent of the Blue Jays. Labatt's was seeking a sports team for promotional purposes because its chief Canadian competitors, Carling and Molson, already had ownership in the Canadian Football League and the National Hockey League, respectively. Moreover, baseball was seen as a better promotional vehicle for beer than the other sports because it is played during the hotter months.[10]

Needless to say, beer is not the only joint product promoted by baseball owners. Bud Selig of the Brewers and Marge Schott of the Reds, for instance, have each promoted their car dealerships in team yearbooks, in game programs, and on stadium billboards. Schott even took the exceptional measure of not allowing competitive dealerships to advertise in Reds-connected media. Media owners such as Ted Turner, John Fetzer, John McMullen, Hulbert Taft, Gene Autry, and the Tribune Company have used their ball clubs to promote their television stations, and vice versa. Indeed, leading sports economist Roger Noll claims that roughly half of baseball's teams are owned either by a broadcaster or by the team's principal broadcast sponsor.[11] The Jacobs brothers are major real estate developers in Cleveland and had invested a small fortune in downtown mall development when news came that the Indians were contemplating a move out of the city. Such an eventuality quite obviously would have placed their investments in profound peril, so in an eleventh-hour deal they bought the team.

Others have had their outside business interests benefited indirectly by the notoriety they gain as owners of major league teams. The examples here are endless, but one prominent case is Eli Jacobs (no relation to the Cleveland pair), owner of the Baltimore Orioles.[12] Jacobs is a venture capitalist who owns many companies. In 1991 two of his largest businesses defaulted on $170 million and $250 million in debt, respectively.[13] A close political acquaintance of Jacobs claims: "Mr. Jacobs' mission is to get the important people of the world to know who he is."[14] He appoints political figures to his boards and entertains them at his ballpark, all with an eye to gaining political capital that will eventually favor his economic interests.

Of course, baseball ownership can be just plain fun as well. Some of the investment return to ownership, hence, is in its value as a consumption good. Principal Yankee owner George Steinbrenner expressed this benefit clearly: "When you're a shipbuilder nobody pays attention to you. But when you own the New York Yankees, they do, and I love it."[15] John McMullen, owner of the Houston Astros, part owner of five regional sports channels in the Liberty/TCI network,[16] including one that carries both the Astros and Rangers on cable, and owner of the New Jersey Devils in the NHL, echoes Steinbrenner's sentiments: "If a person just has $100 million to their name, then they shouldn't buy a baseball team. If he [sic] has $200 million, though, why not? What's he going to do with that money, anyway? And where else are you going to have this kind of fun?"[17]

And sometimes owners can have fun while they get good publicity. Biographers of the Busch family describe how Gussie Busch reveled in and exploited his celebrity status:

> And Gussie, almost overnight, was transformed from a brewer of modest national reputation into a celebrity. . . . He became one of baseball's most colorful curmudgeons, rolling into spring training in his private railroad car, kicking holes in the wall when his team performed poorly, and raging Lear-like against the rise of player militancy. Gone were the days when his public relations flacks practically had to beg for coverage. Reporters now scampered after him by the dozens. The beer baron had become a baseball baron and the copy was good, very good.[18]

THE TAX FACTOR

Bill Veeck, innovator of exploding scoreboards, bat day promotions, and much more, made what was probably his most important contribution to the baseball business in 1959. He reasoned that players were an asset to a baseball team just as machinery was an asset to a manufacturing concern and, like machinery, players had a fixed useful life. By assigning a high share of the purchase price of a baseball franchise to the value of its players (in those days it was typical to assign 90 percent or more), an owner could then depreciate (or deduct from taxable income) a certain share of the purchase price every year.

In his book *The Hustler's Handbook*,[19] Veeck gives a concrete example of how his scheme was used by the group that purchased the Milwaukee Braves for $6.168 million and moved them to Atlanta after the 1965 season. They assigned $0.05 million to the value of the franchise itself (that is, the right to be in the National League) and the rest, or $6.118 million (over 99 percent), of the purchase price to the value of the players, who were amortized over ten years.[20] So each year they got a nominal tax write-off of $611,800. With the top corporate tax bracket then at 50 percent, they saved $305,900 per year. Viewed differently, the government paid half of the purchase price.

To take full advantage of this loophole, however, the group needed to have either baseball profits of over $611,800 or income from other businesses exceeding this amount.[21] Suppose the group had an operating profit from baseball of $311,800; its book profits would then be minus $300,000 (or a loss of this sum). This loss could be applied against income from other businesses,[22] enabling the group to avoid paying taxes on income earned elsewhere. If baseball profits and other income were small, however, the full amount of the deduction could not be used. The ownership of baseball franchises, thus, became especially appealing to individuals, groups, or corporations with already high income.[23] In addition to attracting wealthier owners, the tax shelter also served to induce more rapid turnover of club ownership as its value diminished to zero after the players were fully depreciated (typically over five years).[24] Finally, the actual value of this loophole has fallen over time as the top marginal tax rate for individuals and corporations has dropped, as the maximum share in franchise value ascribable to the players was set at 50 percent in 1976,[25] and as the rules for recaptured capital gains were stiffened in 1976.[26]

When asked to comment on whether he thought his loophole was fair, Veeck replied: "Look, we play the 'Star-Spangled Banner' before every game. You want us to pay income taxes too?"[27] Perhaps if movie theaters also played the national anthem before their main attractions, the Internal Revenue Service would allow Hollywood studios to depreciate their actors.

In fact, from an economic point of view, the loophole makes little sense. First, it is obvious that the overwhelming share of the value of a franchise belongs to the monopoly rent that is generated by belonging to Major League Baseball and the exclusive territorial rights membership confers, not to the players' contracts. The value of these rights does not depreciate over time. Second, baseball players do not depreciate as does a machine. In fact, most players reach their peak performances well after the midpoint of their careers. That is, for five years or more players appreciate in value from their on-the-job training before they begin to depreciate. Third, baseball players do not produce a net income stream unless the additional revenue they generate for a team (their marginal revenue product) is greater than their salary. In this sense, a ballplayer should be considered a depreciable asset no more than a factory production worker. Fourth, players can be replaced simply by promoting a player from the minors. If anything, the depreciable investment in players should be the amount spent on player development in the minor leagues, but this sum is expensed (the related expenses are fully deducted in each year) so it cannot also be amortized.

THE FRANCHISE APPRECIATION FACTOR

As is common knowledge (and is detailed in the next chapter), franchise values have soared since 1976. The introduction of free agency brought rapidly escalating salaries that, in turn, compelled the owners to develop baseball's commercial potential aggressively. New national media and cable contracts, new stadiums with numerous luxury boxes, growing attendance, and licensing income from Major League Baseball properties have all been major new revenue contributors during the last fifteen years. Accordingly, the 1977 expansion teams paid $7 million to enter the American League; the 1993 expansion teams paid $95 million to enter the National League.[28] The established franchise in big-city markets are valued in the $150-to-$250-million range. At these prices, none but the wealthiest individuals in the world can own baseball franchises. Consequently, franchises today are purchased either by sizable groups of individuals or by corporations, with a few exceptions, including Ewing Kauffman, Tom Monaghan, and H. Wayne Huizenga, who had previously amassed riches in the pharmaceutical, fast-food, and entertainment industries, respectively. The lingering small-time operators, such as Bud Selig, bought into baseball prior to the franchise value explosion.[29] They are a dying breed.

GUARDIANS OF THE NATIONAL PASTIME

Anybody who has followed baseball over the last decade or two knows about George Steinbrenner. Steinbrenner, to be sure, stands out in his zaniness and mismanagement, but, according to some, he is more the rule than the exception when it comes to incompetence, insensitivity, or lack of integrity among the owners.

Steinbrenner's story can be told briefly for our purposes.[30] He and several minority partners bought the Yankees from CBS for $10 million in 1973.[31] His reign began with the pledge: "We plan absentee ownership as far as running the Yankees is concerned. I'll stick to building ships." The next year he was suspended from baseball for fifteen months when it was revealed that he made illegal campaign contributions to Richard Nixon in 1972. While managing partner of the Yankees, Steinbrenner traded away star prospects and spent millions on over-the-hill mediocre talent. He went through practically one field manager per year, and the rest of the front office staff turned over with about the same celerity. After firing manager Yogi Berra a few weeks into the 1985 season (having previously proclaimed Berra his man for the entire year), Steinbrenner responded to criticism about the state of his ball club: "I keep hearing about this guy and that guy being unhappy. Well, if they're not happy, let them get jobs as cabdrivers, firemen or policemen in New York City. Then they'll see what it's like to work for a living."

Players and fellow owners were highly critical of his leadership. Third baseman Graig Nettles commented: "When I was a kid, I wanted to join the circus and play baseball. With the Yankees, I got to do both." Chicago White Sox owner Jerry Reinsdorf remarked in 1983: "How do you know when George Steinbrenner is lying? When his lips are moving." And Commissioner Fay Vincent, after evaluating the evidence in the Howard Spira case that resulted in the separation of Steinbrenner from active management of the Yankees, could not restrain himself from noting that Steinbrenner had engaged in "a pattern of behavior that borders on the bizarre."[32]

Steinbrenner's separation from active team management gave him time to concentrate more of his energies on his American Ship Building Company, which had accumulated losses of $21.8 million between 1986 and 1990.[33] Steinbrenner's interim replacement with the Yankees was former chief of the U.S. Drug Enforcement Agency Jack Lawn, who will be remembered by history as the man who praised Panama's General Manuel Noriega on more than one occasion for his exemplary cooperation in thwarting drug trafficking.

Because she does not own a New York team, Marge Schott has received less press for her antics with the Cincinnati Reds than Steinbrenner, but she arguably deserves more. No exam provides credentials for prospective owners with respect to their interest in or knowledge of baseball. If there were, Schott would never have been allowed to own the Reds. In a 1988 interview with her hometown *Cincinnati Post*, three years after she bought the team, Schott shared the following ruminations about her team: "Q: Who do you see as your toughest competition? A: Well, I hope it's St. Louis. Q: I mean in the division. A: Let me see. I don't know. Maybe the Kansas City Royals. Q: I mean your division. A: Well, Pittsburgh's got some young coming, and Los Angeles is going to come back."[34] And when Pete Rose was banned from baseball by Commissioner Bart Giamatti and could no longer manage the Reds, Schott's friend George Steinbrenner suggested she hire the man he had recently fired, Lou Piniella. Her response was: "Lou who?"[35] Schott also revealed that her confusion often extended beyond baseball. To the surprise of everyone at CBS television, moments before the first pitch of the 1990 World Series at Cincinnati's Riverfront Stadium, Schott grabbed the microphone and called for a moment of silence for the U.S. troops "in the Far East."[36]

Since Schott assumed the club presidency in July 1985 there have been four general managers and five traveling secretaries, and more than twenty scouts have quit. In one area, though, she distinguishes herself clearly from Steinbrenner. In parsimony she ranks a close second to Charles Comiskey. Examples of her cheapness abound. Once she tried to sell doughnuts left over from a group meeting to her office employees. In 1990, on the Reds' chartered plane to California for the World Series, she made players pay their wives' plane fare even though the cost to her was the same for the charter whether or not they came. In Oakland the players with wives had to pay half their hotel costs.

But sometimes Schott's tightness with money has manifested itself in weightier matters, and it has gotten her in deep trouble. In 1989 four of the Red's limited partners filed a lawsuit against her for improper behavior and withholding funds. The lawsuit charged that Schott used her position as general partner to order the production and placement of advertising for her Chevy and Buick automobile dealerships in the Cincinnati Reds yearbook and program, on the stadium scoreboard and plaza signboard, and during Reds' radio broadcasts, without discussing the terms of the arrangements with the partnership. The advertising was prepared by Reds' employees at no cost to her. Further, she failed to make any payment for this advertising until after the baseball season was over, and then only upon demand and applying rates well below those charged other advertisers. Even these rates were further discounted and not paid in full, since they were offset by charges for the use of dealership cars. And, according to a 1990 plaintiff's memorandum, she has advertising in the team yearbook for which she had never paid.[37]

Schott has refused to allow other auto dealerships to advertise in Reds' media outlets. She has threatened action against Reds' players who wished to participate in advertising for other dealerships. One case she turned to her advantage was that of Eric Davis, who was offered a contract by a Cincinnati BMW dealer. Schott first attempted to prohibit Davis from accepting the deal, but when challenged by Davis's agent, she offered Davis instead a Corvette gratis from her Chevy dealership and then charged the cost of the car to the Reds. She relocated the Reds' spring training camp from Tampa to Plant City, Florida, in connection with a special real estate option granted to her business associate Robert C. Martin.

The limited partners' suit further charged that during 1986 to 1988 she improperly allocated herself general partnership distributions from profits without the limited partners first having received their distributions as stipulated in the partnership agreement. And in every year she used accounting trickery and dishonesty to avoid properly distributing cash to her partners. In 1986 she failed to include $5.61 million in revenue from the major league central fund in her accounts, and she omitted $620,500 in income from interest and dividends. She set aside a full reserve of over $5 million (reduced net partnership receipts by this sum) to finance a new scoreboard in 1986 and then charged net partnership receipts for the scoreboard again in 1987. The charge in 1987 meant that her calculation showed a net partnership receipts deficit of $2.06 million, but she nonetheless distributed $3.75 million to her units of general partnership. Similar duplications in reserve charges were made for computer installation, Astroturf replacement, the 1988 All-Star game, improvements to the spring training facility, unspecified capital improvements, and an unspecified contingency fund. Overall, the limited partners claimed $6.9 million should have been distributed in 1987 but was not; and, during the four-year period from 1985 to 1989, the Reds enjoyed a net income of $37.54 million, but Schott distributed only $18.85 million, for a shortfall of $17.69 million.[38] Schott settled the suit with the limited partners on May 13, 1991, but the terms of settlement were not made public.

Then, in early October 1991, Tim Sabo, who had served as the Reds' controller but was fired by Schott after testifying on behalf of the limited partners, filed his own lawsuit against the Reds' owner. Sabo's suit charges, among other things, that Schott "asked him to fiddle with Reds' books and report expenses in the wrong years, so that Schott could derive tax advantages."[39] Sabo also claims that Schott instructed him not to hire any blacks in his department, saying, "I don't want their kind here." Of the forty-nine employees in the Reds' front office, only two are minorities.[40]

The issues of integrity raised by the suit against Schott have surfaced frequently enough among other owners: Fred Saigh's tax evasion; George Steinbrenner's proclamations on absentee ownership or dealings with Howard Spira, a small-time gambler and convicted extortionist; Charles Finley's breach of contract with Catfish Hunter; Ted Turner's suspension for tinkering with player contracts; Lou Perini's repeated assurances to the people of Milwaukee that he had no intention of moving his team to Atlanta,[41] and so on.

Thomas Monaghan, owner of the Detroit Tigers and the Domino's Pizza chain, seems to fancy himself as a spiritual leader. His Catholic lay organization, Legatus, has chapters across the United States, Central America, and Mexico and strives, among other things, to bring moral values into the workplace. Yet Monaghan's pizza company has been sued for religious discrimination and for instigating wreckless driving in over one hundred cases.[42] Domino's guarantees pizza delivery within thirty minutes. Its drivers are paid minimum wage in most areas, use their own cars, buy their own insurance, and pay for their own repairs. In a 1987 suit, Monaghan twice failed to appear for deposition after court orders had been filed.[43] He seems to exhibit the same disdain for Detroit's mayor, Coleman Young, as he does to the court system. According to Mayor Young, Monaghan did not return his phone calls about new stadium construction between March 1989 and October 1991.[44]

Gussie Busch was as unscrupulous as any of them. His longtime executive vice president for marketing at Anheuser-Busch, Edward Vogel, assessed his boss: "He had no morals. None! What he did have was charisma. Hitler also had charisma. So did Al Capone."[45] Another of Busch's executives concurred: "Gussie was one of the most ruthless, immoral, terrible despots who ever lived."[46]

Buzzie Bavasi, who spent forty-five years as a baseball executive with the Dodgers, Padres, and Angels, commented on one of his former employers, the first owner of the San Diego Padres, banker C. Arnholt Smith: "He was in trouble with the law over income tax evasion and grand theft . . . and was ignorant about baseball matters."[47]

In his autobiography, Hall-of-Famer Hank Greenberg explained why after three decades in the game, the last fourteen years in management and ownership, he left professional baseball in 1961: "For me it was the end of the road for baseball. I had lost interest in the game. I was completely dissatisfied with the Commissioner and with the other owners. I found their word wasn't worth their bond."[48] He added, "There was no integrity at all among the owners. They were egotistical as far as their other businesses were concerned. Most of them owned their own businesses and came into baseball as more or less a lark, like Tom Yawkey. He was very wealthy and bought the Red Sox and you couldn't talk to him. He just felt that his judgment, because of the millions of dollars that he controlled, was much better. . . ."[49] And: "The only owner I ever knew who gave a damn about his players was Bill Veeck."[50]

Three years later there was ample cause for another owner's disgruntlement. The CBS purchase of the Yankees in September 1964 needed to be approved by a three-fourths vote among the AL owners. At issue was baseball's prohibition against one individual participating in the ownership of more than one team. Joseph Iglehardt was the Baltimore Orioles' board chairman and part owner, as well as a holder of a large portfolio of CBS stock (40,000 shares worth roughly $1.66 million at the time) and chair of the Finance Committee at CBS. Further, according to James Edward Miller: "Press inquiries revealed that a number of league owners had financial ties with the giant television network."[51] Only after an affirmative decision on CBS's purchase was made and Bill Veeck published an article on the affair in *Sports Illustrated* charging duplicity did Iglehardt decide to sell his stock in the Orioles. Arthur Allyn, the owner of the White Sox at the time, unsuccessfully resisted CBS's bid and was scandalized by the behavior of the other owners in the case. Veeck reports on a conversation in which Allyn told him: "I always thought you had gone overboard in what you said about these guys and I want to apologize. You didn't go far enough. These creeps are even worse than you ever said they were."[52]

Is there any reason to believe that the owners have reformed themselves in more recent times? Perhaps, but there is still cause for concern. Consider the following.

Item.   In 1980 AL owners voted 11 to 3 against allowing Edward De Bartolo, owner of football's San Francisco 49ers, to assume ownership of the White Sox. The reasons given: He owned racetracks and was from out of town. But other baseball owners had one or both of these traits. One dissenting owner commented: "The AL unfairly and ruthlessly turned down a fine offer from a fine man. I am embarrassed."[53]

Item.   In 1987 the owners' television committee recommended a rule that team owners not be allowed also to own television stations. Their purported concern was over the growth of superstation coverage. Commissioner Ueberroth opposed the rule, arguing that superstation coverage would occur with or without an ownership linkage to baseball.[54] The rule passed over his objection and has been honored only in the breach. It is now considered a guideline.

Item.   In 1990 Joan Kroc tried to give her Padres to the city of San Diego. The old boys' club of owners disallowed the gift, claiming municipal ownership would be too cumbersome and give the business of baseball too much exposure.

Item.   During 1986 to 1988, the owners engaged in collusion against free agents. Collusion-related damages to players were fixed at $280 million.

Item.   Some have questioned the owners' motives behind their choice of the NL's 1993 expansion franchises. The owners passed by an able ownership group in St. Petersburg with a new domed stadium in rainy south Florida in order to award a franchise to H. Wayne Huizenga in Miami. Huizenga, owner and chief executive officer of Blockbuster Video, was already under contract with MLB to produce all of its official videos.

If integrity has been lacking in the ownership ranks, what can be said about the intelligence of management practices? Back in 1946 a special Steering Committee composed of prominent baseball executives (Will Harridge, L. S. MacPhail, Thomas Yawkey, Ford Frick, Sam Breadon, and Philip Wrigley) was set up by Commissioner Kenesaw Mountain Landis to report back to the owners on the state of the game. The committee concluded: "[Professional baseball] is big business, a $100,000,000 industry. . . . Through the years, however, the business of baseball has been run in the most haphazard way imaginable."[55]

Again, it is not clear that matters have improved much since then.[56] Commenting on the cause of the 1972 players' strike, owner Charles Finley stated: "Very few owners knew there was any surplus in the pension fund. That was the main problem. . . . The owners didn't understand what it was all about."[57]

In a 1983 interview Roy Eisenhardt, executive vice president of the Oakland A's and son-in-law of owner Walter Haas, Jr., commented: "So you always have this mega-ego out there, who's got a lot of money to burn. And this bigger fool is going to come along and pay those salaries. Those people are in it for self-aggrandizement purposes. They're in it for short-term hits. And the game suffers from it." Eisenhardt went on to elaborate that these remarks pertain to perhaps twenty of the twenty-six owners.[58]

Commissioner Ueberroth was demonstrably unimpressed with the owners' competence, repeatedly denigrating their intelligence and referring to them as "dumb," "stupid," and "whining, sniveling malcontents."[59] Economist Gerald Scully is not optimistic on this score either: "All these rapid increases in franchise values and revenues over the years just made it easier for baseball owners to be stupid."[60]

Pete Bavasi, former executive with the Padres, Indians, and Blue Jays, finds cause for optimism in the trend toward corporate ownership. He sees the idiosyncracies in partnerships and sportsmen owners diminishing as more systematic and accountable management styles are introduced by corporations. Certainly, Labatt ushered in sound management of the Toronto Blue Jays when Bavasi was general manager,[61] but one could hardly make the same claim for the Cardinals under Anheuser-Busch.[62] The Cubs under the Tribune Company has not distinguished itself as a trailblazer of a new era. Their 1991 moment of glory notwithstanding, others have raised critical questions about the efficacy of the Atlanta Braves' management under Turner Broadcasting Systems. More significantly, however, for the moment corporate penetration of ownership has affected only a handful of teams. It is still more common for a wealthy executive to have bought into baseball as an individual owner rather than through his corporation or for a group of owners to form a partnership.

Structural tensions on ownership in baseball are rising. The skyrocketing of salaries together with the dim prospects for growth in media revenues in the near future once again have many small-city franchises crying out that their teams are not financially viable. They argue that the only way to bring economic stability to the game is through greater revenue sharing among the teams. Compounding this historical source of friction, the large bounty from 1991 expansion fees produced a bitter conflict between AL and NL owners. If owners have had difficulty behaving in the best interests of baseball during a protracted boom, how will they fare as MLB growth decelerates?

ATOP THE PYRAMID?

The other element in baseball's self-governing structure is the commissioner. By design, the commissioner is supposed to rise above ownership struggles and act in the best long-term interests of the game. The individuals selected for the job have not always inspired great confidence. Judge Kenesaw Mountain Landis, who served as commissioner from November 12, 1920, until his death on November 25, 1944, occasionally challenged the owners on their excesses,[63] but he was so prone to excesses himself that he was not able to provide consistent leadership.[64] As baseball's first commissioner, Landis was regarded by fans and owners alike as a historical fixture of the game; subsequent commissioners did not enjoy the same perception and consequently had little independence from their employers. When they exercised such independence, they placed their jobs on the line.

Happy Chandler (1945–1951) succeeded Landis but was booted after one term because he alienated owners with his support for umpires' unionization and his admission of blacks into the game. He did not get the then-required three-quarters vote for reappointment.

The owners selected Ford Frick (1951–1965), longstanding president of the NL, to succeed Chandler. Frick served two terms and docilely presided over the move of the Dodgers and Giants to California, the suppression of the Continental League, and the sanctioning of CBS ownership of the Yankees. Many argue that the real commissioner, the *éminence grise*, during Frick's years was Dodgers owner Walter O'Malley. Judging by his parting words, fourteen years as the owners' henchman apparently left a sour taste in Frick's mouth: "So long as the owners and operators refuse to look beyond the day and the hour; so long as clubs and individuals persist in gaining personal headlines through public criticism of their associates; so long as baseball people are unwilling to abide by the rules they themselves make; so long as expediency is permitted to replace sound judgment, there can be no satisfactory solution."[65]

The owners' next choice put an even greater premium on servility. Prior to announcing the selection of retired Air Force Lieutenant General William Dole Eckert (1965–1968), one owner confided in a reporter: "We want a guy who won't be too big."[66] According to baseball historian David Voigt: "Eckert was a bumbler. He knew, and learned, little about baseball, and he feared his masters."[67]

Bowie Kuhn (1969–1984), previously one of MLB's lawyers, came next. Kuhn's mission was sanctimoniously to rid baseball of its immorality: drugs, extravagant player sales, gambling, and so on.[68] His policies were imposed inconsistently and erratically. In the end, Kuhn was ineffective in defending the owners' economic interests and in aggressively marketing the game. Ironically, after Kuhn left baseball he joined a law partnership that was sued for various improprieties by its clients. After the suits were filed, Kuhn moved from New Jersey to Florida, allegedly to protect himself and his $2-million investment account from his creditors.[69]

Peter Ueberroth (1984–1989) stands out among baseball's commissioners in his ability to discipline and galvanize the owners behind a clear economic project. Unfortunately for the owners, the project involved collusion and left them saddled with a $280-million settlement. Ueberroth always seemed more interested in his other business ventures, and left baseball after his first 5-year term.[70]

Bart Giamatti's five-month term was too short to assess. His apparent obsession with the aesthetic purity of the national pastime, however, led some to question his potential for effectiveness as a chief administrator or leader.

The owners appointed Fay Vincent, Giamatti's associate commissioner, to serve out the rest of Giamatti's term (through 1994). Opinions on Vincent have varied. His two major decisions through 1991 were the separation of Steinbrenner from operational control over the Yankees and the assignment of a minority share of the $190-million expansion reve-nue to the AL. The Steinbrenner decision was very popular with New York fans and easily digested by baseball's owners. Vincent's allowing Steinbrenner to retain 49 percent ownership of the team and Steinbren-ner's subsequent acquittal in the Spira extortion case, however, make the decision a curious one.

Vincent was under great pressure from both the NL and the AL regard-ing the division of NL expansion money. Previously, league expansion revenue stayed within the league, but earlier sums were diminutive in comparison to the 1991 windfall. Vincent opted for a compromise, giving the AL teams 22 percent of the money but requiring them to provide players in the expansion draft. His middle-of-the-road solution seemed to please no one. Twins' owner Carl Pohlad stated: "I haven't spoken to anyone who thinks it's a good decision." Jerry Reinsdorf of the White Sox affirmed the AL owners' point of view: "The commissioner made an incorrect decision. . . . It should have been a 50–50 split." Another owner, requesting anonymity, was more threatening: "That's it. Fay Vincent is history. Every American League owner I've talked to . . . has serious doubts about renewing Vincent's contract."[71]

Under current rules, election of a new commissioner requires a three-fourths vote (twenty supporters) by the owners, but reappointment needs only a simple majority (fourteen affirmative votes, with at least five votes in each league). Sanctions by the commissioner against individual own-ers, particularly unpopular ones, are palatable. Any general decision, however, such as the Vincent expansion fee allocation, is likely to alien-ate a substantial bloc of the owners. If the AL owner just quoted is correct, then Vincent will have a hard time finding five AL owners to support his reappointment. More generally, over the course of a five-year term, too many controversial decisions by a commissioner are likely to create too many enemies for reappointment.[72]

Given the structural fragility of the job, it is difficult to envisage even the most enlightened of commissioners successfully leading MLB through its maze of economic and political challenges in the 1990s. And even if baseball's internal challenges are confronted effectively, how can the owners' employee be depended on to respond fairly to the rights of the fans and the cities?[73]

C H A P T E R   3

Franchise Finances

Professional baseball is on the wane. Salaries must come down or the inter-est of the public must be increased in some way. If one or the other does not happen, bankruptcy stares every team in the face.

—Albert Spalding, former player, baseball executive, and entrepeneur,
January 1881

You go through The Sporting News *of the last 100 years, and you will find two things are always true. You never have enough pitchers, and nobody ever made money.*

—Don Fehr, Director, Players' Association

Baseball's owners must be the only U.S. citizens whose parents never told them the story of the boy who cried wolf. Their perennial cry of evaporating profits and imminent catastrophe in the presence of rapidly growing revenues and escalating franchise values is hard to take seri-ously. Marvin Miller ridicules the owners' plea for economic sympathy: "People are worrying about an industry where nobody is getting laid off, where jobs are not being reduced and where there is no foreign competi-tion. It's an industry where records are being set every year for revenues and profits."[1]

But are franchise values assured of continuing their ascent to the heavens? If baseball is profitable in the present, does that mean it will be profitable in the future? If some teams are profitable, but others are not, what does this do to the competitive balance of the game?

These questions defy simple answers. Indeed, Major League Baseball itself set up a joint player-owner economic study committee following the 1990 lockout to explore these issues. One must begin by understanding the game's current economic condition.

THE STRUCTURE OF REVENUES

Major League Baseball has three main sources of revenue: broadcasting revenues, gate and stadium revenues, and licensing revenues.

Broadcasting Revenues

Until 1945 almost all of a baseball team's revenue came from ticket and concession sales. Since then radio and television broadcast revenues have grown rapidly, accounting for roughly 3 percent of total revenues in 1946, 10 percent in 1950, 17 percent in 1956, 28 percent in 1970, 38 percent in 1985, 42 percent in 1988, and 50 percent in 1990.[2]

Broadcasting revenues come from both local and national sources. Since the early 1960s the local component of television broadcasting has grown at 13.0 percent annually, while the national component has grown at 19.9 percent (see table 3.1). Accordingly, the national share in total broadcasting revenues has risen from 25 percent in 1960, to 30 percent in 1971, to 44 percent in 1979, and to 49 percent in 1990.[3] It is likely that this trend will begin to reverse itself in 1994, if not earlier (see chapter 7).

The significance of the trend lies in the fact that national broadcasting revenues are distributed equally among the franchises,[4] while the distribution of local broadcasting revenues is unequal and growing more so. Table 3.2 shows that the ratio of the top to the bottom team in local media receipts increased from 5.3 to 1 in 1964 to 18.5 to 1 in 1990. Perhaps more significant than the ratio is the absolute disparity, which grew from $1.3 million in 1964 to an estimated $52.6 million in 1990. The latter sum is more than twice the size of the most expensive team payroll ($23.3 million) in 1990, or 1.35 times the size of the largest team payroll ($38.9 million) in 1991.

TABLE 3.1
National Television Broadcasting Revenues
(millions of dollars)

Year	Amount Per Year	Annual Amount Per Club
1950	1.2[a]	0.1
1960	3.3	0.2
1970	16.6	0.7
1976–79	23.2	0.9
1980–83	47.5	1.8
1984–89	187.5	7.2
1990–93	365.0[b]	14.0[c]

Sources: U.S. Congress, House, 1952, p. 280; Michener 1976, p. 360; Ross 1989, p. 679n; Broadcasting Magazine, 7 March 1988, p. 54, 6, March 1989, p. 40, 5 March 1990, p. 35.

[a] Numbers are rounded to the nearest decimal.
[b] Income from the national radio contract during this period is $12.5 million a year. It is not included in this figure.
[c] The average amount over the four-year period. According to the 1989 10-K Report (p. 11) of Turner Broadcasting System, Inc., the actual annual amounts will be $12.77 million in 1990, $13.35 million in 1991, $14.27 million in 1992, and $15.27 million in 1993.

TABLE 3.2
Local Broadcasting Revenues
(millions of dollars)

Year	High	Low	Major League Total
1964	1.6 (Houston)	.3 (Senators)	14.3
1965	1.8 (Houston)	.3 (Senators)[a]	15.8
1984	11.7 (Yankees)	1.2 (Mariners)	105.4
1985	14.0 (Yankees)	1.6 (Mariners)	116.9
1990	55.6 (Yankees)	3.0 (Mariners)	342.1

Sources: Berry and Wong 1986, vol. 1, p. 62; Paul Kagan Associates, Media Sports Business, 30 June 1991, p. 2. Figures for 1990 are estimates from Financial World, 9 July 1991.

[a] Tied in 1964 and 1965 with the Kansas City Athletics.

These disparities are somewhat mitigated by a modest revenue sharing of "net receipts" from pay television that has been in place in each league since 1982.[5] In the National League, each team pays its opponent 25 percent of "net receipts" from any pay television contract prorated per game. One problem in implementing this agreement is that "net receipts" is not clearly defined. To determine "net receipts," teams can deduct a variety of actual or imputed costs from their gross revenues: rent for the broadcast booth, electricity, production costs, team promotion, or other expenses. The American League changed its formula in September 1991, retroactive to the entire 1991 season. The new system calls for paying 20 percent of net receipts into a league pool to be divided equally among the clubs. But the AL concept of net receipts remains ambiguous. The Yankees, for instance, are arguing that not only can broadcasting-related costs be deducted, but also a good share of their contract with the Madison Square Garden cable network is for the rights to rebroadcast Yankee games and for the use of the Yankee insignia. The Yankees claim net receipts should apply only to revenue from the rights for live game broadcasts.[6] At this writing, the matter was still unresolved.[7] For major league teams that have ownership ties with their broadcasters, the formulas in both leagues are subject to further manipulation in an effort to minimize shared revenue.

Since 1985 there has also been an agreement between those teams carried on a superstation (Braves, Cubs, Mets, Yankees)[8] and MLB to make compensatory payments to the central fund.[9] The size of these payments is proportional to the number of homes that receive the rebroadcasted signal around the country and the number of games televised. The most widely distributed superstation is WTBS, which carries the Braves (both WTBS and the Braves are subsidiaries of Turner Broadcasting). The Braves paid MLB $7.5 million in rights fees in 1989, $9 million in 1990, and $10 million in 1991. At the Braves' election, the agreement can be extended to 1992 and 1993 for $12 million and $15 million, respectively.[10]

Gate and Stadium Revenues

In 1950, 76 percent of all team revenues came from ticket sales and an additional 14 percent came from concessions, stadium clubs, stadium advertising, and parking.[11] Since then these shares have drifted steadily downward: In 1975 ticket sales accounted for 61.5 percent of all revenues, while stadium-related revenues came to 12.8 percent of the total;

by 1988 ticket sales had fallen to 40.6 percent and stadium-related income remained around 13 percent.[12]

Although the share of ticket sales in total revenue has been falling, gate revenue has grown handsomely in absolute terms. This increase owes to rising attendance, higher ticket prices, and new income from luxury boxes.

As shown in Table 3.3, attendance has grown steadily since 1960 and in six of the last seven years has set new records. In 1991 attendance reached 56.9 million, or 3.1 percent above the previous record set in 1989. The 1991 record is all the more impressive because it was accomplished despite the late-season closing of the Montreal Expos' domed Olympic Stadium due to structural damage. Games were rescheduled at the last minute for the ballpark of the opposing team; the Expos' home attendance in sixty-seven dates was only 978,045, and the unscheduled away games were poorly attended.

Ticket prices have also increased, but over the last forty years they have not gone up as rapidly as consumer prices in general. Thus real ticket prices (adjusted for inflation) were 9 percent lower in 1990 than in 1950 (see the last column in table 3.4).

Baseball executives have been quick to point out that the sport has kept itself affordable to the U.S. working class. Indeed, the public relations value of this reality is hard to overestimate given baseball's special status as exempt from the country's antitrust statutes. On more than one occasion MLB has reminded Congress of its reasonable ticket prices. Former commissioner Kuhn, for instance, testifying in the House in 1982, stated: "I believe that baseball continues to be the very best bargain in sports entertainment."[13] A glance at Table 3.5 strikingly confirms this point.

Nonetheless, three qualifiers are necessary. First, baseball ticket prices have been increasing in real terms since 1980, albeit at a modest pace. Second, parking and concession prices at the ballpark have been increasing very rapidly. For an average family, ticket prices are less than half the cost of attending a ball game.[14] Anyone who has tasted a $6 special hot dog at Toronto's SkyDome can attest to this. Third, the average ticket prices publicized by MLB do not include the premiums paid on luxury boxes. For example, the average luxury box seat at a Yankee game costs $69, but when the Yankees publish their average ticket price, they count that luxury box seat as costing $12—the price of a normal box seat. The differential of $57 is considered to be the value of amenities, not the actual admission price. Were this peculiar practice rectified, average ticket prices would increase substantially. (The figures shown in table 3.4 do not reflect this adjustment.)

TABLE 3.3
Attendance
(in millions)

Year	Number of Clubs	Total Attendance	Attendance per Club
1950	16	17.5	1.09
1955	16	16.6	1.04
1960	16	19.9	1.24
1965	20	22.4	1.12
1970	24	28.8	1.20
1975	24	29.8	1.24
1976	24	31.3	1.31
1977	26	38.7	1.49
1978	26	40.6	1.56
1984	26	44.7	1.70
1985	26	46.8	1.80
1986	26	47.5	1.83
1987	26	52.0	2.00
1988	26	53.0	2.04
1989	26	55.2	2.12
1990	26	54.8	2.11
1991	26	56.9 [a]	2.19

Sources: Markham and Teplitz 1981, p. 67; *Statistical Abstract of the United States*, various years, and *Official Baseball Guide*, various years.

[a] This is a preliminary figure.

TABLE 3.4
Average Baseball Ticket Prices

Year	Box	General Admission	Overall	Overall (1990 prices)
1950	n.a.	n.a.	$ 1.60	$ 8.74
1960	n.a.	n.a.	$ 2.05	$ 9.11
1970	n.a.	n.a.	$ 3.18	$ 10.79
1980	n.a.	n.a.	$ 4.53	$ 7.23
1984	$ 7.71	$ 3.33	$ 5.93	$ 7.51
1985	$ 8.19	$ 3.48	$ 6.21	$ 7.60
1986	$ 8.57	$ 3.61	$ 6.70	$ 8.04
1987	$ 8.95	$ 3.96	$ 6.89	$ 7.98
1988	$ 9.60	$ 4.53	$ 7.17	$ 7.98
1989	$ 9.84	$ 4.59	$ 7.61	$ 8.07
1990	$ 10.26	$ 4.47	$ 7.95	$ 7.95

Sources: Unpublished data from MLB; *Economic Report of the President, 1990*, p. 362; Scully 1989, p. 105.

TABLE 3.5
Comparative Entertainment Ticket Prices
Best Seats in the House

Event	1970	1980	1990
Yankees	$ 4.00	$ 7.50	$ 12.00
Knicks	$ 8.50	$ 14.00	$ 45.00
Rangers	$ 8.50	$ 15.00	$ 45.00
Broadway	$ 15.00	$ 30.00	$ 60.00

Source: *New York Times*, 20 October 1990, p. 45. Copyright © 1990 by The New York Times Company. Reprinted by permission.

With or without these qualifiers, general admission prices are still relatively low, and, at least compared to other team sports, admission to baseball games is affordable for most families. Why do baseball executives follow these ticket-pricing policies? Are they concerned that they will lose their antitrust exemption or invite regulation if they charge higher prices? Are low admission prices a loss leader in order to get people into the ballpark so they will spend money on concessions and souvenirs? Or are baseball executives simply behaving uneconomically and not maximizing profits?

The answer most probably is none of the above. First, baseball distinguishes itself from other team sports in that it plays many more games during the course of a season and/or the seating capacity of its ballparks is much greater than that of an indoor arena. Second, the additional (marginal) cost to the home team of one more fan attending a game is very close to zero. Hence, a profit-maximizing team will try to set ticket prices to maximize total gate revenues (ignoring costs). Gate revenues are maximized at that price where the price elasticity of demand for tickets is equal to one; that is, when the percent change in price (in one direction) is equal to the percent change in attendance (in the other direction). Business strategy is actually a bit more complicated because what the team will really try to maximize is gate revenues plus net income from concessions and parking.

Consider the following illustration. Assume a team has one ticket price ($10) and an annual attendance of 2 million. Its gate revenues will then be $20 million. If it lowers the price by 10 percent to $9 and the attendance grows 5 percent to 2.1 million, then the total gate revenues will fall to $18.9 million. Economists say that demand is inelastic at a price of $10, suggesting that the team could increase profits by charging a higher price. In reality, however, since the cost of tickets is around only half the cost of attending a game, when ticket prices go down by 10 percent, the cost of attending a game goes down by only some 5 percent. Thus, in this example, the price of the product goes down by approximately the same percent that the demand (attendance) goes up. If these two percentages are the same, then total revenue will not change (the additional 5 percent or 100,000 people at the ballpark will increase spending on concessions),[15] and the team is charging a profit-maximizing price for its tickets.

Statistical (econometric) techniques can be used to estimate whether teams are setting ticket prices at a profit-maximizing level. Although the evidence we have is inconclusive, it is consistent with the claim that owners are maximizing their profits.[16]

Other evidence on the economic effect of ticket pricing can come from pricing experiments. During June 25–27, 1991, seat prices at the Houston Astrodome were reduced by $4 across the board (between a 33 percent and an 80 percent reduction depending on the seat) and parking was reduced from $4 to $2. During the three-game experiment attendance was more than double the season average, and it rose with each game. Concession prices were also cut in half, but food sales increased less than 20 percent.[17] The outcome with ticket prices and attendance suggests a high demand elasticity, but as a three-day experiment it tells us little about what would happen if the lower prices were applied over a full season. Certainly a good part of the result was from novelty and promotion; another part was from people who chose to attend their yearly ball game during the discount period rather than at another time during the season.

Whether most fans would react positively or negatively to a change in ticket prices, it has become increasingly clear that some corporations and wealthy individuals are willing to spend a lot more than $10 or $12 for a seat to a ball game. People have variously attributed the concept of luxury boxes to Roy Hofheinz, who owned the Houston franchise in the mid-1960s when the Houston Astrodome was built, to former Dallas Cowboy owner Clint Murchison, or to former Miami Dolphins owner Joe Robbie, but luxury boxes in baseball can be traced back to 1883 when A. G. Spalding built a new stadium in Chicago with a seating capacity of 10,000 and complete with a "row of 18 private boxes above the grandstand replete with cozily draped curtains . . . and luxurious arm chairs."[18]

Luxury boxes' modern incarnation as a major revenue source for sports franchises, however, owes a lot to the efforts of Hofheinz, Murchison, and Robbie. Their physical decor and comfort bears little resemblance to what Spalding provided. Michener described an ostentatious luxury box he visited in the mid-1970s:

It consists of two large rooms plus bar and bathroom on one level, three bedrooms and two baths on the next. . . . The entire floor area is covered with expensive carpeting from Belgium, on which have been placed massive pieces of Renaissance furniture providing seats on the main floor for some sixty guests. The wall decorations are paintings from Europe. . . . The bar was imported from London, a stupendous affair along which forty or fifty of the guests can stand comfortably. At convenient spots are pull-out tables on which the guests can place their trays while dining from the lavish smorgasbord. The upstairs bedrooms are done in French provincial style with ornate furnishings of considerable value. The bathrooms are marble and gold.[19]

Albeit typically more modest, luxury boxes are an essential accoutrement to any modern stadium. In 1991 all but two baseball stadiums offered luxury boxes, with a wide variety of availability, design, and price. Table 3.6 provides a partial sampling of luxury boxes rented by teams in 1990.

Generally, the more modern the stadium, the more important are luxury boxes in generating gate revenue for a franchise. Shea Stadium, built in the 1960s, has forty-seven "Diamond View Suites" rented at an annual rate of $73,000 each and yielding a potential $3.43 million in revenue, or roughly 14 percent of Mets' gate revenue. The White Sox's new 1991 park contains eighty-two skyboxes with annual rental rates going from $60,000 to $90,000, adding a potential $5 million to team revenues, or roughly 25 percent of gate receipts. Revenues produced by the luxury boxes at Toronto's SkyDome are more difficult to estimate because there are 160 such boxes with dozens of different leasing and purchasing arrangements. Many boxes were sold privately at a minimum price of $250,000; others are leased up to ten years, others by the game.[20] The Detroit Tigers are hoping their new stadium will yield an additional $10 million in annual revenue.[21]

Food and beverage service to the luxury suites, of course, provide additional income. The Houston Astros publish a "Luxury Suite Menu" that in 1990 included the following dishes[22]:

Fajitas $75.00
Tenderloin of Beef $160.00 ($45 extra for a carver)
Smoked Salmon Platter $150.00
Guacamole $25.00

New limitations on business deductions in the 1986 tax reform do not seem to have deterred noticeably the growth of income from luxury

TABLE 3.6
Luxury Boxes: A Sampling, 1990

Team	Type	Number Seats/Unit	Total Price	Implied Price/Seat/Game
Astros	Suite	18	$720/game	$ 40
Athletics	Suite	12	$740/game	$ 62
	Suite	18	$860/game	$ 48
Braves	Suite	24	$750/game	$ 31
Cardinals	Suite	12	$198,000/5 yrs.	$ 41
Cubs	Suite	12	$1750/game	$ 146
	Suite	12–15	$135–195,000/3 yrs.	$ 46–$54
Expos	Suite	12	$350/game	$ 19
Giants	Suite	12	$360/game	$ 20
	Suite	8–20	$30–40,000/yr.	$ 25–$46
Mariners	Suite	6	$5,000/27 games	$ 31
Mets	Suite	15	$365,000/5 yrs.	$ 60
Pirates	Suite	10	$20,000/yr.	$ 25
Rangers	Suite	8	$23,100/yr.	$ 36
Red Sox	Suite	14	$45,000/yr.	$ 40
	600 Club	4	$25,000/yr.	$ 77
	Super Box	28	$2,000/game	$ 71
Toronto	Suite	16	$4,500/game	$ 281
	Suite	16–22	privately owned	
Yankees	Suite	14	$78,000/yr.	$ 69

Source: Compiled by the author based on information from team ticket offices.

Note: Arrangements vary: Some suites include two parking spaces; a few include snacks and beverage; some include passes to special concerts. The total suite capacity also varies markedly from one park to the next.

boxes. Since that reform, businesses with luxury boxes leased annually can deduct only the cost of a box seat for each seat in its suite (plus food and beverage expenses). Luxury boxes leased on a per-game basis still can be deducted fully.

The growing popularity of luxury boxes despite the restricted deductions seems to be linked to the dramatic shift in U.S. income distribution since the late 1970s; namely, the after-tax real income of the bottom three-fifths of the population fell by approximately 10 percent between 1977 and 1991, while the real income of the top fifth rose by over 20 percent and of the top 5 percent by nearly 60 percent during this period.

That is, the principal patrons of luxury boxes have seen their incomes soar in recent years, despite overall economic malaise.

Similar to revenue from national network and local pay television, MLB has long practiced revenue sharing from gate income. The NL practiced gate sharing in the last century. According to Voigt, there was a "struggle between rich and poor franchises . . . over the division of gate receipts. In this struggle the impoverished faction . . . succeeded in forcing a fifty-fifty division of gate receipts."[23] The initial even split resulted in each team receiving 27.5 cents per admission. As the base ticket price rose over time, the share going to the visiting team fell to 40 percent in 1892, 21 percent in 1929, 14 percent in 1950, 12 percent in 1977, and around 9 percent today.[24] The current formula requires each NL team to share 71 cents per admission; of this, 22 cents goes to the league office and 49 cents goes to the visiting team.

The AL began gate sharing at its inception as a major league in 1901, with the visiting team getting 30 cents for each grandstand seat and 20 cents for each bleacher, or 40 percent of revenues at the time.[25] Gradually, with increasing ticket prices, the visitors' share fell to 21 percent by 1953, when Bill Veeck proposed a return to a 40 percent share but was voted down with five in favor and three against (requiring two-thirds or six votes to pass). In 1965 the AL voted to give 20 percent of ticket receipts (after sales tax) to the visiting team, where the share remains today. Since ticket receipts do not include the premium paid for luxury boxes, neither league shares luxury box revenue. Concession revenue is not shared.

Licensing

Following the lead of basketball's David Stern and NBA Properties, MLB licenses rights to card companies, clothing manufacturers, game producers, and others.[26] These rights are for the use of MLB's insignias. MLB established a separate entity, Major League Baseball Properties, in 1987 to market and contract these rights.[27]

Total retail sales of goods licensed by MLB grew from $200 million in 1987, to $1.5 billion in 1990, and to a projected $2 billion in 1991.[28] In 1991 MLB Properties contracted with over 300 licensees that market 3,000 different items. MLB Properties has a standard royalty rate of 8.5 percent on net sales.[29] If the value of wholesale sales is 60 percent of retail and we apply an 8.5 percent royalty, this implies licensing revenues to MLB of $77 million in 1990 and $102 million in 1991.[30] These estimates exclude other income sources, such as approximately $1 million from Hollywood for the use of baseball uniforms in films.[31] This licensing income (minus management costs of MLB Properties, which could not reasonably exceed $5 million, and should be considerably less) would then go to MLB's central fund for equal distribution to the teams. Thus we might estimate that each team received roughly $2.7 million from licensing in 1990 and $3.7 million in 1991. In addition, individual teams are generating some of their own sales, such as the New York Yankees outlet on 59th Street, which sells cracked baseball bats at anywhere from $75 to $350, depending on the player.[32] Luxury items and designer clothing have been recently introduced, and their sales are growing rapidly. Foreign market retail sales grew from $10 million in 1990 to $34 million in 1991. A dozen specialty shops are slated to open in Japan over the next eighteen months, and in 1992 licensing will expand to include baseball's 152 minor league teams. MLB Properties expects annual growth of 15 to 20 percent in sales over the next several years.

Overall, team revenues in baseball have grown at 11.7 percent per year over the last twenty-one years. As shown in table 3.7, estimated average team revenue in 1991 of $58 million is over ten times what it was in 1970.[33]

Back in 1977, according to MLB's own records, in the AL 18.8 percent

TABLE 3.7
Growth of Average Team Revenues
(millions of dollars)

Year	Revenue
1970	$ 5.7
1977	$ 9.0
1983	$ 20.1
1989	$ 47.7
1990	$ 51.9
1991	$ 58.0[a]

Sources: Noll 1988, p. 17.34; Markham and Teplitz 1981, p. 85; USA Today, 28 November 1990, p. 2c; Media Sports Business, 30 June 1991, p. 3; Financial World, 9 July 1991, p. 36; Seattle Times, 8 September 1991, p. A1.

[a]Estimate.

of average team revenues came from shared sources; this share in the NL was 12 percent.[34] Today, due to three rapidly rising shared revenue sources (network television, licensing, and local pay television), these proportions are considerably higher. Netting out the expenses for operating MLB's central office and other central costs (for example, the $55-million annual contribution to the players' pension fund), we estimate that in 1991 the average AL team received 36.5 percent of its income from shared sources and the average NL team received 34.9 percent. Of course, these are only averages. Low-income teams receive considerably more of their income from shared sources (the Seattle Mariners received approximately 55.5 percent of their near-$36 million total revenues in 1991 from shared sources) and high-income teams considerably less (the New York Yankees' share would have been around 17.2 percent on 1991 total revenues of close to $110 million).[35]

THE STRUCTURE OF COSTS

Between 1970 and 1989 average team costs grew at 9.5 percent per year. Although data is not available for 1990 and 1991, total costs must have grown rapidly in these years because player salaries exploded with the end of owner salary collusion—the average salary growing by 20.2 percent in 1990 and by 42.5 percent in 1991. Player salaries were 17.6 percent of team revenues in 1974, grew steadily with the 1976 introduction of free agency to 41.4 percent in 1983, fell back to 31.6 percent in 1989 with collusion and rapid revenue growth, and increased again to an estimated 42.9 percent in 1991.

In addition to average major league payrolls of approximately $24.9 million in 1991 (ranging from a low of $12.0 million for the Houston Astros to a high of $38.9 million for the Oakland Athletics), teams spend anywhere from $4.5 million to $8.5 million on player development (minor league salaries, team expenses, and scouting).[36] Major league team expenses (transportation; road meal expenses; salaries for coaches, trainers, and managers) can run another $2 to $4 million. Player disability insurance is carried in varying amounts, with a typical policy costing $500,000 or more.[37] Stadium and front office expenses can also be several million dollars each, with considerable variation from team to team. The details of team costs are considered proprietary and are not available for recent years, but a rare look at a cost breakdown for the late 1970s was provided by MLB in conjunction with a congressional hearing. The data

TABLE 3.8

Growth of Average Team Total Costs

(millions of dollars)

Year	Total Costs
1970	$ 7.0
1977	$ 10.3
1983	$ 22.6
1989	$ 39.5

Source: Noll 1988, p. 17.34; Markham and Teplitz 1981, p. 85; *USA Today*, 28 November 1990, p. 2c; *Media Sports Business*; 30 June 1991, p. 3; *Financial World*, 9 July 1991, p. 36; *Seattle Times*, 8 September 1991, p. 41.

in table 3.9 are for all major league teams (twenty-four in 1976 and twenty-six in 1977).

There is an important distinction to be made between operating costs and total costs. Operating costs refer to incurred expenses in the actual operation of the team. Additional costs not directly related to the functioning of the team include player depreciation (discussed in chapter 2) and interest expenses (discussed later).

A significant part of baseball's operating expenses is paid for out of the central fund. The largest such expense is the players' pension and benefit plan. Annual payments into this plan increased from $8.3 million in 1978, to $33 million in 1986, and $55 million in 1990.[38] Also paid out of the central fund are the salaries, benefits, and expenses of MLB's sixty umpires. In 1991 umpire salaries ranged from $70,000 to $195,000 including bonuses.[39] Together with meal money and transportation costs, total central fund payments for umpires must come to around $12 million. A not-insignificant expense is Commissioner Vincent's handsome 1992 salary of $1 million.[40] In light of Vincent's repeated refrain regarding the game's economic difficulties, it is interesting to note that his salary was raised 67 percent from $600,000 in 1991. MLB also added a new director of its Player Relations Committee (PRC) for 1992, while retaining the services of former director Chuck O'Connor and his law firm as chief legal counsel. The new PRC director, Richard Ravitch, will earn $750,000.[41] Deputy Commissioner Steven Greenberg and other executives in the central offices probably command salaries in the neighborhood of $500,000. Nor can their expense accounts be trivial: Flying the commissioner first class to each major league city so he can

TABLE 3.9
Team Cost Structure, 1975–79
(millions of dollars)

	1975	1976	1977	1978	1979
Operating Costs	144.0	161.7	206.5	230.3	266.9
	(100%)	(100%)	(100%)	(100%)	(100%)
Team Expenses	52.3	60.6	82.7	97.7	118.7
	(31.5%)	(32.4%)	(35.0%)	(36.8%)	(39.3%)
Of which:					
Player Salaries[a]	n.a.	n.a.	n.a.	59.9	75.8
	n.a.	n.a.	n.a.	(22.6%)	(25.1%)
Player Development	22.1	22.9	26.8	29.0	33.4
	(13.3%)	(12.3%)	(11.3%)	(11.0%)	(11.1%)
Stadium Operations	28.4	32.0	37.9	41.6	45.6
	(17.0%)	(17.1%)	(16.1%)	(15.7%)	(15.1%)
Ticket Dept. and	12.4	13.9	19.0	19.4	22.4
Promotion	(7.4%)	(7.5%)	(8.1%)	(7.3%)	(7.4%)
General and	23.0	27.0	33.6	35.4	38.8
Administrative	(13.9%)	(14.5%)	(14.2%)	(13.3%)	(12.8%)
Other	4.7	4.2	5.5	6.1	6.6
	(3.5%)	(2.8%)	(2.7%)	(2.7%)	(2.6%)

Source: Calculated by the author from data presented in Markham and Teplitz 1981, pp. 85 and 159.

[a]Does not include workmen's compensation or pension payments, which in 1979 totaled approximately $9.5 million.

watch a ball game and accommodating him in four-star hotels, not to mention spring training facilities and the venues of quarterly owners' meetings, doubtless add several million dollars more to central office expenditures.

PROFITS

Before attempting to decipher profitability figures, it is necessary to understand exactly what is being measured. Profits are intended to be a return on investment. Investing in baseball teams, as we suggested in the last chapter, yields both measurable and unmeasurable returns. Sometimes owning a team benefits another business, sometimes it makes the owner famous, and sometimes it is just plain fun. Insofar as baseball ownership is fun, part of the investment return takes the form of utility from consuming the pleasure of ownership.

If measured profits of a franchise are negative, the team is not necessarily a bad investment. Indeed, if one considers only the negative book profits reported by MLB for practically every year between 1974 and 1985, it would be impossible to explain the eruption of franchise values that took place over this period. The value of a franchise will approximate the discounted value of future estimated profits, where profits are conceived broadly to include all forms of return. If these values are high and rising, there must be (an expectation of) a significant and growing return. The value of companies in an unprofitable industry simply does not rise over time.

Measured profits, then, tell only part of the story. No condolences should be sent to the owners on their basis alone. But measured profits can also be revealing, so it is important to quantify them as accurately as possible.

The pitfalls in measuring baseball profits are well known. While serving as vice president of business operations for the Toronto Blue Jays, Paul Beeston described the dilemma: "Anyone who quotes profits of a baseball club is missing the point. Under generally accepted accounting principles, I can turn a $4 million profit into a $2 million loss, and I can get every national accounting firm to agree with me."[42]

For most of its history under the reserve clause, MLB by its own records was profitable. Table 3.10 shows that the industry even made profits during the depression. During 1945 to 1950 the industry's return on net sales reached a lavish 20 percent.[43]

In connection with congressional hearings, MLB released detailed data

TABLE 3.10
Average Annual Profits per Team, 1920–50

Years	Current Prices	1990 Prices
1920–29	$115,000	$863,100
1930–39	$14,375	$137,804
1940–49	$116,250	$849,800
1950	$47,813	$261,300

Sources: U.S. Congress, House, 1952, pp. 1321–42, 1417–29, 1599–1609, 1636; Andreano 1965, p. 156.

on profitability during the late 1970s. We can see the Beeston principle in action in table 3.11. Despite reported book losses in every year between 1975 and 1979, MLB had substantial and growing operating profits. Player depreciation as it is practiced in baseball (explained in chapter 2) has no economic rationale. The category of "interest expense" corresponds in large measure to loans made for the purchase of a franchise. It is properly interpreted as a return to capital.

Consider the following example. Suppose the City of New York were to arrange with George Steinbrenner and his partners to buy the Yankees for $250 million (with any existing debt canceled), and the city financed this by issuing stock at $1 a share of up to $1,000 per person to residents of the city and its surrounding suburbs. The new owners of the Yankees would have no debt and no interest expense.

Alternatively, suppose the city still bought the team but retained it as municipally owned and financed the purchase by issuing $250 million in revenue bonds bearing 8 percent interest.[44] The annual interest expense in this latter case would be $20 million. If, during the first year of ownership, the Yankees had an operating profit of $45 million, the team could report a book profit of zero if its purchase was financed by revenue bonds. The city could claim half of the purchase price for player contracts and depreciate them over five years (at $25 million a year). This would reduce profits to $20 million, exactly the interest expense. Of course, such accounting chicanery would do the city little good since it would have no tax obligation in the first place, but it could prove to be quite lucrative to private ownership. If the team, on the other hand, were financed by the issuance of stock to residents, then the team would show book profits of $20 million. In either case, the underlying economic

TABLE 3.11
Baseball Profits, 1975–79

	1975	1976	1977	1978	1979
Reported Book Profit	−5.0	−5.1	−4.7	−1.4	−1.0
Player Depreciation	4.1	4.5	6.5	7.5	8.4
Interest Expense	4.0	4.2	4.3	4.3	5.4
Operating Profits[a]	3.1	3.6	6.1	10.4	12.8

Source: Markham and Teplitz 1981, pp. 85, 159–64.

[a] Equal to reported book profits plus player depreciation plus interest expense. Discrepancies due to rounding.

reality is the same: An investment of $250 million would yield an operating profit of $45 million, a handsome return of 18 percent; only the accounting practices make the results appear otherwise.

Now, it happens in the actual case of the Yankees (and many other teams) that the owning partners got together, established a corporate entity, loaned the entity money, and with the money bought the team. Because of this arrangement, in 1982 the Yankees paid Steinbrenner $2.4 million in interest.[45] Yankees' reported book profits, accordingly, were reduced by a further $2.4 million.

Table 3.12 depicts operating profits reported by MLB to *USA Today.* They show that, according to the industry's own figures, baseball turned profitable during the Ueberroth era. In part, this heightened and increasing profitability was a consequence of collusion. The fall in reported profits in 1990, in turn, is attributable to the end of collusion and consequent higher salaries, as well as partial payment of the collusion settlement.

What about the precollusion years? Are the reported losses meaningful? As part of the 1985 negotiations between the owners and players over a new basic agreement, the owners opened their books (albeit in summary form) to the MLBPA. The MLBPA, in turn, hired Stanford University economist Roger Noll to evaluate these books and the owners' claims of losses. Noll's analysis is sufficiently edifying to warrant pursuing it for a moment.[46]

TABLE 3.12
Reported Operating Profits in MLB,
1983–90
(millions of dollars)

Year	Profits
1983	− 66.6
1984	− 41.0
1985	− 7.1
1986	11.5
1987	103.2
1988	121.6
1989	214.5
1990	142.9

Source: USA Today, 28 November 1990, p. 2c; Associated Press, 19 November 1991.

Noll starts with the clubs' figure of a $56.8 million reported net book loss in 1984 (an average loss of $2.19 million per club). Total reported player amortization was $13.2 million ($509,000 per club for those reporting it explicitly). Net interest payments were $17.9 million (an average of $687,000 per club). Subtracting these two items reduces average losses per team to $998,000, or $25.9 million overall. Noll further adjusts for amortization of other intangible assets when explicitly reported, reducing economic loss per team to $904,000. With these basic adjustments, the so-called operating losses are less than half of reported book losses.

Owners were able to claim a total loss of $1.507 million per team, which, at the 50 percent marginal corporate tax rate then prevailing, created a tax reduction of approximately $753,000. Subtracting this tax gain from the adjusted loss yields an average loss per team of $151,000, or under $4 million for all of baseball.

It is instructive to follow Noll's analysis a bit further. Consider the following examples. The Turner Broadcasting Systems (TBS) owns the Atlanta Braves. In 1984 TBS paid the Braves $1 million for television broadcast rights, well below the league average of $2.7 million. Given that the Braves were the only team in the Southeast, that WTBS operated as a superstation broadcasting across the nation, and that it carried far more games than was the case on average, it is clear that the Braves were getting a terrible deal. Through the transfer pricing scheme, for public relations and tax reasons, Turner was taking money from one pocket and putting it in another. The Braves should have received at least the major league average in their local television contract. Noll conservatively estimates the sweetheart contract cost the Braves $1 million.

The St. Louis Cardinals have been part of the Anheuser-Busch corporation since 1953. The Civic Center Redevelopment Corporation (CCRC), which owns the team's ballpark, is also a division of Anheuser-Busch. In 1984 the Cardinals paid the CCRC rent somewhat below the league average. So far so good. More problematic, however, is the fact that the CCRC keeps all revenues from parking and concessions. The league-wide average for these was $3.2 million in 1984. Since the Cardinals' home attendance in 1984 was 17.9 percent above the league average, it is reasonable to assume that they would have earned at least $3.2 million in parking and concessions if they enjoyed a normal stadium contract. If we adjust this figure for the below-average rent, the Cardinals' net loss from their stadium contract would be approximately $2.6 million. Noll uses a more cautious estimate of $2 million.

The New York Yankees in 1984 had a book loss of over $9 million. The Yankees and the Oakland Athletics in that same year accounted for some 70 percent of baseball's combined operating losses. But the Yankees' reported loss is suspect. It includes $500,000 in charitable contributions;[47] travel expenses of double the league average; administrative expenses far in excess of the league average in practically every category; hidden expenses from the team's Tampa hotel and unusually high interest expenses. There are also reasons to believe some income sources were hidden or underreported.[48]

The Oakland A's had MLB's largest financial deficit in 1984, reporting book losses of over $15 million. Part of this came from a capital loss of $831,000 in purchased stocks and/or bonds. Front office personnel salaries totaled $1.25 million, $400,000 above the league average. Team replacement expense included $800,000 in signing bonuses, compared to an average $80,000, and $1.7 million in amortization of deferred compensation. An additional $800,000 loss from the sale of player contracts was claimed.[49] The A's sales and promotion effort is either highly inefficient or overstated on its books. In 1980 the A's spent $663,000 on marketing with game revenues of $6.59 million. In 1984 they spent $4.16 million on marketing, and game revenues grew to only $7.49 million. Thus, according to Noll's calculations, the team spent an additional $3.5 million in promotion and received an increment of only $0.9 million in game revenues. Poor management to say the least.

The Orioles in 1984 showed a profit of over $800,000; yet this appears to understate profits from baseball operation because their books showed a curious item—$2 million in stadium expenses associated with non-baseball activities.

The Dodgers, with net income over $6 million in 1984, spent a whopping $8.4 million on "general and administrative expenses," compared to $2.8 million on average. The principal cause of this extra expense was the $4.4 million spent on front-office salaries and benefits, more than four times baseball's average. Noll infers that owners are enjoying handsome salary windfalls and excessive perquisites and concludes that the real profit of the Dodgers was $3 million higher than reported.

The Chicago Cubs are part of the Tribune Company, as is their broadcaster, WGN. The Cubs' local media revenues in 1984 were $6.4 million, in the range for large-market teams at the time; what was atypical, however, was that the Cubs paid back WGN $810,000 for advertising, while the baseball average was $260,000 and the crosstown White Sox spent $285,000 on this item. This transfer price mechanism artificially depressed the Cubs' net income by $500,000.[50]

Noll identifies an additional $4.7 million of underreported income or overreported expenses in the statements of the Mets, Angels, and Expos. All told, Noll argues that baseball's combined net income in 1984 was understated by at least $25.9 million. One could quibble with Noll's precise estimates—in some cases they appear too small, in others too large—but on balance his numbers appear cautiously estimated. To be sure, as Noll notes, his list of adjustments is not exhaustive. He could not analyze many cases of corporate tie-ins (banks, airlines, hotels, media, ticket sales, law firms, auto dealerships, concessionaires, consulting firms, and insurance companies) for lack of data. If we compare the $25.9 million in adjustments with the estimated combined loss of $4 million for all teams after the tax shelter benefit is included, the result is an overall industry profit of over $20 million in 1984—a figure in sharp contrast to the figure shown in table 3.12 of an operating loss of $41 million or to the reported book loss of $56.8 million!

The kinds of accounting games that are played in baseball, of course, also can be played in other industries. Transfer pricing techniques, for instance, are widely used by multinational corporations to make their profits appear in countries with lower tax rates. But the presence of player contract amortization and the general lack of separation between ownership and management in baseball as prevails elsewhere in the U.S. economy present an unusual opportunity for accounting legerdemain. A joint stock company wants to report strong profits to affirm its successful management, to facilitate capitalization drives, and to exploit stock options for management. A baseball franchise commonly has none of these motives and concentrates rather on the politics and tax implications of transferring profits from one of the owners' operations to another.

Based on any definition of profits, in MLB there was an underlying trend toward increasing profitability from 1981 through 1989. Driven by gradually increasing attendance, rapidly escalating media revenues, the emergence of significant licensing income, and the retarded growth of player salaries during the 1986–89 collusion years and their aftermath, profits rose to record levels. Consistent with this strong profitability, franchise values reached new heights.

FRANCHISE VALUES

Increasing franchise values is nothing new to baseball or professional sports in the United States. Economist James Quirk estimates that an equity investment in every U.S. professional sport at its beginning would have yielded a rate of return up to 1990 three times as high as that on the Standard and Poor's 500 over the same period.[51]

Table 3.13 shows that average franchise values in the 1980s were 69.6

TABLE 3.13
Growth in Baseball Franchise Values
(thousands of dollars)

	1910s	1920s	1930s	1940s	1950s	1960s	1970s	1980s
Number of Sales	6	9	4	11	10	10	9	12
Average Sale Price	$585	$1,019	$673	$1,563	$3,516	$7,637	$12,622	$40,696

Sources: Davis and Quirk 1975, p. 5; *Official Baseball Guide,* various years.

Note: These averages do not include the price of expansion franchises or ownership consolidations except in the 1980s.

times greater than they were in the 1910s, indicating a compound yearly rate of appreciation of 6.3 percent over the seven decades.[52] The rate of appreciation would be even more dramatic if we were to consider the beginning of the 1910s and the end of the 1980s, rather than the decade averages, or if we were to go back to the commencement of the modern era in 1903. In that year, for instance, the New York Yankees (then the Highlanders) were bought for $18,000; they were sold again in 1915 for $460,000; again in 1945 for $2.8 million; in 1964 for $13.2 million; in 1973 for $10 million; and today are estimated conservatively to be worth $250 million. Between 1903 and 1991 the value of the Yankees has appreciated at a compound annual rate of 11.4 percent.

Several facts indicate the acceleration of franchise values after 1985. George Argyros bought the Seattle Mariners in 1981 for $13 million and sold them in 1988 for $77 million. The team did not have one winning season.[53] The Texas Rangers, previously purchased in 1974 for $10.47 million and consistently a second division team, were sold in March 1989 for a record $79.3 million. Prior to the sale of the Mariners and Rangers, the most expensive sale was of the Detroit Tigers for $43 million in 1983.[54] According to a 1991 survey by *Financial World*, six major league teams are worth in excess of $175 million.[55] Similar figures have been estimated by other appraisers.[56] The Baltimore Orioles, ranking sixteenth out of twenty-six in total revenues, reportedly were being offered for sale in 1991 by Eli Jacobs for $200 million.[57]

THE DISTRIBUTION OF PROFITS

If the baseball industry as a whole has been profitable through 1991, there is still the problem that some franchises are financially very strong while others appear to be quite weak. This inequality is reflected by the disparity in estimated franchise values, team revenues, or profits. Top-team to bottom-team ratios in either franchise values or revenues exceed three to one. Estimated profit disparities are more extreme. *Financial World* estimated New York Yankees' profits in 1990 at $24.5 million[58] and Cleveland Indians' losses at $6.8 million. Despite reported 1990 industry profits of $142.9 million, Commissioner Vincent claims that ten teams lost money in 1990.[59] Indeed, it seems to be an annual ritual that no matter how bountiful the year, MLB proclaims that eight to twelve teams suffered losses.

On the one hand, even if the MLB's reports are credible, there is nothing wrong with some teams losing money in each year. The whole entertainment industry is a gamble. More motion pictures lose money than make it, and roughly only one in five record albums shows a profit.[60] Nobody ever said that capitalism guarantees profit. On the other hand, if it is the same teams that lose money year in and year out, then baseball could have a problem of financial stability or imbalanced competition on the playing field. Even in this case, however, the problem is avoidable if baseball's rich teams are willing to extend the practice of revenue sharing.

But how serious is the problem at the bottom end? Is Vincent's claim credible? Why does *Financial World* report that only six clubs lost money in 1990? Why did Roger Noll state in 1991 that "The leagues aren't in the financial trouble they say they are. . . . Everybody is just fine financially as far as I'm concerned"?[61] Why did an anonymous owner assert, "What all this spending shows is just how healthy the industry really is"?[62]

Let us consider three teams from "small" markets that have been discussed most frequently as financially fragile franchises: the Pittsburgh Pirates, the Seattle Mariners, and the Kansas City Royals. The Pirates are in the seventeenth largest media market in the country and had local television and radio contracts worth an estimated $7.7 million in 1990.[63] The Pirates had book losses in every year between 1985 and 1989 and operating losses four of these five years.[64] In 1990, despite winning their division and setting an attendance record, the Pirates reported a book loss of $7 million. The Pirates' payroll rose from $6 million in 1986 to $15.5 million in 1990. Leaked documents to *Sport* magazine resulted in the details depicted in table 3.14 being published on the team's financial condition.[65]

Since the Pirates were last purchased in 1985 (with the aid of a $20- to $25-million grant[66] from the City of Pittsburgh, which has no equity participation), the team was still amortizing its player contracts. In 1988 it was the large amortization deduction that resulted in the Pirates' operating profit being converted into a book loss. In 1989 the team also reported an operating loss, but here there is accounting gimmickry. The

TABLE 3.14
Pittsburgh Pirates' Income Statements,
1988–89
(millions of dollars)

Category	1988	1989
Revenues		
Home Gate	$ 11.1	$ 11.4
Road Gate	1.0	1.0
Local Broadcasts	4.5	5.8
Central Fund	6.3	6.9[a]
Concessions	2.7	1.9
Other	2.2	3.1
TOTAL OPERATING REVENUES	27.9	30.2
Operating Expenses		
Team Operations	$ 8.7	$ 14.6[b]
Player Development	5.2	5.8
Broadcasting	0.7	0.9
Stadium and Game Operations	4.3	4.5
Promotion and General Administration	6.0	5.7
TOTAL OPERATING EXPENSES	25.0	31.4
Operating Profit (Loss)	2.9	(1.3)
NONOPERATING EXPENSES AND INCOME		
Amortization	(4.2)	(3.4)
Interest Income	1.1	1.1
Interest Expense	(0.8)	(0.7)
Book Profit (Loss)	(1.0)	(4.3)

Source: Sport, June 1990, p. 71. Reprinted from SPORT Magazine, June 1990.

[a]$2,716,000 already subtracted as prepayment for expected collusion expenses.
[b]Of this, $11.3 million for team salaries.

team's revenue from MLB's central fund is reduced by $2.716 million as a set-aside on future collusion payments. Yet the actual collusion payments did not begin until 1991. There is no economic justification for this accounting treatment. If the Pirates wanted to be conservative and put aside funds for a future liability, they could have taken their full income from MLB's central fund and invested it in U.S. Treasury Notes. Thus what is reported as both an operating and book loss in 1989 might be more reasonably interpreted as a profit of $1.4 million.

The claimed loss of $7 million in 1990 is suspect for the same reasons. Revenues actually grew by $10 million in 1990 while the player payroll increased by $5.5 million. How then could reported team book losses increase by $2.7 million? The 1990 loss includes a write-off of $8 million for the eventual collusion settlement. This means that the Pirates wrote off their entire collusion obligation by the end of 1990, the year before payments were to begin and two years before final payments were due. If we are to believe their financial statement, it also means that the Pirates forfeited any interest income on the sequestered balance. A final extraordinary item for the Pirates that made their payroll situation in 1990 atypical is that the club had an obligation to pay released pitcher Walt Terrell $2.1 million under a three-year guaranteed contract. Last, no licensing income is explicitly reported in either year. It may or may not be partially included in the "other" income category. Of course, in 1992 and 1993 the Pirates will benefit from their share of the NL expansion booty, an additional revenue of $12.33 million per NL team.[67]

The Seattle Mariners, though in a somewhat larger media market than Pittsburgh, do not have a city with a baseball tradition; nor, before 1991, a winning team. Their situation is undoubtedly more difficult. New owner Jeff Smulyan bought the team with his partners for $77 million in 1989. Smulyan's chief partner is Morgan Stanley & Co., which owns a $20 million equity stake in the team and lent Smulyan an additional $40 million at no interest to help him buy the team. Smulyan says his team lost $20 million in his first two years.[68] As we detail in chapter 6, however, when appropriate adjustments are made for interest costs and player depreciation allowances, the Mariners' losses during 1989–90 were small. If further adjustments are made for one-time extraordinary expenses and excess budgeting, the Mariners' actually operated with a modest profit despite their poor field performance. Smulyan's real cash-flow problems stem from the large losses in his radio network, Emmis Corporation, not from the Mariners.

But complaining about Seattle's support for his team is a no-lose proposition for Smulyan. Either he will get some of the $16 million in the additional support he seeks from the city or he will have laid the public relations groundwork to move his team to Tampa–St. Petersburg or to sell his franchise. Commissioner Vincent has said that he will not stand in the Mariners' way if they want to move.[69] If the Florida Marlins, one of the two new NL 1993 expansion franchises, are worth $95 million, without a competitive group of major league ballplayers, without a farm system, and without national media money until 1994, then Smulyan can parlay his $77-million investment into a $100-million-plus asset with a franchise relocation.

The Kansas City Royals are in the country's twenty-fifth-largest media market. Their local media revenue is an estimated $3 million, at the bottom of the major leagues, with Seattle.[70] Their owner is pharmaceutical millionaire Ewing Kauffman, perceived by some to be baseball's last big-spending sportsman owner. According to the legend, Kauffman is in baseball to massage his passions, not his profits.

To be sure, Kauffman is a big spender. His Royals have been in the top ten in team payrolls since 1986. But paying high salaries and attempting to attract the best available talent is not the same thing as throwing in the towel on profits.

Whitey Herzog played major league baseball for eight years before becoming one of the game's most respected coaches and managers. He managed three teams, one of which was the Royals.[71] In his autobiography, Herzog ridicules Kauffman's claim that he lost $1.8 million in 1985: "There's no way—if you draw two million people—that you can lose money. Unless you're trying." He goes on to estimate that the Royals in 1985 had $21.1 million in revenues and $13.5 million in operating expenses, or over $8 million in operating profits.[72]

Thus, while it is conceivable that the Mariners and perhaps the Indians and another team or two experience real losses, the losses appear to be manageable. Moreover, with good management, losses in one year can be transformed readily into profits in the next. It is well to recall that in 112 years of major league baseball, there has been only one bankruptcy filing.[73] Repeated losses seem to require several ingredients simultaneously: a smaller market, either no baseball tradition or a tradition destroyed by neglect, a team with a consistently losing record, and perhaps bad management. The Indians may lose money today, but back in the early 1950s, the last time they won a pennant, they held major league attendance records. Since then they have gone thirty-seven years without a division championship and have had more ownership groups (eight) than winning seasons (six). There's nothing wrong with Cleveland as a baseball city.

To argue that the baseball industry has been financially healthy, however, is not to establish that it will always be so. Ominous signs are on the horizon, and in the end the boy who cried wolf was devoured. Most troubling perhaps is the projected drop in national media revenues. While these revenues may begin to fall in 1994, they likely will be offset in the aggregate by increases in local media revenues. The distributional implications of the shift in revenue sources can be dramatic. Since national media revenues are fully shared and local media revenues are scarcely shared, small-city teams, though economically viable in the early 1990s, may no longer be so after 1993. If small-city teams will become more marginal, then big-city teams will become more financially robust. The argument for increased revenue sharing in this case becomes more compelling.

For the moment, though, professional baseball is economically healthy and all of its teams are either profitable or nearly so. Before undertaking an analysis of baseball's economic future, we must first take a closer look at player performance, including its relationship to salaries and competitive balance, at the minor leagues, the teams' relationship to cities, and the media.

CHAPTER 4

Player Performance and Salaries

During the 13 years I have been in the major leagues, I know of no player who has been exploited.

—Bob Friend, 1963, Pirates' pitcher

In my view, what I found [in 1965] was [that baseball players] were the most exploited people I had ever seen . . . worse than Cesar Chavez's grape pickers at the time.

—Marvin Miller, former director of the Players' Association

I personally feel the way the players are being compensated is going to change. It has to, simply because of the trouble the smaller markets are going to have. I do feel the way the players are being paid, the average players won't make as much money. . . . The superstars will always be up there, but the average contract will probably level off quite a bit.
—Paul Molitor, 1991, Milwaukee Brewer and American League representative
to the Players' Association

Players' salaries at the major league level have lost not only all sense of proportion, but sense of reason.
—Charles Bronfman, outgoing owner of Expos at the December 1990 baseball
winter meetings

Basically, all our similarities are different.
—Dale Berra, Yogi's son and former player with the Pirates and Yankees

The expensive settlement of Collusions I, II, and III as well as the proviso in the 1990 Basic Agreement calling for triple damages in future collusion cases sent player salaries skyrocketing again for 1991 and after. Average major league salaries rose from $597,537 in 1990 to $851,492 in 1991, an increase of 42.5 percent.[1] The 1991 season contracts included 123 players with salaries equal to or in excess of $2 million, 32 players with salaries of $3 million or more, as well as the first $5 million average annual salary. Early indications suggest that average salaries in 1992 will surpass $1 million, and the Cubs' Ryne Sandberg will enjoy baseball's first $6 million average annual salary. Even baseball's prodigal prince, José Canseco, has raised his eyebrows in disapproval of Roger Clemens's four-year $21.5-million contract: "He should definitely be paid the highest of all the pitchers, but that much for going out every four or five days, I just don't buy it."[2]

More philosophically, Bob Tewksbury, pitcher with the St. Louis Cardinals, opines:

> As a fan of the game, I'm worried about the state of baseball. I mean, what's the incentive to do well? The salaries, it seems like, are just based on service time. Don't get me wrong. The personal side of me says, "Hell, if these guys can go out and make millions of bucks, I can do it, too. All the better." But I really think something has to be done. . . . You hear about people losing their houses and losing their jobs. Then you look at what is happening in baseball, and it's hard to figure out.[3]

A *New York Times*/CBS News poll of 1,283 adults conducted in April 1991 found that by more than a three-to-one margin the respondents felt that the typical baseball player is paid too much; only 1 percent felt that the typical player was paid too little.[4] Most people, however, do not hold it against the players; a strong majority (56 percent to 21 percent) also feel that the owners make too much.

What does it mean to be paid "too much"? Why would an owner attempting to maximize profits pay a player more than the value he produced for the team? Whether or not the present pay levels are justified, what impact do multimillion-dollar, long-term contracts have on the game?

PERSPECTIVES ON PAY

Depending on one's perspective, practically any salary structure could be rationalized. Consider the evidence that might be assembled by those who believe baseball salaries in the 1990s, to use former Expos' owner Charles Bronfman's words, "have lost all sense of reason."

Item. One of baseball's least fortunate teams economically, the Pittsburgh Pirates in 1988 had a total player payroll of $6.5 million; in 1991 eight Pirates filed for salary arbitration asking for $9.37 million, not in salary but in increases!

Item. In 1869, when baseball's first professional team was formed, the top player, Harry Wright, earned seven times the average income in the country. By 1976 the average (not the top) ballplayer earned eight times the U.S. average income. In 1991 the average ballplayer earned forty-seven times the average income. While Babe Ruth's $80,000 in 1930 was eighty times the average U.S. income, Don Mattingly's $3.4 million in 1991 was 160 times the average.

What might the 1 percent who believe that players' salaries are still too low argue?

Item. When Ruth earned $80,000 in 1930, the Yankees had an estimated gross income of $1 million.[5] That is, Ruth received approximately 8 percent of the team's total income. Don Mattingly, with the Yankees' top salary in 1991, received roughly only 3 percent of team income.[6]

Item. Baseball's leading lights earn considerably less than other stars in the entertainment industry. Compare the top baseball salary of $6.1 million to Bill Cosby's estimated $100 million, Merv Griffin's $80 million, Sylvester Stallone's $63 million, Madonna's $62 million, or Michael Jackson's $50 million. Indeed, by what standard are baseball's top stars worth less than chief execitive officers (CEOs) in major U.S. corporations, such as Steven Ross of Times-Warner, who *Forbes* estimates earned $78.1 million in 1990?

One learns in introductory microeconomics classes that in each of the above cases, the individual is paid according to the value of what he or she produces, the so-called marginal revenue product. Thus, if one movie studio offers Sylvester Stallone less than his market value, he can sign with another studio that pays him what he is worth. One important difference between what happens in the movie business and what happens in baseball is that the former is highly competitive. The prices (tickets, concessions, media contracts) established for consuming baseball, however, are by and large monopoly prices. This inflates the value of what a player produces above what it would be if competitive market forces were at work. (It also reduces the number of major league teams and players, and increases team profits.)

How does one actually measure this value that is produced by employees? How, for instance, does Chrysler ascertain Lee Iacocca's marginal revenue product? How is it that the average CEO in Japan receives an income of $300,000 while the average CEO in the United States earns $2.8 million?[7] It turns out that for many types of jobs, custom, rather than marginal revenue product, is more decisive in determining pay. Peter Drucker, the leading U.S. expert on management, for instance, has said: "There is no correlation between company performance and CEO pay. When you look at it, the people who earn the most money have earned it in companies that have done pretty poorly." Leonard Silk, business columnist for the *New York Times*, concurs: Lee Iacocca got a 25 percent raise in 1990 as Chrysler's earnings slid 79 percent, and the average CEO's pay climbed 8.5 percent as average profits fell 7 percent.[8]

Because a baseball player's performance is much more readily quantifiable than is a corporate executive's or many other workers, it is easier to see if the standard of marginal revenue product applies. Of course, not everything about a ballplayer's contribution to team revenue is quantifiable, but relative to other team sports or other professions, the individual's performance is eminently measurable in baseball. Before considering the evidence on ballplayers' salaries and their marginal revenue products, it is necessary to get a fuller picture of their compensation package and the procedures of salary determination.

FORMS OF COMPENSATION

In addition to their basic salary, ballplayers receive a variety of other forms of compensation: promotional income, individual bonuses, team bonuses, licensing income, perquisites, and employee benefits. They also incur a not insignificant—many would say excessive—cost in the payment of player agents.

Information on promotional income (from television and radio commercials, endorsements, appearances, card signings, and the like) is proprietary and difficult to obtain. Clearly, players on big-city teams will derive more income from this source than those on small-city teams. Top athletes can make several million dollars annually from this source; Michael Jordan and Arnold Palmer each reportedly earned $9 million from promotions in 1990.[9]

Individual bonuses, as opposed to base salary, in baseball are not allowed to be based on measured performance—batting average, home runs, and so on. Rather, player bonuses are given for winning awards (such as most valuable player), making the All-Star team, or number of games played. Typical bonuses run in the $15,000 to $100,000 range per category and might total $200,000 or more for the top players.

Team bonuses come from a team's place in its division and from winning the division, the pennant, and the World Series. These bonuses are based on the World Series and League Championship Players' Pool, which is formed from 60 percent of the total gate receipts from the first four games of each Championship Series and 60 percent of the total gate receipts from the first four games of the World Series. This pool is then divided up as follows:

Third-place teams in each of the four divisions (4)	4 percent
Second-place teams in each of the four divisions (4)	12 percent
Championship series losers (2)	24 percent
World Series loser (1)	24 percent
World Series winner (1)	36 percent

The World Series winning team is guaranteed a minimum of $1,937,500 and the losing team $1,291,700 in the 1990 Basic Agreement.[10] Actual per-player shares among World Series' teams have varied, as depicted in table 4.1.[11]

When Marvin Miller took over as director of the Players' Association in 1966, the association needed an independent source of income. At the time, the only baseball card company, Topps, signed individual contracts with almost all major leaguers and many minor leaguers. A player received $5 to sign and $125 a year while in the majors for Topps's exclusive use of his photo in trading cards, sold either alone or with chewing gum.[12] Miller changed the relationship with Topps so that the company signed with the Players' Association, which then used some of the revenue for office expenses and divided the rest equally among all players and coaches (prorated according to the number of days on the twenty-five-man major league active roster). In 1969 the Players' Association licensing income was $400,000;[13] it grew slowly to around $700,000 in the late

TABLE 4.1
World Series (Full) Shares per Player

Year	Winners	Losers
1950	$5,738	$4,081
1960	$8,418	$5,125
1970	$18,216	$13,688
1980	$28,237	$22,114
1988	$109,741	$87,942

Source: Jennings 1990, p. 211. Reprinted by permission of Greenwood Publishing Group, Inc., Westport, CT, From *Balls and Strikes: The Money Game in Professional Baseball* by Kenneth Jennings. Copyright © 1990 by Praeger Publishers.

1970s.[14] By 1990 the licensing agreement of the Players' Association with Topps, Fleer, Donruss, Score, Upper Deck, and other card companies brought in over $57 million.[15] In 1991, the gross licensing income exceeded $69,000 for every (full share) player, coach, trainer, and manager.[16] (Players also pay union dues equal to $20 per day on the active roster or $3240 per full year.)

Player perquisites are plentiful. For instance, all players receive a half-dozen or so complimentary choice tickets for each game. When they are not given to friends and family, they can be traded for other perquisites. Most players are offered cash incentives from athletic equipment companies to try their goods. Some benefits just accrue to their celebrity status: free concerts, meals, and vacations. Players also receive $59 per day in traveling money before each road trip, even though, according to a sports reporter for the *Boston Globe*, buffet-style meals are provided in the clubhouse after (and sometimes before) each game.[17] All players are guaranteed first-class air travel and hotels on the road as well as at the beginning and end of the season.[18] Juxtaposed to the salaries of veteran players and superstars, these perquisites may seem trivial; for the young players earning near the minimum salary of $109,000 or for the great majority of fans, there is nothing at all trivial about them.

Players receive an excellent package of employee benefits ranging from life insurance, to a comprehensive medical and disabilities plan, to generous termination pay and a superb pension plan (with annuities up to the allowable maximum of $112,221 for players with ten years' service and commencing benefits at age sixty-two). Players can opt to begin receiving their retirement benefits as early as age forty-five. The benefits package is financed by a $55-million annual contribution from the Major League Baseball central fund.

Most players employ an agent. Until 1988 the activities of player agents went unregulated. Since 1988 agents must be certified by the Players' Association. The only requirements for certification, however, are that agents register and that they not work for management. Only one agent, Jerry Kapstein, has ever been barred. Although Marvin Miller says Kapstein was exploitative and unethical in his treatment of players, the reason he was barred was because he worked for the former owner of the Padres Ray Kroc.[19] The only regulations agents must comply with are that they must disclose their expenses emanating from representing each player, that their contracts with players cannot last for more than one year at a time, and that their fee cannot make the player's net salary fall below the minimum salary ($109,000 in 1992).

Although agents have been known to charge a fee as high as 10 percent of the player's total compensation, the more typical charge in the early 1990s is 5 percent or less.[20] Marvin Miller says an agent representing two or three top players could make a million dollars in a couple of days, doing little more than answering the telephone. Miller advises players would be better off hiring a top New York lawyer for $500 an hour; the total cost would only be around $8,000.[21] Lionel Sobel gives an example of possible abuse by agents: Suppose an amateur player signs a three-year deal with a $25,000 bonus, $75,000 for the first year, $90,000 for the second, and $110,000 for the third; since the total compensation is $300,000, the agent working at 5 percent would get $15,000, all paid up front out of the $25,000 bonus. If the contract is not guaranteed and the player does not make the team, the agent would still walk away with his $15,000, or 60 percent of the player's gross pay (his signing bonus in this case).[22]

PROCEDURES OF COMPENSATION

Effectively, there are three labor markets for major league ballplayers: those under the reserve clause without salary arbitration rights, hereafter called apprentices; those under the reserve clause with salary arbitration rights, called journeymen; and those free agents with no reserve restrictions, called masters.[23]

The separation between apprentices and journeymen is defined by the rules for salary arbitration. Under the 1990 Basic Agreement, to be eligible for salary arbitration a player must have completed more than two full years of major league service. Until a player so qualifies, he is basically compelled to accept the salary that his team wants to offer him or not to play baseball.

Journeymen are players qualifying for salary arbitration but not for free agency. Except in special cases, to qualify for free agency a player must have completed six full years in the major leagues.

Procedures for salary arbitration were established in the 1973 Basic Agreement and were put into practice prior to the 1974 season. Initially, the right of salary arbitration was extended to any ballplayer with two years of major league service and without a contract for the next year. In the 1985 bargaining agreement between the owners and the players, it was agreed that the eligibility for salary arbitration would be raised to three years of major league service beginning with the 1987 season. The 1990 agreement changed eligibility requirements once again, beginning with the 1991 season, by granting eligibility rights to 17 percent of the players with between two and three years' experience (this amounted to thirteen players for 1991).

Baseball practices what is known as final offer arbitration. When a case goes before an arbitrator, the player and the club each put forward a salary figure. The arbitrator must select one figure or the other; no compromise salary is permissible. The theory behind final offer arbitration is that it encourages each side to put forward more realistic figures and it fosters resolution of differences before going to arbitration. Reality bears out the theory: Nearly four-fifths of the cases filed for arbitration in baseball are settled before the hearing.[24] Further, a significant share of cases eligible for arbitration are settled before filing.

Arbitration hearings are not only expensive and time consuming, they often end up being acrimonious and divisive. An arbitrator is instructed to pick either the player's or the team's salary figure on the basis of the player's performance in comparison with others at his position and with his service level (that is, number of years in the major leagues). But there are ambiguities in the criteria: The arbitrator can overlook years of service if the player is atypical for his service category; the arbitrator is not allowed to take team finances into account but is allowed to take team attendance into account. Both sides go to the hearing armed with statistics, with the owner's agent typically disparaging the player's contribution. Regardless of who wins, the outcome is often embitterment. Atlanta Braves' general manager John Schuerholz commented on the process: "How can I promote cohesiveness and togetherness on a team when I'm minimizing a guy's talent?"[25]

In the eighteen-year history of salary arbitration through 1991, there were 317 decisions, of which the owners won 173 (54.6 percent). The lowest arbitration award ever went to Jack Heidemann for $15,750 in 1974; the highest went to Ruben Sierra for $5.0 million in 1992. Although the split in cases is roughly fifty–fifty between club and player victories, the owners believe that salary arbitration has proven excessively expensive to them. Arbitration seems to carry little downside risk for the players; the choice almost invariably is between one of two salaries, both higher than the previous year's. Even when they lose an arbitration decision, player salaries seem to go up handsomely. In 1990, for instance, the ten players who lost their cases saw their salaries go up an average of 100 percent.[26] In the history of arbitration, fewer than two dozen players have emerged with pay cuts.[27] Management has expressed two overriding concerns with the structure of the arbitration process: First, since the arbitrator is told to compare the player with the salary and performance of others at the same position, the process makes one team pay for another team's extravagance; second, the arbitrator is instructed

TABLE 4.2
Mean Salary and Years of Service, 1990

Years of Service[a]	Number of Players	Mean Salary
0	172	$108,396
1	90	$154,728
2	68	$262,810
3	67	$593,038
4	66	$760,201
5	55	$1,018,120
6	43	$1,047,719
7	47	$956,515
8	29	$1,191,424
9	20	$1,280,542
10	15	$1,229,979
11	14	$920,940
12	18	$1,320,307
13	7	$1,273,150
14	4	$1,068,764
15+	20	$1,398,812

Source: MLB Players' Association.

[a]Completed years of major league service.

not to consider the market size within which a team operates, making small-city teams meet the pay standards of big-city teams.[28]

There is little question that salary arbitration has provided a powerful boost to journeymen ballplayers. Table 4.2 shows a clear pattern of rapidly rising salaries beginning between the second and third years of service. The effect of salary arbitration is part of the explanation for this trend; the rest is due to the tendency for teams to attempt to sign a player to a long-term contract prior to his eligibility for free agency.[29] Indeed, prior to the 1992 season the Cleveland Indians, attempting to avoid the salary effects of arbitration, signed several first- and second-year players to long-term contracts. We will present more evidence of the salary effects of arbitration later.

The introduction of free agency in 1976 brought rapidly escalating salaries and long-term, guaranteed contracts. Free agency rights accrue to players after six years of major league service. Once attained, free agency comes with two constraints. First, once a player has declared himself a free agent, he cannot do so again, except in special circumstances, for another five years regardless of the length of his contract. Second, the team signing a free agent ranked in the top 50 percent at his position loses either a first- or a second-round amateur draft pick.[30] The draft compensation rule, of course, raises the cost of signing a free agent and, hence, lowers the value of free agents in the market. This market interference is justified by the owners in the name of preserving competitive balance on the playing field.

EVOLUTION OF SALARIES

Measured in 1990 prices, the average professional baseball player earned $34,672 in 1898, $73,635 in 1950, and $119,113 in 1976. That is, real average salaries grew at a rate of 1.46 percent annually between 1898 and 1950, and 1.87 percent annually between 1950 and 1976. Between 1976 and 1991, the first fifteen years of free agency, the real mean salary grew at an annual rate of 13.8 percent, or over seven times the rate of growth of the previous twenty-six years.

Star players have cut the trail for rising salaries. In 1947 Hank Greenberg with the Pirates was the first player to earn $100,000. Mike Schmidt earned $500,000 with the Phillies in 1977. Nolan Ryan earned $1 million with the Astros in 1980. Mike Schmidt was the first $2-million man in baseball in 1985. Robin Yount was the first to reach $3 million in 1990. Will Clark's contract with the Giants was the first to call for a $4 million

TABLE 4.3
Baseball Salaries
(Current Prices)

Year	Minimum Salary	Mean Salary
1898	n.a.	$2,200
1910	n.a.	$2,500
1929	n.a.	$7,531
1933	n.a.	$6,009
1939	n.a.	$7,306
1943	n.a.	$6,423
1946	n.a.	$11,294
1950	n.a.	$13,288
1951	n.a.	$13,300
1967	$6,000	$19,000
1969	$10,000	$24,909
1970	$12,000	$29,303
1971	$12,750	$31,543
1972	$13,500	$34,092
1973	$15,000	$36,566
1974	$15,000	$40,839
1975	$16,000	$44,676
1976	$19,000	$51,501
1977	$19,000	$76,066
1978	$21,000	$99,876
1979	$21,000	$113,558
1980	$30,000	$143,756
1981	$32,500	$185,651
1982	$33,500	$241,497
1983	$35,000	$289,194
1984	$40,000	$329,408
1985	$60,000	$371,157
1986	$60,000	$412,520
1987	$62,500	$412,454
1988	$62,500	$438,729
1989	$68,000	$497,254
1990	$100,000	$597,537
1991	$100,000	$851,492

Sources: Voight, 1983, I, p. 234; *Baseball Encyclopedia*, p. 6; U.S. Congress, House, 1952, p. 1611; Gregory 1956, p. 96; Berry and Wong 1986, vol. 1, p. 48; Lehn 1990b, p. 39; data from Players' Association.

annual salary (in 1992), and José Canseco was the first slated to earn $5 million annually from the A's (in 1994).[31] Canseco, of course, has long since been passed by. Ryne Sandberg signed a four-year contract extension with the Cubs prior to the 1992 season at an average annual salary of $6.1 million. (Annual average salaries will differ from actual yearly salaries due to varying time structures of contracts and signing bonuses.)[32]

As shown in table 4.4, the share of major league salaries in team revenues has fluctuated considerably over the years. In the late 1870s player salaries on the Boston Red Stockings came to over 60 percent of team revenues.[33] This share came down gradually until it went below 15 percent for the average team in the mid-1950s.[34] According to Jennings, in 1958 the players proposed that the salary share should be 20 percent, but owners rejected the proposal as extravagant.[35] As would happen so many more times, what the owners averred was out of bounds came to pass finally in 1977, when the average salary share surpassed 20 percent. After free agency was introduced, average salary share grew to around 40 percent, until collusion brought it back down after 1986 to a low of 31.6 percent in 1989. The share recovered to approximately 33.4 percent in 1990 and an estimated 42.9 percent of total revenue in 1991 (based on the twenty-five-man active roster plus players on the disabled list on August 31).[36] Significantly, the minor league share, primarily consisting of player salaries, did not increase appreciably after 1976. Minor league players, of course, have not been granted any relief from the reserve clause.

There is a natural temptation to compare baseball's salaries with those in other team sports, but the cost and revenue structure in basketball, football, and hockey are different from baseball's and from each other's. For instance, none of the other team sports has an extensive minor league system, and only hockey franchises maintain a minor league team. Further, professional basketball teams have only twelve players, while professional football teams have forty-five plus four on injured reserve.[37] In 1990 average team salaries as a share of team revenues was an estimated 41 percent in both basketball and football, 33.4 percent in baseball, and 30 percent in hockey.[38] Table 4.5 depicts average player salaries and their growth over the last decade. In baseball, basketball, and football salaries increased roughly fivefold between 1981 and 1991; in hockey the increase was half as great.

With baseball's soaring salaries came a change in the structure of contracts. In an effort to secure a stable roster in the context of free agency and the players' greater bargaining strength, after 1976 teams began to offer long-term, often guaranteed contracts.

TABLE 4.4
Salary Share in Team Revenues, Various Years

Year	Salary Share[a] (%)	Minor League Share[b] (%)
1929	35.3	10.3 (8.9 and 1.4)
1933	35.9	10.9 (6.7 and 4.2)
1939	32.4	7.5 (9.6 and −2.1)
1943	28.9	15.3 (11.8 and 3.5)
1946	24.8	5.4 (5.8 and −0.4)
1950	22.1	12.6 (4.1 and 8.5)
1974	17.6	13.3[c]
1977	20.5	11.3
1978	25.1	11.0
1979	28.1	11.1
1980	31.3	11.4
1981	39.1	n.a.
1982	41.1	n.a.
1983	41.1	10.9
1984	40.3	10.8
1985	39.7	10.4
1986	40.0	10.4
1987	35.2	12.2
1988	34.2	13.1
1989	31.6	12.6

Sources: U.S. Congress, House, 1952, p. 1611; Scully 1989, p. 118; USA Today, 28 November, 1990, p. 2C; data from Players' Association; Markham and Teplitz 1981, p. 159.

[a] Salary share through 1950 includes salaries to coaches and managers and is as a share of total expenditures, not revenues. Benefits are not included.
[b] Total expenditures on minor league system. In parentheses are first purchase of minor league contracts and second operating losses of farm system. Through 1979 share is based on total expenditures.
[c] 1975.

The only player to have a multiyear contract prior to 1976 was Catfish Hunter who, as mentioned, was awarded early free agency when A's owner Charlie Finley did not live up to the terms of his contract; in 1975 Hunter signed a five-year contract with the Yankees. By 1980, of 650 players 45.8 percent had guaranteed contracts: 4 percent for one year; 6.9 percent for two years; 8.8 percent for three years; 6.3 percent for four years; 14.2 percent for five years; and 4.5 percent for six years. Prior to

TABLE 4.5
*Average Player Salaries in Professional Team
Sports*

Sport	1981	1991
Baseball	$185,000	$851,000
Basketball	$180,000	$825,000
Football	$90,000	$466,000
Hockey	$108,000	$254,000

Sources: *Business Week*, 3 June 1991, p. 55; *New York Times*,
16 September 1991, p. C9.

the multiyear, guaranteed contract, disabled players received salary for
the rest of the year if they were disabled during the regular season and
nothing at all if they became disabled and were released during spring
training. If terminated due to lack of playing skill, they received thirty
days' pay if terminated during spring training and sixty days' pay if
during the regular season.[39] By 1985 well over 50 percent of contracts
were guaranteed.[40]

At the September 1985 baseball meetings, Lee MacPhail, then head of
the owners' Player Relations Committee, was one of the first to call to
the owners' attention the possible negative performance effects of guaranteed, multiyear contracts. MacPhail claimed that players with three-
year contracts and up experienced an average decline of nearly 20 points
in their batting average and an increase of almost 50 percent in the
amount of time spent on the disabled list.[41] Another study of 104 hitters
and 57 pitchers finds evidence of decreased performance after signing
long-term contracts.[42]

Economist Kenneth Lehn argues that long-term, guaranteed contracts
have increased player disability rates. The average number of players on
the disabled list was 89 between 1974 and 1976; that figure rose to 131
between 1977 and 1980.[43] Part of this increase was due to a rise in the
number of players, from 600 to 650 with baseball's expansion in 1977,
but when that increase is adjusted for, the disability rate still increased
36.5 percent. The new contract structure lowered the cost to the players
of being disabled, so they "consumed" more of it. Players have also
become more careful about protecting their valuable physical assets and
are less willing to play when partially injured.[44]

Many commentators have claimed that today's players, attempting to maximize their lifetime baseball income, put first priority on achieving good individual statistics and not risking injury. As sacrifice bunts, hitting behind the runner, and sliding hard into a base become less profitable, the team player becomes a rarer and rarer species. A sports writer for the *Boston Globe* summarized the matter as follows:

> At the very least, say most seasoned observers, the game has never been so fundamentally flawed in the way it is played. Players are more concerned than they used to be with putting up big individual numbers, because personal statistics—the most heavily weighted criteria in arbitration decisions—translate into more money, rendering virtually meaningless other, more subtle aspects, such as solid defense. Pitchers have entered into tacit agreements with hitters not to pitch inside—a fundamental tenet of pitching—because "It threatens my livelihood," as so many hitters have stated after being hit.[45]

Although this last claim about pitchers seems exaggerated, it is significant even if a small number of players behave this way.

Carrying through with this logic, players benched by managers may think first about their future income stream and second about whether or not the move is good for the team. Players called out by umpires may react as if they have been pickpocketed. Fans, resentful of the players' high incomes and attitudes, may become increasingly abusive, and players may react to the fans. Writing in *Baseball America*, Bob Nightengale asserted that Whitey Herzog gave up managing because he had "become disgusted by the game of baseball, with its greed and money-hungry players. After trying to cope with it for so many years, he finally gave up." Nightengale goes on to quote Herzog: "All of a sudden team baseball is gone. Especially for a guy in his walk [free-agent] year. He doesn't want to give himself up and hit the ball to the right side. Oh, he might act like he's doing it, but it doesn't happen."[46]

Steve Fainaru of the *Boston Globe* concluded a special report on the business aspects of baseball: "Some would say the game is in an increasingly bad mood. Tension between management and players, players and players, players and umpires, and, especially, players and fans, has never been more noticeable, mostly because of the salaries, the focus on which borders on obsession."[47]

Perhaps this interpretation is extreme, but few would deny that there is a tendency toward these tensions, which certainly raises questions about the desirability of modifying the salary determination process. In the next section we look at an element of this problem by exploring the relationship between salaries and player performance.

SALARIES AND PERFORMANCE

In 1974 economist Gerald Scully suggested a two-step method for determining a player's marginal revenue product (MRP), or the value of his contribution to team revenues. First, estimate the impact of team batting and pitching on team win percentage; and, second, estimate the impact of win percentage on team revenue. An individual player's effect on team batting or pitching can be calculated, and then his indirect contribution to revenues can be estimated. Several problems with using this method, such as what measure of batting or pitching performance to use, are discussed in some detail in appendix A. The estimates themselves are not meant to be precise, but they do give a general sense of the value of a player's contribution.

Using a modified version of the Scully model with data from 1986 through 1989, we estimated player marginal revenue products. Some of the results for star players are shown in table 4.6. The basic tendencies that hold for all players is observable from inspecting the results for these players. EXPL stands for exploitation; the more it exceeds 1, the more the player is paid below his MRP or the more he is exploited; the more it is below 1 the more the player is overpaid. Almost all the players with fewer than six years' major league service, or without free agency rights, are exploited; those with fewer than two years—the eligibility cutoff for arbitration in 1989—are exploited most intensely. The large majority of players with six or more years of service are paid in excess of their MRPs, except for those star hitters who enjoyed an exceptionally good year in 1989.

Table 4.7 shows that these patterns hold for all hitters from 1986 to 1989. The table also shows that, by our estimates, there was exploitation on average in each of the years (the value of EXPL exceeds 1.00 in the "All" service category). The appearance of diminishing exploitation, however, is mostly due to a statistical idiosyncracy in our procedure.[48]

If we disaggregate by service categories, we find that, on average, only players under reserve are exploited. Apprentices, without salary arbitration rights, were paid between roughly one-fourth and one-sixth of their net marginal revenue product. Journeymen, with arbitration rights and the imminent prospect of free agency, were paid on average between 50 and 64 percent of their MRP. Masters were paid on average 23.6 percent above their MRP in 1986, 31.6 percent above their MRP in 1987, 27.9 percent above in 1988, and 39.7 percent above in 1989.

Table 4.8 provides a more detailed breakdown on the incidence of exploitation among the players by category. Considering the four years

TABLE 4.6
Selected Star Hitters' Salaries and MRPs, 1989

Player	SER	PROD	SAL ($,000s)	MRP ($,000s)	EXPL	SAL90 ($,000s)	EXPL (+ 1)
Roberto Alomar	1	.723	150	827	5.51	390	2.12
Wade Boggs	7	.879	1775	1811	1.02	1900	.95
Barry Bonds	3	.777	360	1340	3.72	850	1.58
Bobby Bonilla	3	.848	740	2103	2.84	1250	1.68
George Brett	16	.793	1948	1176	.60	1839	.64
Ellis Burks	2	.836	275	1092	3.97	475	2.30
José Canseco	4	.875	1600	1209	.76	2000	.60
Will Clark	3	.953	1125	2839	2.52	2250	1.26
Eric Davis	5	.908	1555	1992	1.28	2100	.95
Andre Dawson	13	.783	2100	877	.42	2100	.42
Shawon Dunston	4	.723	550	510	.93	1250	.41
Carlton Fisk	19	.831	1220	966	.79	1750	.55
Julio Franco	7	.848	1275	1455	1.14	1633	.89
Mark Grace	1	.862	140	1630	11.60	325	5.02
Tony Gwynn	7	.813	1131	1698	1.50	1067	1.59
Rickey Henderson	10	.810	2120	1503	.71	2250	.67
Greg Jeffries	2	.706	100	859	8.55	200	4.29
Howard Johnson	7	.928	773	2888	3.74	1667	1.73
Ricky Jordan	1	.724	95	651	6.85	215	3.03
Wally Joyner	3	.755	975	1071	1.10	1750	.61
Roberto Kelly	2	.786	80	951	11.88	265	3.59
Barry Larkin	3	.821	343	1050	3.07	750	1.40
Fred McGriff	3	.924	325	2287	7.04	1450	1.58
Dave Magadan	3	.760	170	1145	6.74	395	2.90
Don Mattingly	7	.828	2200	1595	.73	2500	.64
Randy Milligan	2	.852	75	112	14.93	155	7.22
Kevin Mitchell	4	1.023	560	3245	5.79	2083	1.56
Paul Molitor	11	.818	1750	1407	.80	2600	.54
Dale Murphy	13	.667	2000	480	.24	2000	.24
Eddie Murray	12	.743	2331	1563	.67	2514	.62
Rafael Palmero	3	.728	212	408	1.92	300	1.36
Kirby Puckett	5	.844	2050	1586	.77	2817	.56
Tim Raines	10	.813	2105	1580	.75	2056	.77
Jody Reed	2	.769	175	726	4.15	300	2.42
Cal Ripken	8	.718	2467	429	.17	1368	.31
Ryne Sandberg	8	.853	925	1806	1.95	1550	1.17
Benito Santiago	3	.664	345	296	.86	1250	.24
Darryl Strawberry	6	.778	1455	1389	.96	1850	.75
Mickey Tettleton	5	.878	300	1399	4.67	750	1.87
Alan Trammell	12	.648	1300	307	.24	1800	.17

Note: SER is years on the 25-man major league roster prior to 1989 season; PROD is "production" or slugging plus on-base percentage; SAL is 1989 salary; MRP is estimated player net marginal revenue product; EXPL, exploitation, is MRP divided by SAL; SAL90 is the player's salary in 1990; EXPL (+ 1) is MRP divided by SAL90. Our measure of years of service differs slightly from the official measure.

TABLE 4.7
Relationship of Salaries to MRPs

Year	Service Category	Number of Players	Average Salary	Average MRP	EXPL
1986	All	199	$459,942	$607,628	1.32
	Less than 2 yrs.	35	$78,786	$361,580	4.59
	2–5 yrs.	95	$322,210	$644,612	2.00
	6+ yrs.	69	$842,914	$681,514	0.81
1987	All	238	$486,205	$638,962	1.31
	Less than 3 yrs.	65	$96,708	$563,573	5.83
	3–5 yrs.	80	$351,781	$670,492	1.91
	6+ yrs.	93	$874,068	$664,530	0.76
1988	All	274	$527,856	$605,948	1.15
	Less than 3 yrs.	67	$125,044	$552,673	4.42
	3–5 yrs.	87	$339,407	$524,415	1.55
	6+ yrs.	120	$889,385	$695,076	0.78
1989	All	277	$629,470	$634,514	1.01
	Less than 3 yrs.	51	$102,471	$421,534	4.11
	3–5 yrs.	92	$420,337	$661,643	1.57
	6+ yrs.	134	$973,628	$696,948	0.72

together, more than three-fourths of apprentices were paid below their MRP and almost three-fourths were paid less than half of their MRP. Roughly two-thirds of all journeymen were paid less than their MRP, but fewer than two-fifths were paid less than half of their MRP. Finally, over 60 percent of masters were paid in excess of their MRP.

As explained in appendix A, there is reason to believe that the formula applied to derive our measure of MRP is downwardly biased and hence may understate the degree of exploitation (or overstate the degree of overpayment). It is also important to recall that 1986 through 1988 were years of salary collusion by the owners; the collusion held down salaries for these years and for 1989 as well. Hence exploitation from 1986 to 1989 should not be construed as exploitation in 1990 or 1991.

One striking though not unexpected result of our estimates, elaborated in appendix A, is that there is a stronger correlation between salaries and service than between salaries and MRPs. Indeed, for apprentices the relationship between salary and MRP is not statistically signifi-

TABLE 4.8
Degree of Exploitation by Player Category, 1986–89

Category	Number	Exploitation[a] (% of players)	High Exploitation[b] (% of players)
Apprentices	255	77.6	71.8
Journeymen	338	66.9	39.9
Masters	418	38.5	11.2

[a]MRP/SAL > 1.
[b]MRP/SAL > 2.

cant at all. For all hitters together in 1989, salary increased by $242 for every $1,000 increase in MRP. In a perfectly competitive labor market, salary and MRP increases would be equal. For every additional year of major league service, salary increased by $78,700. (T-statistics on service were also considerably higher than those on MRP.) Close inspection of table 4.6 reveals another tendency: MRP in 1989 is more closely related to salary in 1990 than salary in 1989. Statistically, every $1,000 increase in MRP in 1989 was accompanied by a $499 increase in salary in 1990. That is, salary in a given year is more related to how a player performed in the previous year than how he performs in the current year. This result is testimony to the uncertainty of the salary determination process and the variability of player performance from one year to the next; it also lends insight into why wealthier teams have not been able to dominate on the playing field since 1976—an issue we discuss at length later.

If our MRP estimates are reasonable, how can we explain why a franchise owner would be willing to pay a player, particularly a free agent, above his marginal revenue product? There are, in fact, several possible explanations. Perhaps the most obvious explanation is that owners can misgauge a player's worth. This could happen for a number of reasons: poor judgment, unpredictability of performance (particularly when a change of venue is involved), pride and competitive pressure, and so on. Once a player attains free agent status, the monopoly relationship is in many senses reversed. The player under reserve competes with all major and minor league players for his job but can sell his services to only one owner. Yet from the standpoint of an individual owner, a free agent often has unique skills fitted for the team's needs. In this case, the player is a monopolist selling his services to competing teams. Even under these circumstances it would still not be in the interests of an owner to pay a player above his expected net MRP, but the competitive pressures of the market might well compel risk-taking and lead to errors.

A second explanation is that a player's value to a given team may be more than his actual physical product. Winning, of course, is a function of one team's performance relative to the opposing team's performance. By hiring a star, a team not only is buying that player's hits and RBIs but is assuring that its opponents do not benefit from the same. Our measure considers the player's value only in what he adds to his team, not what he takes away from the opposing team. The more a player's performance stands out relative to others at his position, the stronger will be this effect.[49]

Another reason is that owners seek team stability, and in the post-1976 era this necessitates long-term contracts. For tax and other reasons these contracts are usually structured to have higher pay in later years. Yet the average player reaches his peak performance years well before his contracted salary peaks. According to Scully, the average hitter's profile shows increasing performance until his sixth or seventh year in the major leagues and then trails off until his twelfth year when average performance is the same as it was in his first year.[50] Further, as already indicated, many analysts have claimed that long-term contracts reduce a player's motivation to perform and increase his motivation to protect his valuable physical equipment.

A fourth explanation is that owners may not attempt to maximize profits. If owners are "sportsmen," then they may satisfice[51] or even accept losses in order to assemble a winning team. A variation on this explanation is that owners may joint profit maximize rather than maximize on their baseball operations alone. Baseball may be a vehicle to enhance other business ventures. The better a team performs, the more it promotes the individual or corporate owner and, hence, the more it promotes other activities. Looking out for his or her reputation, an owner may be unwilling to risk the public opprobrium of letting go a star player or failing to sign a free agent.

Finally, it may be argued plausibly that the worth of an aging star player goes beyond what he actually contributes on the field. Such a player may draw fans to the ballpark whether or not he continues to lead the league in batting or home runs.

FREE AGENCY AND COMPETITIVE BALANCE

With the exception of Bill Veeck, prior to 1976 all baseball owners took strong stands on the necessity of the reserve clause to preserve competitive balance in baseball. Indeed, most players agreed. The stated fear was that the wealthy teams would get all the good players. Economist Simon Rottenberg published an article in 1956 that explained why such fears were unfounded.[52] As long as player sales and trades were permitted, he argued, the distribution of player talent across teams would be the same with or without the reserve clause.[53] With the reserve clause, poor teams could trade away or sell their expensive, talented stars to rich teams. Without the reserve clause, players would still tend to move from poor to rich franchises, but the players, not the club owner, would capture their economic rent or value. Thus, reasoned Rottenberg, eliminating the reserve clause would not by itself create a competitive imbalance and the rationale given for keeping it was spurious.

Rottenberg's argument was basically solid. There are nuances, however, that require qualifications in his conclusions. For instance, with poor clubs no longer as able to sell off their stars, an important source of revenue for these clubs is curtailed.[54] Other things being equal, this curtailment can create a greater revenue imbalance, which could lead to greater competitive imbalance. Further, Rottenberg did not consider the possibility that free agency might raise transactions costs (the costs of making and enforcing a contract), which, in turn, might affect competitive balance.[55]

By 1991, Major League Baseball had lived and flourished through fifteen years of free agency. It no longer has to rely on economists' theoretical arguments to know the impact of free agency on competitive balance. By any measure, competitive balance has not only not become more unequal since 1976, it has become noticeably more equal.

During the first fifteen seasons with free agency, twelve different teams won the World Series and sixteen different teams made it to the Series; only three teams (the Mariners, Indians, and Rangers) failed to win division titles. This equalizing tendency also manifests itself in a notable narrowing of team win percentages over time.[56] The contrast could not be sharper to the earlier period: From 1903 to 1970, teams from the four largest cities won forty-nine of sixty-eight pennants; from 1903 to 1964, a New York team won thirty-nine of the sixty-one World Series; and, from 1926 to 1964, the Yankees had thirty-nine consecutive winning seasons and finished first twenty-six times.[57]

Why has baseball's playing field competition become more balanced since 1976? Will this balance be preserved, or are forces at work to undo it?

First, the end of baseball's dynasties dates back more accurately to 1965, the year the amateur draft (described in the next chapter) was introduced, not to 1976. Between 1949 and 1964, the Yankees appeared in twelve World Series and won nine of them. Between 1965 and 1976, Baltimore appeared in the most World Series, four, and won two. Three consecutive Series victories for Oakland from 1972 through 1974, followed by two in a row for Cincinnati and then two in a row for the Yankees, led some to believe that dynasties were reappearing, but since the Yankees' repeat in 1978 no other team has won the World Series two years in a row. The amateur draft, mandating a selection in reverse order of finish, made it impossible for wealthier clubs to dominate the signing of top amateurs; not so coincidentally, it also eviscerated the "bonus wars" of the 1950s and early 1960s. (The highest signing bonus to an amateur prior to the introduction of the 1965 draft was $205,000 paid to Rick Reichardt by the California Angels in 1964. This sum was not exceeded until 1980, when the Mets paid Darryl Strawberry $210,000. The 1965 draft, then, whatever its contribution to competitive balance, seems to have made a major contribution to the owners' bank accounts.)[58] But since predicting the major league performance of an eighteen- or twenty-one-year-old out of high school or college never progressed far beyond dumb luck, the leveling effect of the amateur draft could not have been strong enough to account for the stunning reversal of baseball's dynastic patterns.

Second, team owners since 1976 have done a singularly unimpressive job of signing top-performing free agents or of paying a player according to his output. Consequently, average team salary has been related only tenuously to team performance: From 1984 to 1989, average team salary explained less than 10 percent of the variance in team win percentage ($r = .303$) and less than 12 percent of the variance in team standing ($r = .334$). Put differently, it has not been possible to buy a winning team. Evidence from earlier years, however, suggests that buying a winning team was not only possible, but likely.[59]

Why was it possible to buy winners in the past when it has not been possible in recent years? One reason might be the variable effect of long-term contracts on player performance.[60] Another might be the increased importance of players' emotional character as the game becomes more charged by money and scrutinized by the media. Insofar as emotions become a more crucial factor, player performance is bound to become more unstable. A complementary explanation might point to the emotional compatibility and/or synergy of members of a team; rich teams purchasing many high-priced free agents may end up with destructive ego conflicts.

Another explanation might lie in the quality of ownership. Economist Gerald Scully, for instance, has argued that all the money flowing into the game has only made it easier for the owners to be "stupid." Columnist George Will resonates to this line of argument: "as the Yankees have recently shown, the absence of baseball acumen in the front office can be a great leveler, regardless of financial assets."[61] Will might have added a few more teams to his list. In much of free agency's first fifteen years, many owners seemed to anoint mediocre players as lifetime stars on the basis of a career year and to expect that paying high salaries would solidify their new status. Was this really owner dimwittedness and arrogance, or was there an unspoken purpose behind some of the signings? Is it possible, for instance, that George Steinbrenner, his compulsive behavior and public utterances to the contrary, did not really want his Yankees to win year after year? If they did, after all, concerns about baseball's competitive balance would be validated and pressure for the Yankees to share more of their $110 million revenue with the Mariners, Brewers, Indians, Twins, and the rest of the impecunious teams would become irresistible.

It seems, however, that a more objective and powerful leveling force is at work, and that is the compression of baseball talent. In 1990, 0.00026 percent of the U.S. population played major league baseball, or 35 percent less than the share who played in 1903. At the same time, the population is increasingly fit athletically, blacks have been allowed in the game, Latins have entered professional baseball in large numbers, and the availability of baseball programs for training youth is far more extensive today.[62] Today's major league ballplayers, then, are a smaller fraction of an increasingly prepared population. The difference between today's best, average, and worst players is much smaller than it was twenty or forty years ago. This results in greater difficulty in selecting dominating players and in greater competitive balance among the teams.[63] It also makes individual season performance records more enduring.

Scully has argued that baseball's growing balance is a function of population dispersion; in particular, there is a tendency for small- and medium-size cities to grow more rapidly than big cities. This dispersion results in a leveling of media markets and hence of potential team revenues. Scully is right about the demographics, but this dynamic has not yet come to baseball. In fact, local sources of income have grown considerably more unequal over the last twenty years. What is true, however, is that there has been an equalizing trend in overall revenues among teams. This has been because MLB's central revenue sources (national media contracts and licensing) have been growing the most rapidly. As explained in chapter 3, these central revenues are shared equally among the teams. The result has been a consistent pattern toward total revenue leveling since 1950, as shown in table 4.9.

As total revenue distribution has become more equal since 1950, the distribution of team average salaries first grew more unequal from 1950 until the mid-1970s (as measured either by the ratio of the top-to-bottom team average salary or by the coefficient of variation) and then began to level, as shown in table 4.10. Although, as we have seen, salaries are not as closely correlated with performance, the leveling of team average salaries is consistent with the increase in competitive balance.[64]

In sum, the era of free agency has coincided with an increase in competitive balance, but the end of the reserve clause probably had little impact on this circumstance one way or the other. An important question for MLB is whether or not the strong competitive balance of the last fifteen years left to itself will be maintained in the future. Many people in baseball think as the richest teams earn revenues three times as great

TABLE 4.9
Distribution of Team Total Revenues

Year	Number of Teams	Mean[a] ($)	Standard Deviation	Minimum[b] ($)	Maximum[c] ($)	Maximum/[d] Minimum	Coefficient of Variation
1929	15	758,324	368,874	357,736	1,668,900	4.664	.4864
1933	15	430,211	185,398	202,880	782,607	3.857	.4309
1939	15	760,980	360,539	249,271	1,355,183	5.436	.4737
1943	16	678,141	192,288	369,850	1,054,988	2.852	.2835
1946	16	1,719,322	682,642	819,075	3,455,173	4.218	.3970
1950	16	2,002,217	821,103	736,778	4,211,964	5.716	.4100
1980	26	12,795,400	5,119,022	5,517,000	26,241,000	4.787	.4000
1982	26	16,224,000	6,235,326	7,961,000	37,340,000	4.690	.3843
1984	26	23,503,600	6,554,525	11,807,000	42,018,000	3.558	.2788
1986	26	28,701,400	9,319,654	n.a.	n.a.	3.161	.3247
1988	26	36,854,000	12,237,700	n.a.	n.a.	3.402	.3320
1990	26	51,715,400	15,837,300	34,000,000	98,000,000[e]	2.882	.3062

Sources: U.S. Congress, House, 1952, pp. 1599–611; Scully 1989, pp. 120–21; Financial World, 9 July 1991, pp. 42–43.

[a]Refers to average team revenue.
[b]Refers to lowest team revenue.
[c]Refers to highest team revenue.
[d]Refers to the ratio of highest-to-lowest team revenue.
[e]This is Financial World's estimate of New York Yankees' total revenue in 1990. It is almost certainly too low by $5 to $10 million.

TABLE 4.10
Distribution of Average Salaries by Team

Year	Number of Teams	Mean ($)	Standard Deviation	Minimum ($)	Maximum ($)	Minimum/ Maximum	Coefficient of Variation
1929	16	235,349	54,330	140,422	365,741	2.604	.2308
1933	16	187,815	43,772	138,758	294,982	2.125	.2330
1939	16	228,312	61,927	144,255	361,471	2.505	.2712
1943	16	201,040	44,204	135,405	301,229	2.224	.2198
1946	16	352,948	78,066	221,789	511,025	2.304	.2211
1950	16	432,562	110,651	234,125	651,605	2.783	.2558
1978	26	100,361	35,783	49,300	188,900	3.831	.3565
1980	26	142,757	49,198	55,000	242,900	4.416	.3446
1984	26	328,129	83,222	159,774	458,544	3.558	.2786
1986	26	415,153	122,036	187,850	657,657	3.500	.2939
1988	26	439,889	128,038	226,392	718,670	3.174	.2910
1990	26	597,001	134,077	279,326	804,643	2.880	.2245

Sources: See Table 4.9 and MLB Players' Association.

as the poorest teams, playing field inequality will inevitably reassert itself. They want more revenue sharing.

Andy MacPhail, vice president and general manager of the Minnesota Twins, is one such person, despite the fact that his small-city team won the World Series in 1987 and again in 1991. MacPhail is aware that the imbalance has not yet come and that people like himself have been predicting it for fifteen years, but he doesn't waiver: "Up to this point, I can't back that [prediction of imbalance] up, but do you have to have a nuclear bomb dropped on you to want some sort of disarmament?"[65]

Will the factors that have promoted leveling since 1965 continue in the 1990s and beyond? Some of the factors were idiosyncratic and can be expected not to return. For instance, one element behind the preservation of the Yankee dynasty through the 1950s and into the early 1960s was a hand-in-glove relationship to the Kansas City Athletics. According to baseball historian James Miller:

At the end of the 1954 season, [Del] Webb and N.Y. partner Topping [Yankees' owners] arranged for the Mack family to sell the financially ailing Philadelphia Athletics to a business associate of the Yankees' owners, banker and real estate magnate Arnold Johnson. The new owner immediately bought the rights to Kansas City from the Yankees and moved his team into the stadium that Webb's construction company had recently upgraded.[66]

In his autobiography, Hank Greenberg elaborated on this relationship: "They traded some forty or fifty ballplayers back and forth between the clubs so the Yankees, instead of losing a ballplayer, would trade him to Kansas City and he'd play there and develop and then come back and play for the Yankees again. This, of course, created unfair competition."[67] Roger Maris was one of the special players Kansas City developed for the Yankees. By the time CBS bought the Yankees in 1964, this special arrangement was over. The end of the Yankee dynasty probably had as much to do with the team losing its major league farm club as with the introduction of the 1965 amateur draft.

The leveling tendency of the amateur draft, according to some baseball executives, has run its course. Until recently, baseball has been able to sign its top draft picks at bargain prices. Selected amateurs have either had the choice to sign with the team that drafted them or not to sign at all and wait twelve months (or longer if they enrolled in a four-year college) for the next draft. With the 1990 signing of Todd Van Poppel by the Oakland A's for $1.2 million and the 1991 signing of Brien Taylor by the Yankees for $1.55 million, it seems that the old myths about the unpredictability of young talent are falling by the wayside.[68] Top amateurs and their agents are becoming more aggressive. Some people are concluding that these high prices are undermining the poor teams' ability to rely on the amateur draft and their farm systems to develop competitive teams. Poor teams will no longer be able to afford first-round picks.

Baseball's general managers reacted unequivocally to the Yankees' signing of Brien Taylor for $1.55 million. Houston Astros' Bill Wood said: "I was disappointed. . . . On one side, every club has to do what it has to do to improve, but there is sadness at the realization of the impact of this [signing] on the industry and other clubs. . . . [In the past small-market teams could choose] not to slug it out in the big free-agent market [and could always turn to the amateur draft]." Joe McIlvaine of the San Diego Padres exclaimed: "That's just scary." Philadelphia Phillies' Bill Giles opined: "You look at the big picture, it's another nail in the financial coffin."[69] Predictions of financial doom are nothing new for baseball executives, and they should be taken with several grains of salt; nonetheless, if the farm system option for developing competitive teams becomes more expensive, the game's playing field balance at the major league level might be affected eventually. (At their quarterly meeting in March 1992, to combat this escalation of signing bonuses, MLB owners voted to attach a drafted amateur to the selecting team for five years instead of one. The legality of this new policy will undoubtedly be tested by the MLBPA or in the courts after the June 1992 amateur draft.)

Another theory about why competitive imbalance has yet to assert itself is that baseball owners have been on a learning curve for dealing with free agency. Some argue that initial expectations of being able to buy a winner and ignoring or undercutting farm system talent development has by now evolved into a more sophisticated understanding of the need to pursue a more balanced strategy. Perhaps. But this theory seems too subjective to hang baseball's future on.

A more troublesome development is the coming reversal in the tendency for central revenue sources to grow more rapidly than local sources. It is expected that baseball's next national media contracts commencing with the 1994 season will be no larger than the current ones and will be divided among two additional teams;[70] at the same time, local revenues from cable television have been growing rapidly. Despite the partially offsetting development of hefty increases in central licensing income, the trend toward revenue leveling will likely be reversed if nothing is done to stop it. This, of course, could engender financial instability.

ECONOMIC THEORY AND COMPETITIVE BALANCE

Speculation on the possible evolution of baseball's institutional structures may be useful, but attention to the actual decision-making processes, incentives, and mechanisms for establishing competitive balance is indispensable. One mechanism of competitive imbalance that has been argued by Scully and others is based on the assertion that a star player is worth more to a big-city team than to a small-city team. The notion here is that if Ken Griffey, Jr., plays in Chicago, he will bring more additional people to the ballpark and enlarge the local media contract more than he will playing in Seattle. Hence, other things being equal, Griffey's MRP or his value to the White Sox is greater than his value to the Mariners, and when his free agency comes along he will be offered more and signed by the White Sox. This expectation would only be reinforced by the likelihood that Griffey's promotional income would be much higher in Chicago than in Seattle.

At issue here is not whether increases in metropolitan population augment team revenues. They do. The regressions in appendix A, in fact, suggest that each additional person living in a team's metropolitan area increases annual team revenues by $2.40. Put differently, every 162,000 people add as much to a team's revenue as an additional win; or a team in a city of 2 million would have to have thirty-seven more victories than a team in a city of 8 million in order to have the same revenue.

Nor is the advantage of winning for both small and big-city teams at issue. Rather, given the revenue advantages of a big population base and a winning team, the issue is whether a big-city team has an *additional* advantage over a small-city team in hiring a star player. That is, controlling for the independent effects of a large population and of star players, does the interaction of star players with large populations have an independent positive impact on team revenues? The presence of such an interactive effect can be tested econometrically in a number of ways. The details of these tests are presented in appendix B. The results do not support the hypothesis that star players are worth more to big-city teams.[71]

How can we explain why a star player would not bring more revenue to a big-city than a small-city team? First, our tests relate team revenues to team performance over a maximum period of three years. It is probable that a team's media value is more a function of the team's tradition of winning than its performance in the last year or two. This is particularly the case since many local media contracts are for three years or more. Second, many big-city teams come close to capacity attendance for most of the season whether or not the teams are in first place or close to it. Small teams, on the other hand, do not have the luxury of mediocre performance if they wish to fill their ballparks.

If it is true on average that stars are not worth more to big-city teams, then city size should not affect the size of contract offers and small-city teams should not be at a disadvantage. For example, if Barry Bonds brings $6 million in additional revenues to both the Pirates and the Yankees, then both teams in a competitive bidding process should be willing to offer him $6 million and not more. Indeed, other things being equal, the Yankees might offer him somewhat less, because were they to sign him they would lose a top draft pick. (Were the Pirates to re-sign Bonds prior to his becoming a free agent, they, of course, would not lose a draft pick.) The loss of a draft pick for the Yankees, or any signing team, would lower Bonds's net value.

This observation needs to be qualified by two factors. First, it assumes that both teams are covering their operating costs.[72] Second, it assumes equal risk aversion on the part of the Yankees' and Pirates' owners. Since a player's precise MRP is not known, there is a substantial risk in offering top dollar. If the two owners have the same psychological disposition to risk, it may well be that the Yankees' owner will exhibit less risk aversion because of the team's greater financial cushion.

The second entry point for economic theory in this discussion is the concept of economic rent. If the Yankees' franchise is worth $250 million and the Pirates' $100 million, this is not because George Steinbrenner has made better entrepreneurial moves than Douglas Danforth and his partners. It is because the New York media market is six times the size of Pittsburgh's. This differential value is properly understood not as return to capital but as a return to "land." The fact that Steinbrenner rather than New York City is able to capture this rent is a function of baseball's exempt monopoly status and of tradition, but it should not affect the investment decisions of owners attempting to maximize their return on capital.

Suppose the Yankees were sold to New York City for $250 million. The city, in turn, made a deal with MLB to bypass the 60/40 rule[73] and floated a bond for the entire sum at 10 percent interest to purchase the team. The city would have a $25 million-a-year interest expense. So if the Yankees had an operating profit of $30 million with a $25 million interest expense and the Pirates have an operating profit of, say, $8 million with a $3 million interest expense, both teams would have book profits of $5 million. Indeed, in this case, the Pirates' owners would be enjoying a higher rate of return on their (smaller) investment.

Steinbrenner, however, has not sold his ownership share of the Yankees to New York City, nor will he. What, then, is the relevance of this hypothetical example? If Steinbrenner makes his investment decisions so as to attempt to maximize his income, then he will reason (assuming he owns the whole team to simplify matters) that if he sold the team and safely invested the money, he could earn, say, $25 million a year in interest income. Continuing to hold the team, then, means he forgoes this income and the $25 million is an implicit (or opportunity) cost of owning the team. This opportunity cost would be included in a rational calculation made about any new investment or reinvestment of operating profits in the Yankees. In the end, the decision about how much to invest in Barry Bonds or another free agent is largely independent of the larger absolute dollar operating profits of the Yankees.

Until now this economic dynamic, talent compression, and performance uncertainty may have been the principal forces behind the maintenance of competitive balance in the face of disparate team revenues. As long as baseball's teams continue to cover their operating costs, this dynamic will continue to operate in the future. While this analysis tends to place less importance on revenue sharing's impact on competitive balance, it must again be qualified by the likelihood of differential attitudes toward risk among rich and poor teams. It is also important to keep in mind that from the cold perspective of joint profit maximization, MLB does not seek perfect competitive balance. Profits will be maximized when there is enough uncertainty for any team to have a chance of winning and when pennant races are close. But it is in MLB's joint economic interest to have the big-city teams rise to the top the most often. Such an outcome will provide the highest television ratings in postseason play and produce more lucrative network contracts in the future.

The foregoing analysis says nothing about the possible importance of revenue sharing to preserve financial stability in the future. Yet financial instability, as we saw in the last chapter, is rarely what it appears to be. It will always be in MLB's self-interest to exaggerate the economic difficulties of its weaker franchises, since this provides a ready rationale both not to expand the number of MLB teams and to allow existing franchises to move to greener pastures.

While some additional revenue sharing from richer to poorer clubs may be appropriate under current conditions, it would certainly be appropriate were the major leagues to relinquish their monopoly restriction on the number of franchises. With or without expansion, as local media revenues grow in relative importance there will be greater pressure on MLB to increase revenue sharing among teams. But it is arguable that the real claim on the large revenues of the big-city teams comes from the source of those revenues—the big cities themselves. Rather than getting a larger share of the baseball pie, big cities increasingly are being confronted with extortionate demands for remodeled or new stadiums constructed at the public's expense. We shall turn our attention to this matter in chapter 6, after considering the changing relationship between the major and minor leagues in the next chapter.

CHAPTER 5

The Minors

He'll get a crappy little apartment with a couple of other guys, eat nothing but greasy hamburgers and fries, and try to have a good time. A lot of them will drink too much, and I have to believe that's where a lot of drug problems get started.
—Whitey Herzog, former player, manager, and executive, on the conditions of minor league ball

Quite frankly, we look at the National Association as a sort of apprentice-type arrangement. The real job is in the major leagues.
—Bill Murray, director of baseball operations for MLB

As Gene Orza, associate general counsel of the Players' Association, puts it, back in 1976 major league ballplayers were granted their "citizenship." Those players with six years of major league experience can now entertain competitive bids for their labor services. In Orza's lexicon, minor league ballplayers are still not citizens.

Players enter professional baseball through the annual June amateur draft when they are selected by a single club that has the exclusive right to sign them. The player has the right not to sign, but if he exercises that right he then has to stay out of baseball until the next June, at which time another club may draft the exclusive rights to bargain with him. (As of March 1992, clubs have exclusive bargaining rights over high school draftees for five years.) Once signed, the player is bonded to the team for at least three and a half years.[1] Beyond that, the major league club can keep the player in the minors and control him for another three years by placing him on the forty-man major league roster and optioning him to a minor league affiliate. A maximum of fifteen such optioned players is allowed per team (twenty-five active players on the major league roster plus fifteen optioned players). After the initial three and a half years, any player not put on the forty-man roster can be drafted by another major league team at the so-called Rule 5 draft held yearly at the winter meetings. But to retain a Rule 5 player, the new team must keep him on the active twenty-five-man major league roster for the entire next season. If he is not kept on the active roster, he must be offered back to his original team for $12,500, half of the Rule 5 drafting price.

Thus a drafted amateur faces the prospect of six and a half years in the minors without the right to offer his services to another team or to accept competitive bids from other teams. Many strong prospects are so constrained as they wait in the wings for their position to open up on the major league club.[2] Of course, if promoted to the big club (approximately one minor leaguer in ten[3] ever plays in the big leagues and only one in fifty stays in the majors for six years[4]), they then face another six years before they can become a free agent. It is quite conceivable, therefore, that a player drafted out of college would be thirty-four or thirty-five years old before he gained "citizenship."

Because they are regarded as apprentices, as the quote from Bill Murray acknowledges, they are paid and treated like apprentices. Salaries begin at $850 per month (paid over two and one half months) for first-year minor leaguers and range up to an average of $5,424 per month (paid over four and one half months) in 1990 for Triple-A players. The median Triple-A salary, however, is probably below $2,000 per month; the average is skewed upward by top draft picks and former major leaguers who sign minor league contracts.[5] In 1990 the average salary at the major league level was 24.5 times the average Triple-A salary. What is perhaps curious is that back in 1950, when minor leaguers were also considered apprentices, the average salary in the major leagues was only 3.37 times the average salary in the highest classification minors.[6] Somehow top-level apprentices in 1990 are worth approximately one-twenty-fifth of a major leaguer, while forty years ago they were worth roughly one-third of a major leaguer.

Working conditions for minor leaguers have scarcely improved in the interim. They can be released unconditionally and without further salary rights or severance pay on the same day.[7] They receive no benefits except for a modest individual health insurance program. Even at the Triple-A level, the typical player must scrape to get by. In 1990 Tim Naehring, a top shortstop prospect for the Boston Red Sox, earned $1,400 a month and shared a two-bedroom apartment with four other teammates in Pawtucket, Rhode Island. One of the five slept on a couch. During the off season, Naehring returned to his parents' home and worked delivering pizza one winter and in a sporting goods store another.[8] He was the starting shortstop in Boston when the 1991 season began but was sidelined with a back injury in April, had an operation, and missed the rest of the year.

With 3,400 "apprentices" diligently and docilely working for low wages, one might assume that Major League Baseball would be delighted with its player development system. Not so. To appreciate the present predicament, it is necessary to review the evolution of the minor leagues and their changing role in the organization of professional baseball.

HISTORY

The first minor league, the International League (IL), was established in 1877. It was not until 1883, however, that the National League recognized the IL's right to reserve—that is, to own, players. Once the reservation right was recognized, the NL could obtain minor league players only by purchasing them from a minor league team. As these purchases proved quite expensive to the major leagues, once the competition for players among the NL, the Players' League, and the American Association was ended in the early 1890s, the consolidated NL announced that it would no longer acknowledge the minors' reservation right. This led to baseball's first draft. The 1890s also witnessed the first major league owners buying their own minor league teams. These early "farm" teams provided both players and profits for baseball's syndicate owners of the 1890s.

In 1901 the National Association (of minor leagues) was formed to protect the minors from the player raids imposed by the majors. The majors were purchasing an unlimited quantity of players at a fixed price. Some clubs were being decimated. The National Association scored a small victory in the 1903 agreement between the American and National leagues, which included an antifarming provision. This provision attempted to regulate team efforts to exceed the limit on optioned players through fake transfers. A more important gain came in 1905 when MLB set the limit that only one player per club could be drafted each year and the draft price was raised from $750 to $1,000 for top-classification minor leaguers (and raised again to $2,500 in 1911). These prices were still below what minor league franchise owners could fetch for their players in open market sales, so the draft primarily served to encourage minor league clubs to sell their players prior to the date of each year's draft.

In addition to the number and price of drafted players, the majors and the minors were in a constant struggle over option limits and fees for player transfers. The majors found it convenient and economical to be able to move players back and forth between their club and a minor league club with which it had a short-term working agreement. The minors objected that frequent optioning undermined their autonomy because they had less and less control over the unstable roster of players on their teams. They also claimed it gave an unfair advantage to certain minor league teams whose major league clubs were less active in raiding minor league players. For a while the option limits were more a symbol of the state of major-minor relations than they were a significant restriction on major league teams. Joint ownership of major and minor league franchises allowed some franchises to hold title to sixty or more players.

A series of gains for the minor leagues culminated after the 1918 season, when the minor league draft was suspended and prices for minor leaguers went way up. MLB then took the offensive, suspending the antifarming rules, lifting a ban in effect since 1913 on major league teams owning minor league teams, and reinstating the draft in January 1921. The new draft included a top price of $5,000, and allowed individual minor league clubs to opt out of the draft with the understanding that if they did not permit their players to be drafted then they could not draft players from teams at lower classification levels. Soon thereafter the top-three minor leagues chose not to participate in the draft system. Player sale prices skyrocketed in 1922. The White Sox, for instance, paid $100,000 ($785,000 in 1990 prices) to San Francisco of the Western League for Willie Kamm, and prices for top minor leaguers remained in the $70,000-to-$100,000 range for the rest of the 1920s.

With draft prices and player sale prices multiplying and with the restrictions on optioning and ownership lifted, Branch Rickey of the St. Louis Cardinals went to work developing baseball's first extensive farm system. While both working agreements and ownership ties previously existed between major and minor league clubs, these relationships involved only the top-classification minors, and they were primarily for the purpose of purchasing players rather than developing them. Rickey's concept was to set up a vast scouting and development system that would enable a relatively impecunious club like the Cardinals to procure top talent more cheaply. It would also stock the franchise with so many attractive players that the Cardinals would be able to reap substantial income from sales of its redundant talent. Rickey started by purchasing a half interest in the Fort Smith, Arkansas, club. By 1928 St. Louis owned five farm teams and had working agreements with several more. Rickey continued buying minor league teams and signing working agreements until the Cardinals' farm system peaked at thirty-three clubs in 1937, controlling six hundred to seven hundred players.[9] The Cardinals' increasing success on the field brought attention to Rickey's methods, and other teams followed his lead. By 1929 major league teams owned twenty-seven minor league clubs. During the 1930s both the Yankees and the Dodgers made substantial investments in building large farm systems, though they never rivaled the Cardinals.

The growth of farm systems took place over the frequent and strident objections of Commissioner Landis. As an old trustbuster, he saw monopolistic tendencies in farming, and he deplored the fact that young prospects got stuck in the minors because their position was occupied by a star on the major league roster. Landis proposed a universal draft that would have allowed any team to pick such a player. He got nowhere with his protestations and recommendations, although he scored moral victories in catching both the Cardinals (in 1938) and the Tigers (in 1940) maintaining secret working agreements with minor league clubs.

Naturally, as baseball's talent procurement process became more complex, the locus of bidding wars and spiraling prices shifted. In addition to paying top dollar to buy players from other major league teams and the minor leagues, the growth of farm systems led to upward price pressure on amateur contracts. The depression years and World War II interrupted the trend toward more expensive amateur signings, but "bonus wars" emerged in full force after World War II. By 1951 total bonus payments came to $4.5 million, over 14 percent of combined MLB revenues.[10]

It was becoming increasingly apparent that the Rickey farm system concept had been taken too far and merely transferred costs from one port of player acquisition to another. From 1945 to 1950 the Chicago Cubs spent an average of $454,550 on player development, or $113,637 per player, counting only players who stayed on the big league roster for two years or more. The Yankees estimated their per-player development costs at $201,118.[11] Both teams claimed that farming was more expensive than buying players.

With some 9,000 minor leaguers in 1950 and the average pay at the top classification level almost 25 percent of the major league average,[12] the minor leagues had overexpanded as a player development system. According to a survey done for the 1951 congressional hearings, two-thirds of minor league teams operated at a loss in 1950.[13] Thus, at the same time that the major leagues decided it was necessary to lower their investment in ownership (major league clubs owned 207 minor clubs in 1951 but only 38 in 1957)[14] and cut back their working arrangements with the minors, the minors themselves were on shaky financial grounds. The majors began to sell off their minor league clubs and demand that working arrangements be made more flexible, reducing the autonomy of minor league operators. This, in turn, made minor league rosters more unstable and reduced the number of ex–major leaguers playing for Triple-A clubs, weakening fan identification with local minor league teams.[15] Simultaneously, the spread of television kept many small-town baseball fans at home to watch their favorite major league team from their living rooms while suburbanization and the growth of the automobile made it easier to drive to the big league park. Both of these developments contributed to the decline in attendance at minor league games.

As a result of these pressures and the exodus of 1,322 players to do service in the Korean War,[16] in 1950 minor league baseball began a period

TABLE 5.1
Minor League Attendance

Year	Number of Leagues[a]	Number of Clubs[a]	Attendance (millions)	Club Average
1949	59	464	41.9	90,301
1952	43	324	24.0	74,149
1961	22	147	9.8	66,438
1968	21	152	9.9	65,048
1973	18	146	10.8	74,170
1975	18	137	11.0	80,451
1979	18	154	15.2	98,731
1983	17	162	18.6	114,562
1988	18	188	21.7	115,212
1989	18	189	23.1	122,222
1990	18	189	25.2	133,333
1991	18	189	26.6	140,741

Sources: Wulf 1990, p. 35; Scher 1990, p. 13; U.S. Congress, House, 1952, p. 1616; National Association of Professional Baseball Leagues.

[a]All leagues and clubs belonging to the National Association, except the Dominican League. Includes 16 teams in the Mexican League and 173 in the United States and Canada in 1991. The excluded Dominican League has eighteen teams.

of dramatic downsizing, as shown in table 5.1. The number of minor league teams fell by more than two-thirds, from 464 in 1949 to 147 in 1961; over the same period attendance at minor league games decreased by over three-quarters.

MLB also made a more direct assault on the bonus wars. The first step was taken in December 1952 with the introduction of a rule that obligated a major league team to bring any bonus player who signed for over a few thousand dollars to the majors within one year and keep him there. Failing to do so would subject the player to an unrestricted draft. The restriction was intended to make it more risky and less attractive to pay big sums for amateur players, but it proved too weak a measure and the bonus wars continued unabated. Subsequent attempts during the 1950s and early 1960s to restrict the market for top amateur prospects were largely ineffective, because they left intact the basic competition among major league teams to sign "bonus babies." It was not until the introduction of the minor league draft in 1965, which granted exclusive rights to a single team to sign an amateur, that bonus expenses were brought under control. As cited earlier, the highest signing bonus to an amateur prior to the introduction of the 1965 draft was $205,000 paid to Rick Reichardt by the California Angels in 1964. This sum was not to be exceeded in nominal terms until 1980 when the Mets paid Darryl Strawberry $210,000; in real terms (adjusting for inflation) it was not exceeded until the Yankees signed Brien Taylor in 1991 for $1.55 million.[17]

MLB claimed that the purpose of the amateur draft, which gave top draft picks to the weakest clubs, was to create a better competitive balance on the playing field. The 1960s were still the days (albeit waning) of the Yankee dynasty, and the argument had some merit. But what is true today about the draft was also true at that time: The absence of a developed system of college baseball and a sufficient scouting apparatus to report systematically on high school prospects made success in the baseball draft, particularly after the first few picks, more a matter of dumb luck than anything else. Consider, for instance, the facts that José Canseco was picked in the fifteenth round of the amateur draft, Roger Clemens the twelfth, Ryne Sandberg the twentieth, and Nolan Ryan the tenth.[18] Nonetheless, it was an advantage to get the very top prospects, and insofar as the Yankees and Dodgers had been able to outbid the other clubs and corner the amateur market, the introduction of the 1965 draft did make some contribution to competitive balance. At the same time, however, it chattelized the amateur players and thwarted the bonus wars.

In the 1950s streamlining of the minors left them financially weakened. Most clubs were still losing money in the mid-fifties and required subsidies from their parent clubs. Commissioner Frick ushered in the era of systematic subsidies in 1956 when he established a fund of $500,000 to aid failing minor league teams. To deal with their financial difficulties, MLB also urged the minors to sell shares of stock to their local communities. Not surprisingly, this turned out to be an effective strategy both to raise needed capital and to reanimate interest in minor league ball. By the early 1960s a majority of the teams in the Triple-A International League were community-owned. Several community-owned teams in the IL are still thriving in the 1990s.[19]

The first standardized Player Development Contract (PDC) between major league teams and National Association teams was adopted in 1962. Among other things, it called for the majors to pay players' salaries in excess of $800 a month at Triple-A, of $150 a month at AA, and of $50 a month at A level. It also set forth regulations about major league payments for equipment, travel, and meal money. In 1967 the minors began receiving a share of MLB television income. The minors limped through the 1960s and 1970s, with only a minority of clubs earning (modest) profits. The PDC was altered periodically to provide increasing subsidies to the minor league franchises.

Table 5.1 also reveals that attendance at minor league games more than doubled between 1975 and 1991. It seems that the heightened commercialization of baseball engendered by the advent of free agency was a boon as well to the minor leagues. Whether this was a product of a greater interest in following the development of a future multimillion-dollar superstar or, indeed, a reaction against commercialization and a return to baseball's simple roots emulated by the immediacy and lack of pretense of minor league parks is difficult to ascertain. Interest in minor league ball certainly got one boost from commercialism as new Hollywood films such as *The Natural, Bull Durham*, and *Field of Dreams* glorified the simplicity and the spirit of the game itself.

With booming attendance came not only profits for minor league operators but also skyrocketing franchise values. Class A franchises, which sold for under $5,000 in the late 1970s, were selling for as much as $2 million in 1990. Double-A franchises, which sold for under $100,000 in the early 1980s, were being sold for up to $4 million in 1990. The Triple-A Vancouver Canadians sold for $5.5 million in 1990. Larry Schmittou, owner of the Nashville Sounds of the Triple-A International League, was said to have turned down a $10 million offer for his club in 1991.[20] And *Baseball America* reported that the owner of the Triple-A Denver Zephyrs was asking $15 million for his franchise rights to Denver.[21]

Needless to say, MLB was somewhat jealous of the minor leagues' newfound prosperity. MLB's expenditures on player development programs (amateur signing bonuses, minor league player salaries, scouts, umpires, team operations,[22] and administrative costs) had grown rapidly. With hopes of cutting scouting expenditures, MLB set up a central scouting bureau in 1985. Although the bureau may have succeeded in slowing the rate of increase, individual team scouting budgets continued to surge in the late 1980s. Total player development expenses for MLB grew from an estimated $10 million in 1958, to $40 million in 1981, $57 million in 1983, $74 million in 1986, and $143 million in 1989.[23] As depicted in table 5.2, the average player development expenditure per club in 1989 worked out to $5.5 million, or approximately 12.6 percent of average club revenues. Having made this large investment, then, MLB felt it deserved some of the emerging financial rewards.

THE 1990 NEGOTIATIONS

When the negotiations between the majors and minors began around a new Professional Baseball Agreement (PBA)[24] in the summer of 1990, the major league owners were still reeling from their defeat in the three collusion cases brought by the Players' Association. With rising attendance, profits, and franchise values in the minor leagues, MLB decided the time was ripe to negotiate a new deal with lower subsidies. Some analysts suggested that having lost their war with the players, MLB was determined to beat up on the minor leagues.

The economic relationship between the major and minor leagues is complicated, to say the least. Consider, for instance, the following elements of the pre-1991 PBA. Each major league team paid each Triple-A

TABLE 5.2
Player Development Expense, 1986 and 1989

Year	Lowest Club Expenditure	Highest Club Expenditure	Average
1986	$1,800,000	$3,900,000	$2,900,000
1989	$4,300,000	$8,900,000	$5,500,000

Source: D. Nightingale 1990; Erardic 1991; see also notes 3 and 19 to this chapter.

affiliate for 100 balls, 300 bats, $8-a-day meal money per player on the road, and for the first nine hotel rooms. Every time a player was moved from one team to another, a $35 transaction fee was paid to the National Association. At the Triple-A level, the major league club paid all player salaries except the first $200 per month per player; of an average Triple-A team payroll of $785,000, all but $21,000 was paid by the parent club.[25] These subsidies varied at the Double-A and Single-A levels. MLB also paid each minor league team a television fee, theoretically to compensate for the lost attendance from major league broadcasts. A total of $1.8 million was paid to minors in television fees in 1990.

Bargaining over these and other provisions began in the summer of 1990 with the two sides far apart. The minors were looking for a fivefold increase from the majors in television rights payments, while the majors sought to eliminate such payments altogether. The majors also wanted to end transaction fee payments to the minors. Further, the majors sought nearly full control over minor league affairs, including the right to approve franchise sales, transfers, expansion, and schedules. The majors also sought to impose a new, rigid set of facility standards, ones that most minor league clubs could not meet. Finally, the majors asked that the minors pay $150,000 per club for the right to receive players.

In August MLB began to play hard ball; Commissioner Fay Vincent instructed all clubs to terminate any expiring working agreements with their affiliates by September 15. The not-so-veiled threat was to end minor league baseball as the 173 host cities across the United States and Canada had come to know it.

The two sides did not meet at all in September, and, as instructed, the major league franchises dutifully terminated fifty-nine working agreements. MLB indicated a contingency plan to relocate the affected players to spring training facilities in Arizona and Florida. Negotiations resumed on October 3 and continued fitfully with escalating threats and brinksmanship from both sides until a new agreement was fashioned in mid-December. According to a weighted league voting formula, the minors ratified the new agreement with exactly the minimum of three-quarters voted required.

One reporter who covered the talks for *Baseball America* offered the following assessment of the negotiations:

> The process nearly fell apart several times, but was saved by a continuing dialogue between Barger (Pirates president) and Louisville Redbirds president Dan Ulmer, a banker who had been involved in business deals with Barger. At one point, Triple-A owners talked openly about breaking off and forming a third major league, and agents and the Players Association began

ruminating over the possibility that minor league players could claim free agency if no agreement was reached.[26]

The principal financial elements of the new seven-year accord were as follows.

1. The National Association (the minors) will pay a flat annual fee to MLB of $750,000 in 1991, a minimum of $1.5 million in 1992, $1.75 million in 1993, and $2 million in 1994. This sum is based on a maximum contribution of 5 percent of revenues for each minor league club, with the percentage declining at higher revenue levels.
2. The National Association agreed to participate in a joint licensing arrangement with MLB Properties and in return will receive a minimum of $2.8 million a year for four years (a sum equal to the estimated trading card royalties accruing to the minor leagues).
3. Minor league clubs will pay travel expenses on the road for a maximum of twenty-nine people (including coaches and trainers) at the Triple-A level, twenty-seven at Double-A level, and twenty-six at Single-A level, in 1991; the maximum will rise to thirty at all levels by 1993. The previous arrangement was for the minors to pay expenses for twenty, nineteen, and eighteen at the Triple-A, Double-AA, and Single-A levels, respectively.
4. Major league clubs will pay all salaries and meal money for players and umpires, and buy all equipment; previously, Triple-A clubs contributed $200 a month for player salaries, and equipment, meal money, and umpire-development costs were shared.
5. The $35-per-transaction payment to the minors is eliminated.
6. Minors will no longer receive a cut of the majors' television rights' fees, previously set at $25,000 per club at AAA, $16,000 at AA, and $11,000 at A level.

Although the agreement is for seven years, it can be reopened by either side after three years (in September of 1993) and terminated after the 1994 season.

Although minor league salaries are extremely low by major league standards and their growth is moderate, the total payroll expense for the average of over 130 players per minor league system is appreciable. Table 5.3 depicts the growth of average minor league salaries at each level since 1979. The averages at the Triple-A level are distorted upward by the relatively high salaries of a few dozen top draft picks and former major leaguers. The median salary at the Triple-A level in 1990 was likely below $2,000 a month.

TABLE 5.3
Average Monthly Salary[a]

Year	AAA	AA	A	Rookie
1979	$2,340	$1,037	$666	$584
1981	$2,984	$1,199	$743	$615
1983	$3,346	$1,322	$769	$620
1985	$4,026	$1,490	$830	$707
1987	$5,168	$1,684	$876	$718
1989	$5,020	$1,637	$967	$840
1990	$5,424	$1,763	$1,074	$868

Source: George Pfister of MLB.

[a]Minor leaguers play for and receive salary over 4.5 months, except those in the rookie league who play for 2.5 months. Bonuses are not included in the above figures. Bonus data is treated as confidential by MLB.

Minor league officials estimate the new package will save each major league club at least $80,000 in 1991 and $106,000 in 1992. The estimated cost to the minor league clubs will vary from $25,000 annually at the Class A level to over $100,000 for some Triple-A clubs.[27] Major league officials denied that the major leagues would receive any economic advantage from this new arrangement. Indeed, MLB claims its minor league costs will rise. If this is so, it is far from clear that the new agreement is the cause. One appreciable new cost is that MLB has created the new post of director of minor leagues. It was filled in 1991 by attorney Jerry Lee Soloman. Another cost comes from MLB's decision to audit the books of all minor league clubs.

Harold Cooper, president of the International League, suggested that the minor league clubs "place on the [admission] ticket whatever the fee is they have to pay the major leagues, so that everybody knows that these cheap bastards are getting 25 cents off the tickets."[28]

Bill Valentine, general manager of the Double-A Arkansas Travellers, dreaded his team's new financial predicament: "That 5 percent [of mandated revenue sharing] isn't going to make a drop in the bucket to them. They pay $2 million to a free agent who doesn't even play a game. To me it's maintenance money. It's the difference between putting in new showers. It's the difference in putting in a new drainage system." To be sure, the price of minor league franchises seems to have leveled off in 1991 after the signing of the new PBA.[29] The economic viability of minor league ownership may have entered a new stage of uncertainty.

THE MINORS AND COMPETITIVE BALANCE

With major league player salaries having surged to occupy approximately 42 percent of revenues for an average team and near 60 percent of revenues for some low-revenue teams, some commentators have characterized expenditures on player development, rather than on free agents, as the only avenue for poor teams wishing to field a competitive or championship team. The inscrutability of high school talent, the reverse-order draft, and the amateur draft pick compensation for losing a free agent have all served to allow the fortunate small-city franchise to develop a winning team. However, in the last couple of years the growth of free agent salaries as well as the variability of free agent performance have led even the rich teams to concentrate more heavily on signing top amateur draft picks. Consequently, high free agent salaries are increasingly rubbing off on the bonuses of the top draft picks.

In 1990 the Oakland A's convinced first-round draft choice and pitching prospect Todd Van Poppel to postpone indefinitely his planned enrollment at the University of Texas. Van Poppel was persuaded to sign with the A's for a three-year deal worth a record $1.2 million, becoming the first high school player to be signed for over $1 million. Van Poppel was also given a major league contract, meaning that he was placed immediately on the forty-man roster and could not be kept in the minors for over three years without first being made available to another team. Just a few years earlier, in 1987, the first-round draft picks had signed initial contracts for between $80,000 and $175,000.[30] The A's attempted to justify Van Poppel's fatter contract by arguing that he was a special case because he had already been accepted to the University of Texas on a baseball scholarship. In 1991 the Yankees had the first draft pick in the first round and chose a fireballing, eighteen-year-old southpaw by the name of Brien Taylor. Because Taylor had no college plans at the time of the June draft, the Yankees said he was not in the same category as Van Poppel and offered only $650,000. Taylor's agent, Scott Boras, and his mother saw through the ruse and arranged for Taylor to be matriculated at a local junior college.[31] The day Taylor was to attend his first class, he signed with the Yankees, as cited earlier, for $1.55 million on a three-year minor league contract.[32]

The baseball establishment was not pleased. Indeed, according to Taylor's mother, a scout who identified himself as being sent by Commissioner Vincent tried to pressure her into having her son sign for under $1 million.[33] To the other owners, the Taylor signing meant that a $1-million floor had been set on the top draft picks for the future. With

Van Poppel there was the fiction of a special circumstance; now the veil on the fiction was lifted, and a new era of bonus wars seemed to be upon them.

It was feared that the leveling effect of the amateur draft would be undermined. Shortly after the signing of Taylor, Kenny Henderson, the first-round draft pick of the Milwaukee Brewers and also represented by Scott Boras, demanded a firm $1 million to sign. The Brewers told Henderson "to take a hike," which he did, enrolling at the University of Miami. He cannot be drafted again until June 1994. The inference drawn by observers was that the Brewers and the other low-revenue teams would no longer be able to afford first-round draft picks.[34]

One of the main factors pressuring the Yankees and other drafting clubs is that under then current rules, they retained the draft rights to a player for only one year, until the next June draft. If the Yankees spent their first-round pick on Taylor and did not sign him, they ran the risk that another club would draft and sign him the following year. Recognizing the modicum of bargaining power that this rule gave the amateur draftees, in early October 1991 the owners directed the MLB Operations Committee to devise a plan that would permit teams to retain draft rights to players throughout their college years.[35] A new rule was adopted in March 1992 allowing teams to retain rights over drafted players out of high school for five years. It will be likely challenged by the MLBPA or in the courts following the June 1992 amateur draft.

There is a certain irony in the 1991 pronouncements of some major league owners on the importance of the player development system for baseball's competitive balance. In 1991 the claim was that the minors were especially important for the poorer franchises. Yet in 1990, prior to MLB's negotiations with the National Association over a new Player Development Contract for the minor leagues, the claim was that the minors as then organized were not an economical means for player development. The major league owners claimed that with average expenditures of $5.5 million per team on their farm and scouting systems and a typical promotion rate of three minor leaguers per year to the active twenty-five-man roster, the cost of developing an average player in the minor league system was $1.83 million.[36] This, said the owners, was too much. Left out of this formulation is the fact that the minors serve other functions for the major leagues besides player development—they provide a cushion for the majors when players are injured, and they serve to generate interest in the parent club in the minor league cities. Also left out is the fact that the minors are not necessarily organized or run as efficiently as they might be.[37]

WHAT IS TO BE DONE

In one sense, it is scandalous that minor leaguers' salaries and benefits are so poor relative to major leaguers: average salaries one-twenty-fifth as high, no job protection, virtually no benefits, and no free agency rights. Certainly in an ideal state of affairs matters would be very much different.

If one compares minor league ballplayers, however, with their counterparts in theater, plastic arts, cinema, academia, and some other professions, it is not clear that minor leaguers have it so bad. Society seems to put up with the struggling apprentice predicament in a panoply of professional endeavors, and baseball is no exception.

It is perhaps too glib to argue that the amelioration of conditions for minor leaguers should be left up to the ballplayers themselves. It does not seem that they are sufficiently motivated or equipped to do much about their employment conditions. They are, after all, generally young, transient, without families to support, and aspiring to greater heights. According to both Marvin Miller and Don Fehr, major league players have evinced little interest in providing the financial and institutional support to initiate an organizing drive of minor league players.

Some owners, such as Eddie Einhorn of the White Sox, have proposed doing away with the minor leagues. Others have proposed doing away with part of it. Whitey Herzog, for instance, believes that Single-A ball could be eliminated with the least experienced minor leaguers working out at the parent clubs' spring training sites under close supervision. Among other things, this would permit clubs to reduce the number of minor leaguers in their systems, reduce subsidies, and apply some of the savings to improved conditions for the remaining players. Improved conditions might include better instruction, better field conditions (for example, leveling and smoothing of the infield), better living situations for the players, and more attention to minor leaguers' dietary habits. An apparent disadvantage of Herzog's scheme is that it would rob dozens of communities of their only direct contact with professional baseball. This disadvantage could, of course, be mitigated were MLB to expand the number of major league teams while reducing the average number of farm teams per parent club.

Another efficiency-seeking proposal has the same defect: Pool all minor league talent and conduct a universal, reverse-order draft. This would end competition among teams over scouting and player development and certainly would allow a major reduction in the size of the minor leagues; it would also take a lot of fun out of the competitive development of player talent.

Other analysts have argued that the bulk of the training should be transferred to college baseball. There are, of course, good reasons why college baseball has not developed as has college football or basketball to date.[38] Foremost among them is that baseball is a summer sport and colleges are not in session at that time. Most schools are not located in a climate that is warm enough to play baseball earlier in the spring. Several dozen schools do have serious baseball programs, but they generate little revenue and operate on tight budgets, tight enough anyway so that since 1974 college baseball has employed aluminum bats. Aluminum bats have larger sweet spots, generate more bat speed, and break infrequently. Major league scouts say that college players have to change their swings to use professional baseball's wood bats.

Proponents of making greater use of college baseball for developing professional ballplayers argue that with the savings on minor league subsidies, the majors could provide sufficient financing to the colleges to enable them to use wood bats, hire better coaches, and play on better fields. Additional financing would allow colleges to play farther into the summer or to expand the eight existing summer leagues.[39] Several difficulties, however, arise. First, if MLB can be persuaded to invest in such a program, would the colleges accept the loss of autonomy over their athletic policies that outside financing would imply? Second, MLB involvement would be another step toward the professionalization of college sports, invoking a legion of knotty issues. Should college athletes be paid? Should they be required to maintain a certain grade average in classes? Do most individuals on athletic scholarships have the motivation or opportunity properly to pursue their studies while in college?[40] Et cetera.

As matters currently stand, the National Football League (NFL) requires an individual to have completed three years of college before he can play professional football, and the National Basketball Association (NBA) requires a special petition from high school graduates to be able to participate in the professional basketball draft. A scandalously small proportion of NFL and NBA players complete their college education before entering pro ball, and many who do graduate are guided through a specialized curriculum of gut courses.[41] Not so in baseball where most players are still drafted out of high school. Indeed, baseball scouts have actively attempted to convince many high school graduates to postpone college and go directly into baseball.[42] The relationship between professional sports and intercollegiate athletics is far from optimal for the NBA, NFL, or MLB. An intermediate arrangement that allows for physical training together with the legitimate pursuit of one's studies should be sought in all three sports.

Most everyone who is familiar with the functioning of baseball's minor leagues believes that they are an inefficient system for player development. Most would also agree that the employment conditions of minor leaguers leave much to be desired. While there are no easy solutions, one policy that would address each of these problems is major league expansion. Expansion in the majors would result in more job opportunities with "citizenship" for minor leaguers, and it would allow a restructuring of farm systems without a decimation in the number of minor league franchises. In the next chapter, in discussing baseball's relationship to its host cities, we shall argue the case for the feasibility and desirability of major league expansion.

CHAPTER 6

The Metropoli

This is what I call the rape of the cities.
—Howard Cosell, broadcaster, testifying before the U.S. House of
Representatives, 1981

*Otherwise it is a pretty rampant case of socialism to say that you [baseball
teams] cannot move.*
—Ted Turner, owner of the Atlanta Braves, testifying before the U.S. House
of Representatives, 1981

Don Drysdale, former Dodgers' pitcher and Hall of Famer, says that had
it been put to a vote back in 1956, all twenty-five players on his team
would have opted to stay in Brooklyn. Certainly had the citizens of
Brooklyn been asked to vote, they too would have cast their preferences
unanimously and emphatically to keep their beloved ball club. But these
votes did not count. What counted was the vote of one man, Dodgers'
owner Walter O'Malley, and the big media contracts that awaited him in
Los Angeles. Sure, California was ready for Major League Baseball, but a
more rational course would have met this historical imperative straight-
forwardly—through expansion.

When the National League invited applications for its two 1993 expansion franchises, eighteen groups from ten different cities made the obligatory $100,000 deposit and filled out detailed questionnaires in September 1990.[1] Some aspirants spent considerably more money. Consider these cases: "Orlando's video presentation to the National League was produced by the local Disney studio. Miami owner candidate H. Wayne Huizenga poured about $500,000 into his presentation, including leather-bound fact books, Tiffany paper-weight gifts, and a slick ode–to–South Florida video."[2]

Originally, at least fifteen cities were interested in landing one of the two new teams, but it soon became clear that many were out of the running.[3] Demand by cities for a professional baseball team outstripped supply at the going price by a factor of at least five to one. Were baseball operated as a competitive industry, supply would expand; that is, there would be more than two expansion franchises—many more. But Fay Vincent says the two new teams in 1993 are it for this century.

Back in 1951, J. G. Taylor Spink, editor of *The Sporting News*, told the Celler Committee in the U.S. House of Representatives that one reason baseball should not expand was that there were not enough qualified umpires.[4] With the possible exception of Lou Piniella, this argument convinces nobody. The rationale for no further expansion articulated by baseball's commissioners and owners is that there are not sufficient quality players.[5] This claim is equally self-serving and dubious.

As long as MLB can keep demand for teams from viable cities greater than supply, then existing teams have greater leverage in bargaining for new stadium construction, new luxury boxes, lower rent, or a greater share of concession and parking revenues. They can threaten to leave. Of course, how many cities are viable depends not only on the size of each metropolitan area's media market but also on, among other things, the effectiveness of a team's management and the degree of revenue sharing among teams.

The Green Bay Packers in the National Football League, for instance, have operated successfully since 1923 out of a home base with a population of under 100,000 in 1991. Their success has been made possible principally by the NFL practice of sharing equally virtually all television revenues and sharing 60/40 all gate revenues. Many also believe that the Packers' success is related to the strong community support, itself a product of local community ownership.[6]

FRANCHISE MOVEMENTS

Franchise movements seem to go in cycles. From 1903 to 1952 there were no new teams and no moves. From 1953 to 1972 ten teams changed their home city.[7] Prior to 1953, team moves required a unanimous vote in the affected league and a majority vote in the other. In 1953 the rule was relaxed to require a three-fourths vote in the affected league and no vote in the other.[8] Between 1952 and 1972 only two owner-proposed moves were rejected: Bill Veeck's proposed move of the St. Louis Browns to Baltimore in 1953 and Charlie Finley's proposed move of the Kansas City Athletics to Louisville in 1964. Both Veeck and Finley, however, were outcasts among owners, and in both cases the moves subsequently were approved: the Browns after Veeck sold the team and the Athletics after the stadium lease in Kansas City expired as well as four years of heavy losses.

Since the Washington Senators moved to Arlington, Texas, in 1972, there have been no team movements. Earlier legal suits from bereaved cities, threatening noises from Congress, new expansion franchises, and nineteen years of booming media revenues and attendance records combined to bring security to baseball's host cities. However, new economic pressures have surfaced in the last couple of years and several teams actively have been threatening relocation. Although Commissioner Vincent has paid public lip service to the importance of geographic stability, he appears ready to sanction team movements. Thus a new phase of carpetbagging by baseball's owners soon may be upon us.

Many fans still feel the pain from the last round of team movements. Perhaps the most ignominious of franchise movements involved the Dodgers' and Giants' relocation to the West Coast after the 1957 season. Dodgers' owner Walter O'Malley was the instigator. After his own plans to move the Dodgers were at an advanced stage, O'Malley persuaded Giants' owner Horace Stoneham to join him in moving to increase the viability of having major league baseball on the West Coast.

Walter O'Malley was "a wealthy lawyer who achieved a position of corporate influence through his effective mortgage foreclosures. As a reward for services rendered, he was made one of three partners in the ownership of the Brooklyn Dodgers."[9] After one owner died, O'Malley convinced the widow to allow him to handle the team for her. From this new position of power, he forced out the team's mastermind, Branch Rickey, and by 1950 had gained operating control over the Dodgers.

O'Malley began expressing disappointment with Ebbetts Field in 1952. He complained of its limited capacity of only 33,000 and lack of

parking, and expressed concern about urban decline with suburbanization. He negotiated with New York City about new land and a new park.
The city made several offers, but none to his satisfaction. Before becoming governor, Nelson Rockefeller offered to buy the Dodgers to keep them
in New York.[10] But O'Malley had his sights set on the West Coast. He
traded his minor league franchise in Dallas for Phil Wrigley's franchise in
the Western League, and thereby obtained both a ballfield and the rights
to a major league club in Los Angeles.[11]

The City of Los Angeles gave the Dodgers 300 acres to build a new
park and agreed to spend $2.74 million to provide access roads and other
improvements. The Dodgers were to cede their minor league park obtained from Wrigley to Los Angeles. The initial plan was to use this park
until the new stadium became ready, but its capacity was only 22,000
and interest in season tickets proved greater than anticipated. Rather
than forgo potential gate revenue, the Dodgers opted to do a facelift on
the Los Angeles Coliseum, built in 1923 and designed for football.
O'Malley's general contractor for his makeover of the LA Coliseum was
none other than Yankee co-owner and construction magnate Del Webb.[12]

The facelift produced a stadium with a massive, 90,000-plus seating
capacity, but it was entirely inappropriate for baseball. The left-field foul
pole was only 251 feet from home plate, and the right-field pole was a
distant 390 feet. To offset the Little League distance in left, a 42-foot
screen extending 140 feet to the 320-foot marker in left-center field was
put up. It came to be known as "O'Malley's Brooklyn Bridge," and
ballplayers had many jokes about it: Some argued that left fielders should
be designated as deep shortstops in the box score; one pitcher said he had
to take care in his windup not to scrape his elbow against it. In his
autobiography, Don Drysdale described the distorted dimensions of the
Coliseum: "The left-field fence was so close, you could practically spit on
it. The right-field fence was so far away, you needed binoculars to see
it."[13] In 1958, the first year of professional baseball at the Coliseum,
there were 193 homers hit; 182 of them went to left field. What was
anathema to Duke Snider and other left-handed power hitters was a
blessing to O'Malley's pocketbook.

Many wondered why O'Malley's pockets were not already fat enough.
Between 1946 and 1956, the Dodgers captured 44 percent of total National League profits.[14] Bill Veeck artfully explained one of the essential
ingredients to the team's financial success:

> The Brooklyn Dodgers were a winning team and a profitable one. The
> Brooklyn fans supported the team when it was a loser, and they had

supported it so well as a winner that over the previous decade the Dodgers had been second only to the Yankees in attendance and profitability.

The Brooklyn fans had become the symbol of the baseball fanatic. They were recognized by ballplayers throughout the league as the most knowledgeable in the country. The Dodgers were a part of the city's identification, a part of its pulse beat. The loyal rooters never doubted for a moment that their beloved Bums were as much a part of their heritage as Prospect Park. They discovered they were wrong. The Dodgers were only a piece of merchandise that passed from hand to hand.[15]

Don Drysdale echoed these sentiments:

But they were great fans, those people in Brooklyn. They were the best. I might be wrong, but I've seen a lot of fans in a lot of cities throughout the years and those Brooklynites are right on top of the pedestal. . . . If you'd have asked the players on the Dodgers to take a vote, it might have been 25–0 to stay in Brooklyn. I was born and raised in California, but I would have voted with the majority. There was complete chaos on the ballclub because of our move and I have no doubt that it affected our performance.[16]

These sentiments notwithstanding, Drysdale buys the myth that O'-Malley's entrepreneurial vision was responsible for bringing baseball to the West Coast. He wrote: "It took a pioneer to bring this about, and Mr. O'Malley was that man."[17] In fact, civic groups in Los Angeles had been pressuring for a major league team since 1939. In 1939 2.5 million people lived within a 50-mile radius of Los Angeles, a total greater than thirteen of the sixteen major league clubs. A variety of teams previously had expressed interest in moving to Los Angeles.[18] The city was obviously viable in itself, but before the days of commercial jet aircraft having a team or two on the West Coast was unworkable. One idea that was pushed by Phil Wrigley, among others, was to convert the Triple-A Pacific Coast League (PCL) into a third major league. In the early 1950s, salaries in the PCL were close to those in the major leagues, and many claimed the quality of ball was not far away either. All the PCL needed at the time was an agreement from MLB to exempt its players from being drafted or called up. MLB refused.[19] Crediting Walter O'Malley with bringing baseball to the West Coast is like crediting Columbus with discovering America.

Even Buzzie Bavasi, O'Malley's right-hand man for over two decades and an unrepenting O'Malley booster, could not cover up the true motive for the Dodgers' flight. In his autobiography Bavasi wrote: "Walter was accused of leaving out of greed; people were saying that he saw the California gold, that he went prospecting. If he did, so be it. He was entitled."[20]

The move of the Dodgers and Giants did create enough outrage to hatch the plan for the Continental League, which, in turn, led to MLB's first expansion since 1903. New York City got back one team, the Mets. But expansion could and should have happened anyway, and with less pain. The West Coast could have received new teams and the Dodgers could have remained in Brooklyn.

Why should an individual like Walter O'Malley, who happened to be in the right place at the right time, be able to rob Brooklyn, as Bill Veeck put it, of a part of its heritage? There is a perfectly clear legal answer to this question. O'Malley had a property right in the team that enabled him to do this without legal reproach. But should not the borough of Brooklyn or New York City at least share in this right? After all, the city nurtured the team during its development, conferred upon the franchise part of its trademark, gave the team what amounted to daily, abundant, free advertising through sports' coverage in its newspapers and media, and provided a variety of subsidies to the club over the years.

Of course, the same questions apply to all cities who have lost their baseball teams. Consider Milwaukee. The Braves' stadium lease expired after the 1965 season. Then, after twelve years in the city, with new owners who had promised to keep the team in Milwaukee, the Braves moved to Atlanta. The new ownership group, headed by Ray Bartholome, claimed that the team was losing money in Milwaukee. Bill Veeck argued this was nonsense, a product of accounting legerdemain.[21] True, after the Braves finished no higher than fifth place from 1962 through 1965, attendance began to fall off, but over the twelve years in Milwaukee they had the second highest attendance in the major leagues. Attendance during 1953, the Braves' first year in Milwaukee, was 1.83 million, and this was followed by four consecutive years of over 2 million attendance, with a record-breaking 2.22 million in 1957.[22]

When Bartholome, lured by an attractive television deal in Atlanta,[23] announced his planned move, a suit alleging violation of state antitrust laws was brought to enjoin the team to remain in Milwaukee. A circuit court in Milwaukee ruled that the Braves could not move to Atlanta, but the Wisconsin Supreme Court reversed this ruling, stating that the 1922 Supreme Court decision exempted baseball from antitrust statutes on both the state and federal levels.

During House hearings in 1981 over a bill to regulate the movement of sports franchises, the Braves' case was revisited. The new team owner, Ted Turner, commented that he saw no reason why the Braves or any

other team should not be allowed to relocate just the same way that a
Coca-Cola plant can relocate at will. Testifying next, broadcaster Howard
Cosell was asked what he thought of Turner's comment. Cosell responded without subtlety: "I find that argument really could not appeal
to anybody over the age of six . . . they talk out of both sides of their
mouths. They have developed an everspinning spiral of hypocrisy and
deceit that ascends up to the heavens."[24] Less poetically, Bill Veeck made
a similar appraisal of the Braves' move, calling it baseball's "latest testi-
monial to the power of pure greed."[25]

Although no MLB team has packed its bags since 1972, a number of
teams threatened to do so in 1990 and 1991, including the Montreal
Expos, the Houston Astros, the Detroit Tigers, the Chicago White Sox,
the Milwaukee Brewers, the Cleveland Indians, the San Francisco
Giants, and the Seattle Mariners. The White Sox talked about moving to
St. Petersburg, Florida, which was offering a generous package of financial incentives as well as a new domed stadium. Chicago rewarded the
White Sox for their loyalty with a new stadium, equipped with modern luxury boxes projected to yield additional revenues over $5 million
annually.

Under the original agreement for a new White Sox stadium, the Illinois State Legislature created the Illinois Sports Facilities Authority
(ISFA) and authorized the expenditure of up to $120 million to build the
new ballpark. After St. Petersburg sweetened its offer, Chicago was compelled to reciprocate. The final plan called for $150 million for stadium
construction, financed by revenue bonds and a 2 percent hotel tax. Strong
neighborhood opposition from the low-income residents who would be
forced from their homes was eventually quieted by offering homeowners
market price for their homes plus a $25,000 cash bonus toward moving
expenses. Renters got moving expenses plus a $4,500 bonus plus $250
per month as a rent differential for one year.[26] The city, of course, bore
these extra expenses. Chicago and the State of Illinois agreed to split any
operating losses on the stadium of up to $10 million per year. From 1991
to 2001 the ISFA will pay the Sox $2 million as a maintenance subsidy,
to be increased in later years; if attendance falls below 1.5 million per
year in the second decade of operations, the ISFA is obligated to buy
300,000 tickets per year.[27] Asked if the White Sox painted the state
legislature into a corner, Representative Jim Stange replied: "Absolutely,
they held us up."[28]

The Tigers are involved in politically charged negotiations with Detroit for a new stadium. Domino's Pizza entrepreneur Thomas Monaghan owns the Tigers and is using ex–Michigan Wolverine coach Bo
Schembechler as his point man with the city. Despite Detroit's $34-

million budget deficit in 1990, the city and Wayne County have agreed to build a new stadium and to float a $200-million bond to finance it.[29] As of early November 1991, Detroit had offered the Tigers two downtown sites, but Schembechler rejected both, alleging insufficient parking and excessive rent.[30] The Detroit media is more skeptical, claiming that Schembechler and Monaghan are holding out for a suburban location that can be a self-contained parking, entertainment, shopping, and eating center—a veritable baseball mall.[31] If the park has a downtown location, the Tigers' stadium club and food outlets in the prospective stadium will have to compete with the restaurants in the theater district and Greektown. Worse yet from Monaghan's point of view, fans may park their cars where they eat dinner and walk to the ballpark. And the less time fans spend in the ballpark prior to the game, the less they will browse around the baseball memorabilia shops. No matter where they locate, the Tigers are expecting $10 million or more in additional revenues from new luxury boxes, according to Bill Haas, Tigers' senior vice president.[32] The Tigers also seek an additional million or more from new advertising on an electronic scoreboard.

Mayor Coleman Young, in an October 4, 1991, press release from his office, claimed that he had been trying to talk to owner Monaghan for the previous two and a half years, but that Monaghan had not returned his phone calls.[33] Mayor Young also claimed that Bo Schembechler had not returned his calls. Wayne County official Michael Duggan says that "[Schembechler's] problem is that he can't deal with anybody."[34]

After Detroit spent $5 million to refurbish Tiger Stadium in 1977, the team signed a thirty-year lease.[35] The Tigers now claim, however, that the city has not lived up to the maintenance clauses in the contract and, therefore, the team is not bound by the lease. In his press release, Mayor Young said that there had been no lease violation by the city and he was prepared to hold the Tigers to the lease.[36] With negotiations between Monaghan and the city going nowhere, Monaghan announced in late February 1992 his intention to sell the club.

The City of Seattle already lost one baseball franchise in 1970. When the Seattle Pilots' owner went bankrupt after one year, businesspeople in the city put together a new ownership group that tried to buy the team to keep it in the city. Commissioner Bowie Kuhn rejected the bid on the grounds that there was "too much of a spread of local ownership."[37] According to U.S. Senator Marlow Cook, the owners' old boys' club wanted at least 51 percent ownership to be in the hands of one person.[38]

When the team was sold to Bud Selig and moved to Milwaukee, the attorney general of the State of Washington brought suit against MLB, claiming that the city had built the 60,000-seat Kingdome at the behest of the American League. The suit was settled out of court when the AL in 1975 agreed to place an expansion team in Seattle.[39]

The Seattle Mariners entered the AL in 1977 after paying an expansion fee of $6.5 million. After a few years the new owners sold out to Los Angeles businessman George Argyros for $13 million. Argyros was a crafty owner who managed to turn a book profit in most of his years despite never fielding a team with a winning record. In 1985, also making carpetbagging noises, Argyros convinced the city to renegotiate the stadium contract. Stadium rent would be free for 1985 through 1987,[40] and thereafter it would be only $1.2 million a year, down from $3.5 million prior to 1985.

In 1990 Argyros sold the team to Jeff Smulyan for $77.5 million, with Smulyan also assuming over $12 million in liabilities. The Mariners had their first winning season ever in 1991 and with 2.15 million attendance broke the team's previous record, but Smulyan says he is "pouring money down a rathole."[41] He claimed a book loss of $6 million in 1990 and projected an $11.6 million loss in 1991.[42] On September 6, 1991, Smulyan said he needed local leaders to come up with $16 million to solidify his team's staying in Seattle, and he gave them forty-five days to gather the funds. He claimed this was the sum he needed to bring in $52 million, or 90 percent of projected 1991 average AL team revenues.

In 1990 Commissioner Fay Vincent set forth his conditions for allowing franchise moves. (As commissioner, he can veto anything decided by the leagues if he deems it in the best interests of baseball.) His conditions: "The franchise has to have a history of substantial losses over a long period. The stadium has to be substandard with no prospects for refurbishment. The city has to have taken some steps to indicate it is not interested in baseball and is no longer going to be supportive. And there has to be some sense that staying with the community and trying to rebuild the franchise would be ultimately futile."[43] By these criteria, the Mariners do not qualify for relocation.

In the summer of 1991, Vincent set up a committee to report back to him in sixty days on new criteria and procedures for team relocation. The commissioner's office seems to be going out of its way to appear deliberative and essentially opposed to club transfers. It would make little sense for Vincent to affect any other posture. If baseball appears glib, it will only encourage the wrath of the people of Seattle and their representatives in Washington, D.C. Indeed, Washington State Senator Slade Gorton introduced legislation in September 1991 to mandate revenue sharing among baseball's rich and poor teams. Meanwhile, Vincent seems to have backed off of his 1990 conditions and has made statements to the effect that he will not stand in the Mariners' way.

Smulyan has been pulling out all stops to convince the world that he is in the poorhouse. He might be. But if he is, it likely has more to do with his 59 percent ownership in Emmis Corporation, a foundering radio chain.[44] His losses in Emmis left him in a cash-flow crunch and appeared to make it difficult for him to cancel some one-time liabilities of his baseball team. But given Smulyan's business partners, it is not clear how real this purported crunch is. Morgan Stanley & Co., a partner of Smulyan's in Emmis, owns a $20-million stake in the Mariners and lent Smulyan another $40 million at no interest to finance the purchase of his controlling interest in the team. The partnership of Smulyan, Morgan Stanley, and Indianapolis developer Michael Browning then borrowed the remaining $17.5 million from Security Pacific Bank. They subsequently borrowed an additional $22 million from Security Pacific to cover operating losses and cancel liabilities.[45] Security Pacific, in mid-September 1991, contributed to the image of an insolvent Smulyan/Morgan Stanley by demanding Smulyan meet his interest obligations, refinance the loan, or sell the team. Smulyan has repeatedly reminded reporters of this convenient ultimatum from Security Pacific, but he has not sought additional loans from any local or national bank.[46]

Smulyan's economic interest is clearly to persuade the baseball world that he has no choice but to relocate his team. Naturally he proclaims a sincere interest in keeping the team in Seattle, but it would be imprudent to do otherwise. Should Smulyan's public relations efforts succeed, then the obvious choice for relocation is Tampa–St. Petersburg with its new domed stadium. The market value of his franchise might jump by $50 million overnight. If the team does not move, then Smulyan will have squeezed additional millions in financial support out of the city and the business community.

But a closer look at the finances of the Mariners suggests that the team itself is not generating operating losses. Consider the figures Smulyan released to the *Seattle Times* concerning his team's operations (table 6.1).

Smulyan's figures show a cumulative book loss of $15.9 million during 1990–91. These figures include the $6.2 million extraordinary cost of cancelling the team's collusion liabilities to the Players' Association and the team's interest expenses. Neither of these items should be included in judging the operating profitability of the team;[47] without them, the operating loss in each year is below $2 million. However, Smulyan's figures for three items (player development, team costs, and administration) are unrealistically high.[48] Since these numbers are proprietary, they are not available for most clubs. But the 1989 figures for the Pittsburgh Pirates were leaked out, as explained in chapter 3. Average club figures for 1984 have also been published.[49] If we compare Smulyan's figures

TABLE 6.1
Finances of the Seattle Mariners
(millions of dollars)

	1990	1991 Projected	1992 Estimated[a]
Gate	$11.5	$12.8	$16.0
Concessions	$2.9	$3.3	$4.0
Advertising, Misc.	$1.8	$2.4	$2.8
Broadcasting			
local radio	$2.3	$2.3	$2.5
local television	$1.2	$1.2	$4.5
national	$13.0	$13.9	$15.5
NL Expansion	0	0	$1.5
TOTAL REVENUE	$32.7	$35.9	$46.8
Player Payroll	$14.3	$16.7	$21.0
Team Costs[b]	$3.6	$4.2	$4.2
Player Develop.	$7.3	$7.6	$7.9
Stadium[c]	$1.8	$1.9	$1.9
Administration	$7.0	$7.0	$7.3
Interest	$3.0	$3.9	$3.9
Extraordinary	0	$6.2	0
TOTAL COSTS	$37.0	$47.5	$46.2
BOOK PROFIT (LOSS)	$(4.3)	$(11.6)	$0.6
OPERATING PROFIT (LOSS)[d]	$(1.3)	$(1.5)	$4.5
ADJUSTED OPERATING PROFIT (LOSS)[e]	$2.3	$1.3	$7.1

Source: McDermott 1991d.

[a] 1992 estimates are from McDermott 1991d, supplemented by author. NL expansion revenue is assumed to be paid in two equal parts during 1992 and 1993. (As an extraordinary item, arguably it should not be included in operating profit. If this were done, estimated 1992 operating profits would be $3 million.)
[b] Travel, spring training, equipment, and so on.
[c] Rent and games costs.
[d] Operating profit = book profit + interest costs + extraordinary costs.
[e] Using 1989 costs of the Pittsburgh Pirates augmented by projected inflation for team costs, player development and administration.

with the Pirates' 1989 figures and 1984 average club figures adjusted for inflation, we find that in 1990 Smulyan's numbers for player development costs were $1.2 million above those of the Pirates and $4.5 million above the adjusted 1984 average; his numbers for administration were

$2.3 million above those of the Pirates and $3.9 million above the adjusted average; and his numbers for team costs were $0.1 million above those of the Pirates and $0.5 million above the adjusted average. In the last row of table 6.1 we adjust Smulyan's cost estimates by substituting those of the Pirates, adjusted for inflation. These figures, we believe, give a truer picture of the Mariners' potential profitability. They show the team could have been quite profitable in both 1990 and 1991, and would be profitable in 1992 even including interest expenses. Were Smulyan's numbers adjusted not by the Pirates' numbers but by the adjusted average club costs for 1984, the Mariners' potential profitability would be substantially greater.

Further, Smulyan included no explicit income from licensing. From our estimates in chapter 3, team licensing income was $2.7 million in 1990, $3.7 million in 1991, and will increase to over $4 million in 1992. It is not clear, however, whether this income is included in another category; to keep our estimates on the conservative side we did not further adjust Smulyan's figures for this item. The Mariners' prospects for 1992 and beyond brighten with the signing of the team's first cable television contract, worth at least an additional $2 million, and a likely doubling of its over-the-air television contract.[50]

At this writing, Smulyan's option date to break his lease with the Seattle Kingdome for the 1992 season has already passed. The lease, which includes the reduced rent of $1.2 million annually through 1996, allows Smulyan to opt out if the team's home attendance is not at least 90 percent of the league average through early August. To assure no difficulty in this regard, the King County Council allotted $200,000 to purchase tickets for the last thirteen home games during the 1991 season.[51] Of course, statistically speaking it is highly improbable that every team be within 10 percent of the average attendance. In fact, between 1984 and 1989 more than one-quarter of the teams had attendance more than 20 percent below the major league average. In guaranteeing an attendance level, Seattle has given Smulyan special status, and this still might not be good enough for him.

Smulyan interprets the Kingdome lease to mean 90 percent of average AL attendance since 1990 rather than in any given year. The Mariners had 92 percent of the AL average attendance in 1991, but they say they had only 70 percent in 1990. Accordingly, in December 1991 Smulyan filed papers to trigger the disputed escape clause in his lease. The lease, however, requires Smulyan to offer the team for sale to local buyers before moving. Smulyan had the team appraised at $100 million and has offered it for sale at this price. The $100-million appraisal was conditioned on additional commitments worth several millions that Smulyan's threats extracted from the city's businesses. Further, Smulyan apparently gave to the appraiser figures on the Mariners' finances different from those he gave to the city.[52]

On January 23, 1992, a group from five local businesses (Nintendo America, Microsoft, McCaw Cellular Communications, Puget Sound Power and Light, and Boeing) offered to buy the Mariners for $100 million and put up an additional $25 million in working capital. The total investment would be $125 million and involves no debt. But Nintendo is a Japanese company, and Commissioner Vincent said it was baseball's "strong policy" to allow owners only from the United States and Canada. Dave Anderson, sports columnist for the *New York Times*, called this thinking as "narrow as a bat handle."[53] He was being generous. Nintendo America's headquarters have been in Seattle for fifteen years. They were approached by Washington state Governor Booth Gardner, Senator Slade Gorton, and Seattle Mayor Norm Rice to participate in buying the club as a public service. Their representative to the proposed partnership is president of Nintendo America. A resident of Seattle for fifteen years, he would be the first majority owner of the Mariners to live in the city, to have raised his family there, and be the first to possess a Washington driver's license. The partnership's proposed chief operating officer is John Ellis, chairman of Puget Sound Power and Light. Covenants in the partnership provide abundant guarantees to the city of Seattle. Nintendo has announced that it does not want to make waves and stated its willingness to withdraw the offer. If it does withdraw, it will have won some political capital and solved a knotty problem for MLB. If it does not withdraw, then, were MLB to stand by Vincent's initial xenophobic utterances, it will seem to be courting a legal suit from Seattle and new legislative challenges from Washington, D.C.

Finally, it should be pointed out that in September 1991 the American League adopted a more generous revenue-sharing package. Twenty percent of net revenues from local cable television contracts for game broadcasting are slated to be pooled and divided equally, retroactive for the 1991 season. The details of this system have yet to be worked out, and we cannot estimate their effect. The expectation though is that the Mariners' revenues will receive an additional fillip.

If our estimates of the Mariners' finances are too rosy, then further revenue sharing would be preferable to abandoning Seattle or any existing major league city. Seattle, after all, is the nation's fifteenth largest media market and before 1991 never had a winning team, much less a division or pennant champion. There is no reason MLB cannot be viable in Seattle. The city should not be subjected to perennial threats of abandonment and extortionate demands. If MLB cannot stabilize the situation, then public authorities should. Several bills to regulate franchise movements in professional sports have come before the Congress, but only one ever made it out of committee, in vitiated form at that, and none has ever been voted on in the full House or Senate.

STADIUMS, BASEBALL TEAMS,
AND CITY FINANCES

What is it worth economically to a city to have a MLB team? It is not an easy matter to pin down an answer to this question. Clearly cities lose money on first building and then leasing public stadiums. This has become a larger and larger cost item as the share of stadiums that are publicly owned has increased dramatically since 1950. In 1950 only one team, the Cleveland Indians, played in a public stadium. Commissioner Ford Frick announced in the mid-1950s that in the future, municipalities would have to assume a greater share of the costs of operating baseball teams by providing publicly owned and maintained stadiums.[54] The cities obliged.[55] Today only five teams play in privately owned stadiums. The tendency of the 1970s and early 1980s toward retrofitting old stadiums with modern luxury boxes, public facilities, and concessions outlets has turned into a trend of building entire new stadiums; since 1986 six new, public baseball stadiums have been built or are being built, with at least three more on the way.[56]

The most careful study on the finances of public stadiums was done by Benjamin Okner in 1974.[57] Absence of reliable data has prevented more recent studies, but the situation has surely become more financially problematic for cities. Among other things, stadium construction costs have increased between 50 and 100 percent faster than the rate of inflation.[58] Okner found that revenues were sufficient to cover the operating costs of the twenty publicly owned stadiums he studied but insufficient to cover both operating costs and amortization and interest charges associated with the loans for construction. Total cost exceeded revenues by $5.9 million annually; plus he estimated that the cities lost another $8.8 million in forgone property tax that would have accrued to them had the stadiums been privately owned. Total losses were 60 percent of stadium revenues. Further, Okner found that the more recently the stadium had been built, the greater were the losses. Finally, when associated expenses for access roads, public transportation, and security were included, Okner conservatively estimated total municipal subsidies to be 3 percent (and rising) of estimated gross revenue of professional baseball and football clubs.[59]

But looking only at stadium costs and revenues gives a partial picture of the economic impact of a baseball team. Teams stimulate additional economic activity, such as the production, distribution, and sale of hot dogs, beer, peanuts, and the like. Depending on the economic geography of the metropolitan area, much of the production activity may be in the city itself. Commercial activity around the stadium (sports memorabilia stores, restaurants, clothing shops) will also be generated. To the extent that the workers in these retail outlets, as well as team employees, live and spend their income in the city, the local economy receives another push. Public transport also gets a boost. All of the direct and indirect income from these activities is connected to the operation of the baseball franchise.

A city contemplating investing in stadium construction should take all of these effects into account; however, it should also consider what alternative investments would bring to the local economy. That is, if the city floated a $200-million bond to renovate the downtown area with a cinema or theater complex, an amusement park, a concert hall, a shopping mall, new street lights, covered parking, and the like, instead of building a baseball stadium, how much economic activity would be generated? How many jobs and what kind of jobs would be created? What would be the level of retail sales and what share of the goods would be produced by the local economy?

In a 1990 study economists Robert Baade and Richard Dye argued that stadium activity brings mostly low-wage, part-time jobs. If surrounding areas are higher wage, stadium construction could actually lower the city's share in regional income. In a statistical test, the authors found precisely this to be the case. "After controlling for the effect of population and time trend, the presence of a new or renovated stadium has an insignificant impact on area income for all but one of the metropolitan areas."[60]

Whether or not having a baseball team computes as a measurable economic asset for a city, it is likely that a city reaps unquantifiable benefits from having a team. Most researchers who have studied the issue agree that having a professional sports team puts a city on the map and gives it a certain amount of prestige. More tourists and businesses are attracted to the city. The city's sense of itself and of community can be enhanced.

On the other hand, cities that have teams and lose them are likely to encounter an image problem. Politicians may face charges of incompetence and more probable electoral defeat. Most important, fans would lose a source of enduring pleasure and entertainment. Thus, whether or not having a baseball team produces a measurable economic gain, politicians work hard to attract or retain a team.

Together with MLB's controlled supply of teams, this demand for teams from cities engenders sizable public subsidies to the franchises and income transfers to their owners. One author found that "the cost to taxpayers of subsidizing sports teams' facilities runs into the hundreds of millions of dollars annually."[61]

A few examples underscore clearly the franchises' upper hand in dealing with the cities, even the largest ones. Consider New York's 1975–76 refurbishing of Yankee Stadium. The original stadium, opened in 1923, cost $2.3 million to build.[62] The refurbishing was originally scheduled to cost $23 million but ended up costing over $100 million.[63] According to Berry and Wong,[64] when it came time to collect the rent, the city was alarmed to discover that with deductions allowed in the new lease, it actually had to pay the Yankees $10,000.[65] According to the 1991 audits conducted by the New York City Office of the Comptroller, the Yankees made no rent payments to the city in 1989, and in many years the team's maintenance deductions have resulted in rent payments below $200,000.[66] The same audits found that the Yankees, who are obligated by their lease to submit a rental statement with payment by March 10 each year for the previous year, did not submit rent statements for 1988 and 1989 until November 1990.[67] All told, the audits found the Yankees owed the city $1.12 million in rent on admissions and concessions and electricity payments and $931,827 in rent on cable and luxury box income for the period 1987 to 1989.[68]

Many teams enjoy subsidized annual rent below $2 million.[69] Others, as we have seen, have lease clauses that oblige their city to buy up tickets if attendance falls below specified levels. Still others, such as the Pittsburgh Pirates and Montreal Expos, receive outright grants from their host cities in order to keep the club. When the Pirates were purchased in 1985 for $41 million, thirteen owners put up $2 million each and the city kicked in $15 million.[70] When the Expos sold for $98 million in 1990, only $65 million could be raised from a group of private businesses, so the City of Montreal and the Province of Quebec put up the remaining $33 million.[71] Despite their capital contributions, these cities are still barred from equity ownership by MLB and have no voice in management.

There is only one team, however, that threatened to move and thereby pressured the city to sell it a municipal ballpark. In the mid-1980s Anheuser-Busch bought the Civic Center Redevelopment Corporation (CCRC) from the City of St. Louis. The CCRC owned Busch Stadium and had been receiving all concessions and parking income; it also owned a riverfront hotel and two undeveloped parcels of land and had $15 million in investments. A Wall Street investment firm appraised the CCRC at between $75 and $90 million, but August Busch manipulated behind the scenes to eliminate a competitive bidder and bought it for $53 million. The Cardinals then pressured the city council into prohibiting independent souvenir and refreshment vendors from selling in the area surrounding Busch Stadium.[72]

Bud Selig, owner of the Milwaukee Brewers, is trying a variation on the St. Louis theme. After intimating relocation, Selig convinced the city, county, and state governments to contribute $67 million toward the construction of a new stadium that he and other private investors will own. Selig plans to finance his share of the construction costs by selling luxury boxes in advance.[73]

Some authors have suggested that a return to the days of privately owned stadiums would be desirable. On the one hand, there is evidence that they are constructed at lower cost than publicly owned stadiums.[74] On the other hand, it is alleged that teams would be less likely to migrate if they owned their own stadium. Both points seem plausible, but elementary political economy says it will not happen under current conditions. MLB has the monopoly power to restrict the number of franchises and largely to dictate its own terms to municipalities. Why give up a good thing if you do not have to?

Another plausible scenario that will not come to pass is municipal or community ownership. In the 1950s MLB actually encouraged community ownership in the minor leagues to deal with their financial crisis. Several viable operations were spawned that still thrive today. One such team is the Rochester Red Wings of the International League. In 1957, to stave off bankruptcy, 40,000 nonnegotiable shares were sold at $10 apiece to local residents to buy the team from the St. Louis Cardinals.[75] Another community-owned team is the Toledo Mud Hens, also of the International League. The Mud Hens have made a profit every year since 1965. As much as $75,000 of this has gone yearly to pay for public services in the city.[76] The Scranton/Wilkes-Barre Red Barons and the Columbus Clippers of the International League also are community owned. The Clippers were purchased by Franklin County, Ohio, in 1976, with funds from a budgetary surplus. Clippers' general manager Ken Schnacke credits community ownership with giving the club an economic boost: "We find when we meet with corporate clients, that it's a little easier to sell advertising and sponsorships when they know that the money stays here in the community and is not going to one individual owner in town or to an absentee owner."[77] In 1989 the Clippers were named by *Baseball America* as the Triple-A organization of the decade.

But MLB does not want municipal ownership at the major league level. In 1990 they prevented Joan Kroc, then owner of the San Diego Padres, from giving the Padres to the city. MLB also prevented Montreal and Quebec from buying the Expos. The usual public explanation for this prohibition is the messiness of public ownership. The owners do not want to deal with politicians. Listen to co-owner of the Boston Red Sox Haywood Sullivan: "We've got enough politics as it is now. You don't want elected officials to be involved in your industry because you don't know how long they're going to hold their elective office."[78] If Sullivan inquired about the way community ownership works in the International League or in other industries, he might have his anxieties laid to rest. The IL clubs do have public oversight boards, but they are run by appointed general managers with their staff. The Toledo ball club's general manager, Jim Rohr, comments: "We've never had any political headaches. Matter of fact, the county pretty much leaves us alone."[79]

Sullivan's remarks, though, are representative of the owners' desire to control who their fellow owners are. Allowing the choice of top executives to be made by political officials undermines this control. More important, public ownership also leads to open books and public scrutiny. A private club, after all, is a private club. Why open it up unless you have no choice?

EXPANSION

The travesty of the Dodgers' and Giants' migration to the West Coast after the 1957 season immediately provoked efforts to form a new major league. The fledgling Continental League was stillborn by MLB's decision to undertake its first expansion since the national agreement of 1903. The American League expanded by two teams in 1961 and the National League by two teams in 1962. Sporadic congressional pressure, a lawsuit, and the possibility that if too many viable cities are deprived of having a team a new league might form have led to a policy of periodic expansions. Table 6.2 depicts the expansion process through 1993.

Notable in the expansion timetable is the sixteen-year gap between 1977 and 1993. It took the near formation of a third league involving Donald Trump, among others, aborted by the October 1987 stock market crash, and the establishment of the Congressional Baseball Expansion Task Force involving seventeen senators and representatives in November 1987 to shake MLB out of its complacency. In April 1988

TABLE 6.2
Major League Baseball Expansions

Year	League	Team	Price (millions)[a]
1961	AL	Los Angeles Angels	$2.1
	AL	Washington Senators	$2.1
1962	NL	Houston Colts	$1.9
	NL	New York Mets	$1.9
1969	AL	Kansas City Royals	$5.6
	AL	Seattle Pilots	$5.6
1969	NL	Montreal Expos	$12.5
	NL	San Diego Padres	$12.5
1977	AL	Seattle Mariners	$6.5
	AL	Toronto Blue Jays	$7.0
1993	NL	Colorado Rockies	$95.0
	NL	Florida Marlins	$95.0

[a]Dollar amounts rounded to the nearest 100,000.

the task force threatened to introduce legislation revoking MLB's anti-trust exemption.[80]

The 1993 expansion process produced a surfeit of strong applicants. The eventual winners, Denver and Miami, seemed obvious enough in hindsight. The Denver group is headed by John Antonucci, an owner of beer distributorships, with Coors Brewing Company as the principal investor. As discussed earlier, baseball ownership has a long and lucrative association with the beer industry. Moreover, Denver is 606 miles from the next closest baseball city, Kansas City, and is the country's nineteenth-largest media market. The Miami group is headed by multimillionaire H. Wayne Huizenga, principal owner of Blockbuster Entertainment, 50 percent owner of Joe Robbie Stadium, and 15 percent owner of the Miami Dolphins. Huizenga already had a business relationship with MLB as the exclusive producer of videos for MLB Properties and the sole distributor of its tapes. Board chairman of the Pirates Doug Danforth and his president, Carl Barger, were principal boosters of Miami. Barger holds more than 100,000 shares of stock in Blockbuster Entertainment. Not surprisingly, Huizenga named Barger the president of the new Florida Marlins. The closest major league city, Atlanta, is 663 miles away, and Miami is the sixteenth-largest media market in the United States.

The expansion price tag is $95 million per team, yielding $190 million in revenues for MLB ($12.3 million to each NL team and $3 million to each AL team). Most sources estimate that initial startup costs (establishing a front office, a minor league system, advertising, and so on) will add another $25 million or more per club. By agreement Denver and Miami will not receive any of the revenues from the national media contracts in 1993 (worth over $15 million to each of the existing twenty-six teams), and by previous experience neither franchise can look forward to winning baseball until the second half of the 1990s.

Not so coincidentally, the two most active members of the congressional task force were Senators Connie Mack of Florida and Tim Wirth of Colorado. As of October 1991, the task force had not met for a year.[81] Meanwhile, Commissioner Vincent has announced that no further expansion will be considered in this century.[82] Rather than calling for more expansion, Senator Mack hopes to attract the Mariners and another existing franchise to settle in St. Petersburg and Orlando. One has to question whether such a war among cities is really in the public interest, and whether it is necessary.

Why should MLB not continue to expand? MLB itself would give two answers: first, the number of quality ballplayers is insufficient for further expansion; second, the economics of the game would not support further expansion. Neither of these answers is convincing.

Consider player quality. How would Fay Vincent or any other baseball official measure the absolute quality of the level of play? Of course, it is true that the level would fall somewhat immediately after an expansion, but the same was true in 1961, 1962, and so on. Such a short-term drop is inevitable, but it has nothing whatsoever to do with an acceptable or desirable level of play. The problem is that there is no empirical measure available of the absolute quality of play. Baseball performance is an outcome of opposing forces. If batting averages do not rise, it does not mean that hitters have not improved; it means that pitchers and fielders (and their gloves) have improved by as much as hitters have improved.

But how do we know that hitters and pitchers have gotten better? Common sense. Athletic records in all sports where individual performance is independently quantifiable have improved continuously over the years; for instance, the record for the 100-meter run stood at 12 seconds in 1896 and fell steadily to 9.92 seconds by 1988; the high-jump record increased gradually from 5 feet 11 inches in 1896 up to 8 feet in 1989.[83] Further, the physical stature of ballplayers has increased: Average player height was 69.9 inches in the 1880s, 71.6 inches in the 1930s, and 73.2 inches in the 1980s; average weight was 170.5 pounds in the 1880s,

TABLE 6.3
Baseball Players and Population

Year	Major League Players	U.S. Population	Population/Player
1890	480[a]	63,000,000	131,250:1
1903	320[a]	80,000,000	250,000:1
1990	650	250,000,000	385,000:1

[a]Based on assumption of an average of 20 roster players per team.[84]

178.8 pounds in the 1930s, and 186.8 pounds in the 1980s.[85] Cursory inspection reveals that the weight increase does not owe anything to increased obesity. On the contrary, players today are visibly more physically fit than ever before.

Another indication of quality improvement is that the share of the U.S. population playing major league baseball has fallen over the years.- Based on the ratios in table 6.3, the current U.S. population would support 40 major league teams using the 1903 ratio or 76 teams using the 1890 ratio. Indeed, baseball expert Bill James estimates that there is sufficient talent for 60 major league teams.[86]

Some fans would argue that these ratios overstate potential baseball talent because today baseball has to share the best athletic talent with football, basketball, and other professional sports to a greater extent than ever before. This is true, but the number of individuals who possess the talent and physical stature for both baseball and another sport is questionable. Of those who do, it is not clear that the other sport is often chosen.[87] Length of career expectancy is greater in baseball than either football or basketball, and baseball salaries are above those in football. Nonetheless, some young athletes probably do choose football or basketball over baseball, in part because football and basketball offer a more attractive apprentice stage. In particular, the conditions and social status of university athletics along with the opportunity to gain a college degree contrast sharply with the unglamorous and often penurious life of a minor league ballplayer.

It is also noteworthy that professional basketball and hockey have expanded at a decidedly more rapid pace than baseball. In 1967 there were ten teams in the NBA and six teams in the NHL; in 1991 there were twenty-seven and twenty-two teams respectively. That is, the NBA has expanded by a factor of 2.7 and the NHL by 3.7 over the period, while

MLB expanded from twenty to twenty-six teams, by a factor of 1.3. The NFL has also expanded more rapidly, but the existence of so many quasi-major football leagues (for example, the World League of American Football, the World Football League, the United States Football League, the Canadian Football League, and arena football) over the years makes a direct calculation more problematic.

But more important, an offsetting factor makes using the population-player ratios underestimate potential baseball talent, not overestimate it: namely, until 1946 blacks were excluded from MLB and today they comprise 28 percent of all major league players, and increasingly over the last forty years Latin players have been incorporated into the game.[88] Further, not only is general physical conditioning far superior today than it was during the early decades of the twentieth century, baseball conditioning and training has advanced enormously over the years. Little League baseball, for instance, did not even exist before the late 1930s, and it has expanded steadily since then.[89]

The fact that a smaller proportion of a more athletically talented population is playing baseball produces another statistical outcome—compression of talent at the top end. The variation among players in performance statistics has narrowed steadily over the years. One of the reasons why some longstanding records, such as sixty-one (or sixty) home runs, 190 runs batted in (1930), 177 runs scored (1921), 257 hits (1920), .424 batting average (1924), 1.01 earned run average (1914), or 41 wins (1904), are not only not broken but not even approached nowadays is that the variance in pitching skills is smaller. Today's top sluggers face fewer weak pitchers and more excellent hurlers with a broader array of dazzling pitches than did Babe Ruth, Jimmy Foxx, and Hank Greenberg, and today's top pitchers face fewer weak hitters.[90] One salutary effect of expansion would be more approaches to such records.

Further, if MLB expands it will mean more attractive job opportunities. When making career choices, young athletes will perceive a greater chance of playing in the plush major leagues and a lesser chance of being stuck in the penurious minor leagues. Eventually the supply and quality of players will increase. Pee Wee Reese made this point in his testimony before the Celler Hearings in the U.S. House of Representatives in 1951, and Larry MacPhail, a successful baseball innovator and top executive of three clubs, agreed: "I think the creation of additional major leagues would support and strengthen the whole minor league structure . . . , and there would be greater inducements to young players."[91] MacPhail went on to tell the House hearings that baseball would be better organized if there were an expansion to six major leagues instead of two.

Consider economic viability. It is convenient to MLB to have a few franchises each year that appear to be struggling. MLB can point to them and say that it has already overexpanded. But there is no reason why all companies in a business should be profitable every year, particularly if they are poorly managed. Further, as we have demonstrated in chapter 3 and above, what appears to be a struggling franchise is not always a struggling franchise.

At present, the Cincinnati Reds operate profitably in baseball's smallest media market, the thirtieth largest in the country.[92] Without incorporating any smaller media markets, since four metropolitan areas have two teams each and two teams are in Canada, it would be possible for MLB to expand to thirty-six teams. Another six media markets are within 14 percent the size of Cincinnati; at a growth rate of 2 percent a year, by the year 1997 they would all be larger than Cincinnati was in 1990. More cities could be added gradually after that.

Some observers will say that certain cities are not good for baseball. There is plenty of evidence, however, that baseball cities are made, not born. Cities that during some years appear apathetic toward baseball appear passionate in other years, depending on team performance. Within cities there has been a sharp year-to-year variation in a team's share in league attendance; for instance, between 1910 and 1950, the share of the Chicago White Sox in American League attendance varied from 23.9 percent in 1917 to 7.0 percent in 1948; the share of the Washington Senators from 15.6 percent in 1943 to 7.1 percent in 1947; the share of the Cleveland Indians from 23.5 percent in 1948 to 6.5 percent in 1915; and the share of the Philadelphia Athletics from 18.1 percent in 1911 to 3.4 percent in 1950.[93]

The cost structure of the game is not immutable and, if necessary, will respond to market changes. It may be possible to demonstrate, for instance, that if player and executive salaries continue to grow at recent rates and media and licensing revenues stagnate, several teams will be making regular losses, even without further expansion. If MLB does expand and smaller media markets host franchises, however, then baseball salaries would have to adjust to the new economic conditions. Salaries may not grow as rapidly but there would be more players earning major league, instead of minor league, salaries. To the extent that expansion produces some small-city franchises that exhibit real financial difficulties year after year, MLB can always redistribute some of the excessive profits from the big-city franchises.

Expansion to thirty-five or forty teams by the end of the century would mean that more cities have their demand for a team satisfied, a more equitable relationship would develop between existing teams and host cities, and there would be a greater number of MLB players. This outcome sounds like something economists call a welfare maximizing solution. But economists never claimed that welfare maximization was a property of unregulated monopolies. A public policy is called for, and we shall discuss some options in chapter 8.

The Media

What is the point of having a national pastime if we can't even have a national game every Saturday afternoon?
   —Senator Howard Metzenbaum, November 1989, Senate hearings on cable
industry

I live in northeast Tennessee, approximately 300 miles from Cincinnati. At 7:30 P.M. June 18 the primary game shown on ESPN was Cincinnati at New York. Why is it that Kentucky, Tennessee (except the Memphis area), western North Carolina, most of West Virginia and Ohio, western Mississippi, Indiana, most of New York and New Jersey were shown the alternate game, Oakland at Detroit? It seems to me that these areas are where the primary game needs to be shown.
   —Fan in Kingsport, Tennessee, writing to the editor of *USA Today Baseball
Weekly*

When the contract with CBS runs out [in 1993], no network is ever going to pay that much money again. The owners, who threw away all the television money, most of it on bad ballplayers, in the first 15 minutes after the checks cleared, are going to ask the players for a giveback. And the players, who have every reason to believe all owners are rich idiots, are going to laugh at them.
   —George Vecsey, sports columnist of the *New York Times*, October 1991

Professional sports franchises are quasi-public institutions. They derive much of their value from the support of the community, the goodwill of the

fans, the publicity of the media, and to ensure their stability, government has granted anti-trust exemptions to sports leagues, given tax incentives to sports franchises and built public facilities for sports teams. In exchange for this publicly created value, it only seems fair to require public access.
—Senator Herbert Kohl of Wisconsin, November 1989, Senate hearings on
cable industry

If New York is at the cutting edge of Major League Baseball's relations with the media, fans are in for some disappointments. The Yankees went from broadcasting 130 games on over-the-air television in 1965 to 75 games in 1987 and 55 games in 1991, while the Mets went from 129 off-air games in 1965, to 82 games in 1987 and 75 games in 1991.[1] Generally, the games lost to free television have gone to cable, but since cable rate deregulation in December 1986 (a product of the 1984 Cable Broadcasting Act), average cable subscription prices have increased at an annual rate of over 12.6 percent. Moreover, in many regions baseball coverage on cable has been tiered (put on a higher price category of service) or sold separately. To understand why this has happened, what the future holds, and what, if anything, can be done about it, we must look at the ongoing technological revolution in telecommunications and the ever more concentrated and interlocked structure of the broadcasting industry.

The annual value of MLB's national media contract grew by 600 percent during the 1980s, but are the halcyon days of media revenue explosion over? Despite the media success of the closely contested seven-game World Series in 1991, CBS has been making loud noises about massive losses in its $1.06-billion contract with MLB for 1990 through 1993. Has television become oversaturated with sporting events, and, if so, what does this portend for baseball media revenues? What alternative income sources can MLB turn to, and how might these affect fans' access to (and the price of) viewership?

BACKGROUND

Baseball broadcasting began innocently enough. During the 1890s, telegraph services paid for the privilege of relaying game reports to saloons and poolrooms. Not all owners were enthusiastic about this arrangement; many claimed that such contemporaneous information on the games would keep people away from the ballpark.[2] In 1913 Western Union offered each team $17,000 a year over five years for telegraph rights.

Meanwhile, in 1910, the motion picture industry paid MLB $500 for the right to film and show the World Series. In 1911 this rights' payment increased to $3,500.

MLB's early relationship with radio was equally ambivalent. In early 1920 a New York Giants' executive commented that radio coverage of games was "impossible and absurd" because "it would cut into our attendance. . . . We want fans following games from the grandstand, not from their homes."[3] This and other voices of protest notwithstanding, MLB's first radio broadcast of the Pirates/Phillies game at Forbes Field occurred on August 5, 1921. The 1921 Yankees versus Giants World Series was radio broadcast by relay. The sports editor of a Newark newspaper reported the games from a telephone in the Polo Grounds to WJZ, a Newark station, which then repeated the information over the air.[4] The following year some 5 million Americans listened to the first live radio broadcast of the World Series. In 1925 William Wrigley decided that radio broadcasts might serve as a kind of free advertising and actually promote interest in his team. Despite the protests of his fellow National League owners, Wrigley invited any radio station to cover any or all of the Cubs' games. Though the Cubs' attendance did not suffer, it still took several years before other teams followed his example.[5] As late as 1932, the three New York teams banned all radio broadcasting, even re-creations. This policy held until 1938, when it was broken by Larry MacPhail of the Dodgers. In 1939 all MLB teams broadcast games on radio for the first time. Radio rights for the World Series sold for approximately $400,000 during the late 1930s.[6]

The first baseball game ever televised was a battle for fourth place in the Ivy League between Columbia and Princeton on May 17, 1939.[7] Local television broadcasting of MLB games began in 1946 with a Yankees' contract for $75,000. When NBC provided the first live network coverage of the World Series in 1949, fewer than 12 percent of U.S. households had television sets. By 1953 fifteen of the sixteen clubs had local television contracts, and ABC introduced the first network game-of-the-week format. The share of U.S. households with televisions grew rapidly throughout the 1950s, reaching 67 percent (34.9 million households) in 1955 and 87 percent (45.8 million households) in 1960.

Radio and television broadcasting revenues together contributed only 3.0 percent of MLB revenues in 1946, but that figure rose to 16.8 percent by 1956.[8] MLB revenues from broadcast rights to the All-Star Game and World Series rose from $275,000 in 1947 to an average of $1.195 million during the years 1951 to 1956. Local team revenues during the early 1950s averaged just above $200,000 per team, ranging from a low of $9,000 in St. Louis to a high of $580,000 for the Brooklyn Dodgers.[9]

With the rapid growth of television, broadcasting revenues increased geometrically after the network contract expired in 1956. MLB's annual television network revenues rose to $3.25 million in 1960 (almost triple the figure of four years earlier), $16.6 million in 1970, $47.5 million in 1980, and $365 million in 1990. National television revenues grew at an annual rate of 17.0 percent from 1960 to 1990, while local revenues grew at a somewhat slower, albeit impressive, annual rate of 13.0 percent. MLB's national radio income is $12.5 million a year between 1990 and 1993. The estimated share of radio and television broadcast revenue in MLB total revenues rose from 16.8 percent in 1956, to 28 percent in 1970, 38 percent in 1985, 42 percent in 1988, and 50 percent in 1990.[10] These figures exclude "substantial" income from foreign broadcasting contracts in Japan, Canada, the Caribbean, and elsewhere.[11]

Since network broadcast income grew more rapidly than local income, the share in total broadcast revenues from national (in contrast to local) contracts rose over time from 25 percent in 1960, to 30 percent in 1971, to 44 percent in 1979, and to 49 percent in 1990.[12] The significance of the trend lies in the fact that national broadcasting revenues are distributed equally among the franchises[13] while the distribution of local broadcasting revenues is highly unequal. Further, the disparity of local media revenues among the teams is growing. The ratio of the top to bottom team in local media receipts increased from 5.3 to 1 in 1964 to 18.5 to 1 in 1990.[14] Perhaps more significant than the ratio is the absolute disparity, which grew from $1.3 million in 1964 to an estimated $52.6 million in 1990. The latter sum is roughly one and a half times the size of the most expensive team payroll in 1991. As explained in chapter 3, these disparities are somewhat mitigated by the introduction of modest revenue sharing out of local pay-television receipts since 1982.[15]

Since 1985 there has also been an agreement with those teams carried on a superstation to make compensatory payments to MLB.[16] The size of these payments is proportional to the number of homes that receive the rebroadcasted signal around the country and the number of games televised. The most widely distributed superstation is WTBS, which carries the Atlanta Braves (both are subsidiaries of Turner Broadcasting). The Braves paid MLB $7.5 million in rights fees in 1989, $9 million in 1990, and $10 million in 1991. At the Braves' election, the agreement can be extended to 1992 and 1993 for $12 million and $15 million, respectively.[17]

ANTITRUST EXEMPTIONS

During the 1950s the Justice Department and the courts several times indicated their disapproval of the professional sports leagues' attempts to bargain as a single entity over broadcasting contracts. But in 1961 Congress passed the Sports Broadcasting Act (SBA).[18] The SBA gave sports leagues the right to act as a cartel and sell package deals for the entire league to television networks. During the hearings on the SBA the National Football League (NFL) argued that the league needed to package television rights in order to equalize club revenues. Without such equalization, the league feared that unbalanced competition would result. Through 1991 at least, the NFL has employed its exemption judiciously. Public Law 93-107 of 1973 obligated the NFL to offer all sold-out games of home teams on free television; when the legislation expired at the end of 1975, the NFL was unwilling to risk adverse public reaction from a policy change.[19] Also, the NFL has split revenues equally among its franchises. This policy, together with the 60/40 gate split between home and visiting teams, has provided for financial stability and balanced competition in the NFL. It has allowed franchises such as the Green Bay Packers, despite a home base population of under 100,000, to survive and often thrive over the years.[20] MLB also shares equally its central media revenues among its twenty-six teams, but unlike football, the teams of MLB receive some $340 million in local media contracts, most of which is not redistributed.[21]

On the negative side, sports economist Roger Noll has claimed that the SBA had the expected impact; namely, by creating monopoly power within two years of the SBA's passage, the NFL and MLB had their revenues triple while the number of broadcast games was cut in half.[22] Whether or not Noll's finding was accurate for the 1960s, the SBA is clearly behind one other set of restrictive practices that exists today in sports broadcasting: In order to preserve the value of their package deals, the sports leagues have found it in their interests to restrict the number of local broadcasts. The National Basketball Association (NBA), for instance, restricts the number of locally broadcast games per year per team to forty-one (of which only twenty-five can be carried by a superstation, according to NBA rules).[23]

MLB has an arrangement whereby each team, in exchange for its share of the major league central fund revenues from the package deals, agrees not to allow pay television transmission outside of its designated geographical area.[24] Thus, in western Massachusetts, for instance, where there are many New York Mets' and Yankees' fans, it is not possible to subscribe at any price to either New York SportsChannel or to Madison Square Garden (MSG) network. Technology is available and inexpensive to provide such service, but MLB's restrictive practices preclude this commerce.

The 1961 SBA includes a phrase that says the right of the leagues to pool television rights applies only to "sponsored telecasting." From the hearings on the SBA to the present day, the phrase "sponsored telecasting" has always been interpreted to mean "over-the-air free broadcasting." During the hearings in 1961, when the counsel to the House Anti-Trust Subcommittee said to then–NFL Commissioner Pete Rozelle, "Do you understand, Mr. Rozelle, that this applies only to over-the-air free broadcasting?" Mr. Rozelle, who had his own counsel at his side, replied, "Absolutely." Thus the SBA was intended to apply only to the right to make package deals for over-the-air broadcasting. This raises an interesting question: Are the various package deals that have been made by the sports leagues in recent years with cable television illegal?[25]

In the case of baseball, of course, the matter is made more complicated by the 1922 Holmes decision. That is, it could be argued that baseball does not need the 1961 SBA to make a package deal with ESPN. MLB has a blanket antitrust exemption from the 1922 decision and its subsequent affirmation in the 1953 Toolson and 1972 Flood decisions.[26]

The other antitrust exemption affecting the broadcasting of baseball is the de facto monopoly power that the 1984 Cable Broadcasting Act granted to cable companies. The 1984 Cable Broadcasting Act underwrites the process of cable-ization or sports siphoning as well as the trends toward placing sports programming on higher tiers ("tiering") and rapidly increasing cable rates.[27] The hearings that came before this act essentially promised the legislators in Washington that within the course of one year (this was back in 1984!) a significant amount of competition to the existing cable franchises would develop throughout the United States. The competition was to come from direct broadcast satellite (DBS), from MMDS (microwave or "wireless" transmissions), and from the telephone companies (telcos).[28] This competition, however, still had not materialized at the end of 1991.

The 1984 Cable Broadcasting Act, anticipating imminent competition from new technologies, allowed cable companies facing "effective competition" to set their own rates and empowered the Federal Communications Commission (FCC) to define effective competition. Until the 1984 Cable Act, local boards had the power to regulate rates and services. Under the provisions of the act, rates were deregulated as of December 29, 1986. Cable companies are free to charge whatever price the consumer will pay in their monopolized markets.

The FCC's definition of effective competition left cable executives laughing all the way to the bank. A cable company was deemed to have effective competition if households in the area could receive three over-the-air broadcast signals with roof antennas. Essentially, this meant rate deregulation for the entire industry.[29] A new FCC definition of effective competition in 1991 has done little to alter the situation.[30] Senator Joseph Lieberman of Connecticut commented on the FCC definition: "The cable companies complaining of competition from three broadcast channels is like the 19th-century railroad barons complaining of competition from the Pony Express."[31]

The competition promised in the hearings prior to the 1984 act has not been forthcoming, save in 65 out of the 9,400-plus cable systems in the country. In those 65 local cases where there are competing cable delivery systems, rates are lower, the number of channels is greater, and the quality of service is superior.[32] One study has found that having competition in all cable systems would lower rates by nearly 50 percent and save consumers $6 billion annually.[33]

Why has the competition, promised prior to the 1984 act, not developed? A small part of the reason is that the alternative technologies have some remaining problems. Wireless, MMDS transmissions, for instance, do not work well if the signal's line of sight is interrupted. Most signal-quality questions of DBS have been resolved (DBS is used extensively in Japan), but decoder capabilities are subject to piracy. In the case of telcos, the regional telephone companies are awaiting legislative approval to operate television services. Once approved, an extended period of massive investments of over $200 billion, converting their trunk and feeder systems from copper to fiber optic cable, will be necessary.[34]

The more important reason why local cable companies today face little competition is because of vertical and horizontal integration[35] in the cable industry. The principal companies that are behind direct broadcast satellite and other projects are the major cable companies or MSOs (multisystem operators). The MSOs operate cable delivery services not in one community but in hundreds or thousands. Indeed, the two largest cable companies, TCI (TeleCommunications Inc.) and ATC (American Television and Communications Corp.), seem to control from 32 percent to 48 percent of all subscribers in the country, depending on the source. Since the major MSOs control most new technological initiatives for alternative delivery services that would compete with cable, and since there is no reason for the MSOs to compete with themselves, the DBS technology has not been deployed in the United States. Indeed, John Malone, TCI's chief executive officer, and the executives at some of the other MSOs have made it quite clear that they envision DBS as a complementary system, not as one that would enter into competition with existing cable companies.

In the few instances where independents rather than the MSOs have initiated DBS or other ventures, the independents have had a great deal of difficulty obtaining cable programming. Cable companies are vertically integrated as well. TCI, for instance, is the nation's largest cable delivery company, and it owns controlling shares of the American Movie Channel, Discovery, QVC, United Artists Entertainment, Home Sports Network, and Showtime, and substantial shares of the five Turner networks as well as the Black Entertainment Network. It also operates and mostly owns Prime Network, the dominant operator of regional sports networks (RSNs). So TCI effectively can limit programming availability to any independent DBS or other delivery technology effort. Viacom, which is one of the larger MSOs in the country, in fact, in 1990 brought a suit against ATC, of which Time-Warner owns 82 percent (Time-Warner also owns HBO, Cinemax, Manhattan Cable, and a 19-percent stake in Turner Broadcasting Systems). In that suit Viacom charged ATC with antitrust violations, including "engaging in integrated series of predatory and exclusionary acts and strategies designed to increase the costs of their rivals."[36] As movie studios have been prohibited since 1948 from owning movie theaters, why are cable delivery companies allowed to own cable programming? At the very least, the law is inconsistent here.

What does all this have to do with sports and sports siphoning? The cable companies have two sources of revenue. One source is the advertisements (which is, of course, the source that the broadcast networks rely on), and the other source is subscribers. To the extent that more and more of the nation is cabled, the difference in potential advertising revenue between cable and the networks diminishes. Over time, then, cable companies will develop a growing comparative advantage in the purchase of sports programming. Once purchased, their unregulated monopoly status enables them to charge excessive prices and to tier programming virtually at will. As Senator Howard Metzenbaum of Ohio stated during cable hearings in November 1989: "All this sports programming is moving into the control of an industry which is an unregulated monopoly."[37]

Congressman Chris Shays of Connecticut has expressed concern about this monopoly pricing potential. He argued in Congress as follows: "Why would a sports programmer pay a team over half a billion dollars, far more than most franchises are even worth, for the rights to broadcast its games for the next twelve years? Isn't it because the programmer knows that it can pass the cost onto the cable operator who, in turn, can pass the cost onto the consumer, who ultimately will pay this five hundred million dollar bill?"[38]

Shays went on to say that if one compares the contract the New York Mets received before cable deregulation (pre–December 1986, when the rate provisions of the 1984 Cable Act came into play) and the contract the Yankees received after the deregulation of cable, there is a tremendous disparity. The Mets signed a contract for less than $4 million a year, while the Yankees signed a contract for nearly $42 million a year. Thus, allowing local cable systems to be monopolies has permitted more revenue eventually to go to the professional sports clubs, which, therefore, are increasingly attracted to contracting with cable. In this way, the 1984 Cable Act is promoting the sports siphoning process.

Realizing the advantages of cable, the parent companies of ABC (Capital Cities) and NBC (General Electric) have been taking major interests in cable programming and systems. ABC is 80 percent owner of ESPN, and NBC is a major player in Sportschannel America's RSNs. In late 1991 CBS jumped in as well, purchasing a controlling interest in Midwest Sportschannel. This tendency of networks to buy into cable will likely reduce competition between off-air and cable networks for sports programming and further reduce the number of games broadcast over free TV.

The reduced competition over rights' bidding will also provide a countertendency to the positive effect that cable's monopoly power has had to date on broadcasting revenues of sports' leagues. The mid-1991 consolidation of the two regional sports channels in San Francisco and the talks between NBC/Cablevision's Sportschannel America and TCI's Prime Network possibly adumbrate reduced competitive bidding over sports programming. These developments may induce sports teams to opt for controlling their own programming and marketing. That is, the sports teams may attempt to sell the broadcasting of their games directly to fans without using a television station or a cable channel as an intermediary. The San Diego Padres already do this, and MLB has considered setting up its own baseball channel on more than one occasion.[39]

The growing vertical integration between cable programmers (for example, the regional sports channels) and the cable systems (for example, TCI or Cablevision) may make it difficult and expensive for MLB or its teams to move significantly into their own programming. One safeguard against getting squeezed out by the big media companies is for MLB to interlock with them. Baseball is doing this. TCI, the nation's largest cable operator, owns a 22 percent stake in Turner Broadcasting Systems, which owns the Atlanta Braves. Time-Warner, the nation's second largest cable operator, owns a 19 percent stake in Turner Broadcasting. The

Tribune Company owns the Chicago Cubs, WGN-TV (which broadcasts both Cubs' and White Sox's games), WGN-RADIO (which covers the Cubs), WPIX (which broadcasts Yankees' games) and KTLA (which broadcasts the Angels, and used to be owned by Gene Autry, singing cowboy and Angels' owner). John McMullen, owner of the Houston Astros at this writing, owns sizable action in four RSNs in the Prime Network system, including the station that carries the Astros' games. The Red Sox own 48 percent of NESN, the cable station that carries their games. MLB has set up a partnership for international ventures with NBC, thus linking to the NBC/Cablevision network. And this is not all.[40] It is curious that despite these various entanglements MLB still pretends to adhere to its 1987 guideline against cross-ownership between baseball franchises and television companies.[41]

VIEWERSHIP

Cable-ization (or sports siphoning) reduces baseball viewership both voluntarily and involuntarily. At the end of 1991, around 60 percent of U.S. television households had cable. People without cable obviously have reduced access to baseball broadcasting as games are shifted from off-air to cable coverage.[42] Others voluntarily restrict their viewership because they choose not to pay for cable installation or for the cable services that include sports programming. The trend has been for sports programming first to be "siphoned" from free television to cable, then to be moved from basic cable to expanded basic service, and then to be moved to higher or exclusive service tiers. Some fear the next step is pay-per-view (PPV), wherein it may cost anywhere from $3 to $15 to watch a game, depending on the package and the team. With each step, baseball viewership becomes more expensive and larger numbers of fans opt out.

There has been an animated dispute among sports columnists as well as between fans and baseball executives about exactly how much baseball siphoning has gone on. Commissioner Vincent has argued that the growth of baseball on cable has been in addition to, not instead of, off-air television. To a large extent, Vincent is right—for the moment.

As shown in table 7.1, considering the six-year period 1987 to 1992, the total number of broadcasts did indeed rise, as the commissioner suggests. There has, however, been a modest diminution (of 110) in the number of games broadcast on local television between 1987 and 1992. More important perhaps, the number of broadcasts on over-the-air net-

TABLE 7.1
Television Coverage of Baseball
(number of games)

	1987	1988	1989	1990	1991	1992
Local Television	1,632	1,591	1,580	1,577	1,604	1,522
Superstation[a]	466	474	417	451	435	436
Local Cable[b]	914	966	1,006	1,097	1,144	1,105
National Television	41	39	40	16	16	16
National Cable	0	0	0	175	162	156
TOTAL	2,587	2,596	2,626	2,865	2,926	2,799

Source: Paul Kagan Associates, *Media Sports Business,* various issues.

[a] Included in local television total.
[b] In 1982, there were only 328 local cable broadcasts.

work television has fallen sharply, both because CBS has reduced the number of nationally telecast weekend games and because ABC's Monday night baseball has been replaced by ESPN (cable) coverage five nights a week. These developments preclude viewership for fans without cable and/or without a local team. For fans in New York and other cities where over-the-air telecasting of games has been sharply reduced, the averages are of little comfort.

In addition to the issue of the viewership "rights" of these fans, there is the question of what will happen to the vast majority of fans over the coming years. Although local over-the-air broadcasts have held steady over the last five years, the new large cable contracts signed by the Yankees, Mets, and other teams, together with the financial advantages of cable already discussed, lead to the expectation of ongoing cableization. Vincent proudly states that free television broadcasts have held their ground, but he is not willing to guarantee this will be true in the future. MLB, unless otherwise deterred, will follow the economic imperative. Although not all of baseball's owners are so indiscreet, White Sox co-owner Eddie Einhorn probably spoke for most owners when he called free television "a stupid giveaway to spoiled fans."[43]

Do baseball fans have an inalienable right to watch games on free television? Certainly not; nor does it make sense from the standpoint of social welfare to encourage more sports television viewing than already exists. It does, however, make sense to guarantee some level of "free" access to baseball games on television. Such access will not only protect the fan without a home team or without cable, but it will prevent baseball from returning to its pre-1882 status of catering principally to the middle and upper classes.[44] As Senator Kohl is quoted at the beginning of this chapter, baseball teams are quasi-public institutions whose survival and flourishing are dependent on numerous public subsidies. A balance should be struck between private economic imperative and public access. Limits and controls need to be placed on cable-ization, and this is the job of public policy.

PROGNOSIS FOR MEDIA REVENUES

Any sound public policy will need to concern itself with the financial solvency of baseball and other professional sports. Since media revenues have been the most rapidly growing source (and have come to account for more than half) of baseball income, it is important to explore what the future holds. Bill Veeck once argued that baseball was a bargain to television, providing a three-hour show (though two to two and a half hours in Veeck's day) with its own location, actors, props, ushers, audience, writers, and so on. At his level of generality, Veeck was completely right. Baseball will always be profitable for television, at some price. The question is: at what price?

There is now a deafening, unanimous chorus that the prices paid by CBS and ESPN for their 1990–93 contracts are too high. CBS signed a deal giving it exclusive rights to 16 weekend games during the regular season, the All-Star game, the playoffs, and the World Series for an average of $265 million a year. ESPN signed a deal for 175 regular-season games a year, with exclusive rights only on Sunday night, for $100 million a year. The first year of the contracts produced large losses for each network.

The problem for CBS in 1990 was fourfold. First, that year's playoffs and World Series did not involve teams from baseball's largest media markets. This fact helped to reduce playoff ratings by 9.4 percent for prime-time games and by 3.4 percent for weekend day games below their levels in 1989. The ratings for the 1990 World Series' games improved by 26.2 percent compared to 1989, but the 1989 Series, which was interrupted by the earthquake in San Francisco, had the lowest ratings of any World Series of the decade. The 1990 World Series' ratings were still significantly below what they had been in any year between 1982 and 1988.[45] Few television executives have forgotten the 1978 or the 1981 World Series between the New York Yankees and Los Angeles Dodgers, teams from the two largest media markets, that attracted an impressive

56 and 49 percent of households with televisions in use (or ratings of 32.7 and 30.0) respectively.[46]

Second, the 1990 American League playoffs lasted only four of a possible seven games, while the National League playoffs lasted six games. Even worse, in the World Series Cincinnati beat Oakland in four consecutive games. By one estimate, CBS lost $5 million for each playoff game not played and $15.4 million for each World Series game not played.[47] Third, the United States was in the midst of its first recession since 1982 and company advertising budgets were crimped. CBS had asked $300,000 for 30-second spots during the World Series but ended up filling some of its inventory for $240,000.

Fourth, and this was at the heart of ESPN's difficulties as well, the market had become oversaturated with baseball and sports broadcasting. The total number (cable and free television) of broadcast baseball games increased from 1,777 in 1982 to 2,836 in 1991, and the total number of live sports programming on television increased by 57 percent between 1980 and 1989. National programming by ESPN and CBS has proven to be decidedly less popular with fans than local teams' programming. On a typical day, most fans have the option of watching their home team on over-the-air or cable television or watching a national broadcast on ESPN, CBS, or a superstation. Understandably, most fans chose their home team. Fans without a favorite team, fans displaced from their favorite team's media market, fanatics of the Rotisserie League, and gamblers are the main potential audience for nationally telecast games.[48] ESPN's regular-season telecasts during 1990 averaged just under 1.15 million viewers per game.

Overall, ESPN's estimated losses in 1990 were at least $36 million.[49] CBS claimed after-tax losses of $55 million for 1990 and estimated a total after-tax loss of $170 million for the four-year contract. CBS was hurt financially not only by manifestly overbidding for the contract but by negotiating for exclusive rights to all postseason games. In previous years, the networks split the contract and thereby split the risks. CBS's aggressiveness (or greed) obviously did not pay off.

ESPN's and CBS's regular-season baseball ratings were down 4.7 percent and 14 percent respectively in 1991. ESPN lost an estimated $40 million (roughly $24 million after taxes) in 1991. Their ratings were hurt by the existence of only one tight divisional race, and in this case ESPN had to compete with superstation WTBS, which carries the Braves.[50]

The 1991 All-Star Game ratings were 17.4 (roughly 16 million households), up 7 percent over 1990. The ratings for the playoff games that did not compete with Clarence Thomas's confirmation hearings for the U.S. Supreme Court were also substantially improved from 1990. Although played by teams from two smaller markets, the closely contested, seven-game 1991 World Series between the Atlanta Braves and Minnesota Twins had the highest ratings since the 1986 Series between the New York Mets and Boston Red Sox. Not only did CBS achieve the highest weeklong rating of any network since January 16–22, 1989, and gain its highest weeklong rating since February 20–26, 1984,[51] but each of the Series' last three games were estimated to have brought CBS an additional $15 to $20 million in advertising revenue.[52]

After claiming after-tax losses of $170 million on its four-year MLB contract in 1990, CBS took an additional after-tax loss of $194 million in 1991 on all of its sports contracts.[53] CBS refused to specify how much of this sum it attributed to baseball. The network's sudden diffidence might arouse some suspicion about whether it is engaging in a public relations game in a bid for smaller contracts the next time around. Even though CBS wrote off additional losses, it is highly unlikely that in 1991 it lost more than the average annual $38 million (after-tax) loss for 1991 to 1993 already claimed in 1990. Conservative estimates are that CBS took in $105 million in advertising revenues from the World Series, $95 million from the playoffs, $10 million from the All-Star Game, and $40 million from the regular season, for a total of $250 million (compared to the $265 million CBS paid MLB). To this apparent loss of $15 million should be added production costs, but the promotional advantage CBS gained during the playoffs and World Series for advertising its fall shows must be deducted. It is hard to see how CBS could have lost more than $38 million (even before taxes) from its MLB contract in 1991; and it is well to remember that advertising revenues continued to be affected by the U.S. recession and that ratings were hurt by the absence of a big-city team in the playoffs and World Series.[54]

Ratings decreases on nationally televised games and pessimistic predictions for future contracts are not new phenomena in MLB. In 1971 *Forbes* magazine warned that falling ratings might lower the value of the next network contract.[55] And in 1985 *Fortune* magazine, noting a drop in Neilson ratings between 1984 and 1985, warned "when baseball negotiates a new TV contract for 1990, it may get less than it earns now."[56] Of course, neither drop came to pass.

Nonetheless, projections that the next national contracts will not be as rich seem credible in the current context of broadcast saturation. Adjusting for the various factors that have affected the ratings during 1990–91, it would seem prudent for baseball executives to anticipate a drop of up to 20 percent for the next national contracts. Moreover, whatever contract materializes, it will have to be shared by twenty-eight, not twenty-six, teams. How will MLB adjust?

In terms of media-based income alone, offsetting increases in local broadcasting revenues seem probable. Baseball is not losing popularity. Attendance at the ballpark continues to grow, and overall viewership is up. The increase in the number of games watched more than makes up for the lower ratings per nationally televised game. Ratings for local over-the-air games have held up from 1989 to 1991, and although they are down slightly from 1985 to 1988, this drop is again more than compensated for by the increased viewership of local games on cable and the increase in the number of television households.[57]

In 1990 six teams had no local cable contracts and several others had over-the-air or cable contracts that promise to increase substantially when renegotiated. The Mariners, for instance, received $1.2 million in local television revenues in 1991 but are projected to more than triple that sum, up to $4.5 million, in 1992.

Many analysts have pointed to PPV as baseball's ace in the whole. Economist Gerald Scully has been quoted as claiming that PPV could bring a tripling of television revenues and an increase in player salaries up to the $8 to $9 million range.[58] Pirates' pitcher Neal Heaton is even more sanguine, predicting PPV by the late 1990s could raise salaries to "tens of millions of dollars."[59] Robert Wussler, chief executive officer of telecommunications giant COMSAT and owner of the Denver Nuggets in the NBA, predicts that PPV packages for "jewels," complementing regular game broadcasting, could add up to 50 percent to television sports revenues.[60]

Whereas PPV may indeed prove valuable as an additional revenue source to baseball, whether it will be a major contributor in the near future is far from clear. Several teams have experimented with PPV formats since the mid-1980s, and many of them have returned to standard cable contracts. Fans are not accustomed to paying for individual (or packages of) games on television. New habits can be created, but not quickly or without cost. As of early 1992, only 20 million homes are equipped to receive PPV. With this number growing by 2 million a year, eventually the potential market will be there to undertake new efforts to sell PPV for baseball. But it must be recalled that baseball has few jewels, and those are already accounted for by national network contracts. It is questionable whether even the complacent U.S. Congress would allow the All-Star Game, the playoffs, and the World Series to be shifted to PPV in the near future.

What appears more plausible is that by the late 1990s PPV will combine with other new technological options, such as fiber optics and cable compression, to offer fans the option to purchase viewership of any MLB game on any day. New technology will also permit viewing enhancements, such as high-definition television (HDTV), compact disc–quality audio, and interactive viewer controls of angle shots, replays, statistics, and so on. All this will undoubtedly mean more television revenue for baseball, but these options are unlikely to be developed by the time the current CBS and ESPN contracts expire after the 1993 season. Among other things, such a development would require MLB to drop its long-standing restrictions on market areas for each team, enabling fans any-where to take full advantage of what technology allows.

The greatest likelihood, then, is for some income growth in local media contracts helping to neutralize an expected decrease in the na-tional television contracts after 1993. MLB's television revenues overall can be expected to stagnate or creep upward until the late 1990s, when a new growth period is possible. Continued growth in MLB licensing and luxury box income will also help. On a smaller scale, increased revenues from stadium advertising, concessions, parking, and higher ticket prices can be anticipated as well.

From a commercial point of view, the revenue potential of PPV is great. Consider the following. In 1989 an average of 560,000 households watched each New York Mets game broadcast on WOR-TV in the New York City inner market.[61] At this rate, over a 162-game season, 91 million households would watch Mets' games. If the Mets were to estab-lish their own PPV station and cautiously charge just $1 to view each game, even assuming viewership fell 50 percent, there would still be $45.5 million in revenues before counting any advertising income. The Mets' total revenue from local television and radio in 1989 was around $21 million.[62] Alternatively, consider a team at the other end of the scale. Using the same assumptions, the Seattle Mariners could have earned $7.4 million in PPV sales alone, without including any revenue from selling advertising. Actual Mariners' income from local media in 1989 was $3.0 million. If MLB ever gets its foot in PPV's political door, any early pricing discounts are sure to disappear and regular-season per-game prices in the $3-to-$10 range are more likely.

Should Congress allow it, even greater gains would accrue to MLB if its jewels were put on PPV. For instance, if only 10 percent of the country's 92.5 million television households paid $10 a World Series game, then each game would gross $92.5 million before advertising revenues. On this basis, a seven-game series would gross nearly $650 million. The commercial imperative has defined MLB's path until now, and without a concerted political effort it is likely to do so in the future.

In the meantime, an interesting issue is how baseball will deal with the shifting balance between local and national media revenue sources. As national sources decrease and local sources increase, under existing regulations the share of media revenues that are distributed equally among the teams will go down. The sharp inequalities in local revenue sources will then become more decisive in determining a team's financial position, and greater pressures for revenue sharing out of local media income are certain to surface.

Procedures for changing MLB's revenue-sharing rules vary from requiring three-fourths vote in a joint meeting of the two leagues, to a three-fourths vote in each league, to a simple majority in each league, depending on the revenue source being shared. Complicating matters further, these revenue-sharing regulations are defined in different sections of Article Five of the Major League Agreement as well as in separate National and American League documents. These documents include sufficient cross-referencing and ambiguity in the language to provide fertile ground for dissension among the owners regarding the proper procedures.[63]

In September 1991 the AL altered its revenue-sharing formula out of local pay television monies. The former formula set an amount to be paid into a league pool, later divided equally among all the teams. The amount paid into the pool was based on the number of subscribers to the team's pay television channel, with varying contributions per subscriber depending on whether the service was carried on basic, premium, or pay-per-view cable. The end result reportedly involved sharing roughly 10 to 15 percent of local pay-television revenues. The new formula calls for sharing 20 percent of "net receipts" (the NL formula calls for sharing 25 percent of "net receipts").

The 1991 modification in the AL formula required only a majority vote, according to a change in voting procedures voted at an AL meeting in December 1984.[64] There is, however, some dispute about whether the AL owners actually voted at that 1984 meeting to make this change. Thus the 1991 modification in AL revenue-sharing rules could have been challenged by a big-city team, but the Yankees, for one, agreed not to challenge it, hoping for a lenient interpretation of "net receipts." As we pointed out in chapter 3, "net receipts" is not clearly defined, and teams can deduct a variety of actual or imputed costs from their gross revenues: rent for the broadcast booth, electricity, production costs, team promotion, or other expenses. For major league teams having ownership ties with their broadcasters, this definition becomes even more malleable. The Yankees also argued that "net receipts" referred not to the entire cable contract but to that part of it related to original game broadcasts.

The Yankees claim that a good part of their $42 million annual contract with MSG is not for the original game rights but for rebroadcast rights and the rights for the use of the Yankee logo. In July 1991 the New York City Comptroller's Office produced a tax audit that claimed the Yankees owed the city over $1 million in back taxes for 1987 to 1989; one of the main areas of contention was precisely the Yankee's interpretation of net cable revenues.[65]

Given these conflicts and ambiguities, MLB seems ill-equipped to adopt policies for greater revenue sharing. If the commissioner's office tried to force the issue, citing the "best interests of the game" clause, it is a sure bet that the big-city owners would seek to defend their property rights in court.

With a more rational course of action apparently beyond its grasp, MLB is likely to seek revenue-enhancing options that do not produce conflicts of interest among the teams. These options, however, all lie in greater commercialization and produce a conflict of interest with the fans. For example, the advertising time between half-innings of a ball game has already been expanded from one minute to two minutes and ten seconds; in consequence, the average length of games has increased from just over two hours to close to three hours; perhaps advertising time will be stretched a bit more.

The World Series is already played exclusively at night (at least for East Coast viewers), excluding most children from viewership. It is difficult to see how this is in baseball's long-run business interests. Curt Smith, expert on baseball broadcasting and author of *Voices of the Game*, laments: "What they've done is write off an entire generation of Americans. . . . If you don't learn to love baseball as a kid, you never will."[66] But with short-term profits beckoning, perhaps this nocturnal prejudice will be extended to all playoff games as well.

To the chagrin of Ernie Banks and millions of baseball fans, scheduled doubleheaders have become exceptionally scarce; perhaps they will become extinct. Postseason playoffs have already been expanded from a best-of-five to a best-of-seven format; perhaps we will see an NFL-type playoff system that involves more teams in an effort to preserve broader fan interest during the season as well as to generate more postseason revenues.

The biggest commercialization threat looming on the horizon appears to be pay-per-view. In a new telecommunications environment and with a permissive government, PPV can be a major source of new revenues, but it may also progressively alienate low-income fans from the game.

To paraphrase genteelly White Sox co-owner Eddie Einhorn, it is plausible to contend that baseball viewing should not be unlimited and free.

But it is equally plausible to argue that in return for the significant government subsidies and public patronage that are bestowed upon MLB, the political process has the right to place some constraints on MLB's propensity to commercialize.[67] Public policy should pursue a balance between the private economic interests in the game and the importance of preserving access to our national pastime for all fans.

CHAPTER 8

The Future

It is time the Congress acted to solve this problem.
—Chief Justice Warren Burger, referring to baseball's antitrust exemption in the concurring position in the 1972 Flood case

It is disgraceful for Congress to remain inactive when injustice and confusion are so prevalent in American sports, and something should be done promptly.

—James Michener, author, 1976

Baseball's exemption is an anachronism and should be eliminated. I know of no economic data or other persuasive justification for continuing to treat baseball differently from the other professional team sports, all of which are now clearly subject to the antitrust laws.
—Deputy Assistant Attorney General Abbott Lipsky, testifying before House Subcommittee on Monopolies on April 28, 1981

Disaster is coming.
—Jerry Reinsdorf, co-owner of the Chicago White Sox, 1991

When you come to a crossroads, take it!

—Yogi Berra

We began our exploration of the business of baseball by quoting Commissioner Fay Vincent's premonition of catastrophe. We have seen, however, that dire economic predictions are as much a part of the baseball tradition as the seventh-inning stretch. The economics of baseball in the 1990s is indeed in flux, as it has been for most of the sport's professional lifetime, but there is no natural catastrophe in its path.

Baseball's popularity and, more so, its revenues continue to increase. Although it is widely anticipated that Major League Baseball's national media contracts will be smaller next time around (commencing in 1994), local media contracts should be sufficiently richer to compensate for any shortfalls from the national deals. Further, licensing revenues are large and soaring. In 1991 licensing revenues per team probably surpassed $3,500,000 and give every indication of growing at 15 to 20 percent or more per year in the immediate future.[1] Income from the sale of luxury boxes is another important new revenue source, as is the increase in concessions income that these boxes stimulate. A more modest but interesting revenue growth potential lies in international media and licensing contracts. The astronomical growth in franchise values that has characterized the last fifteen years may well abate, but average franchises are still profitable even before considering their synergy with jointly held companies, tax advantages, and the consumption value to their owners.

MLB has been the beneficiary of public subsidies worth tens of millions of dollars annually, a blanket antitrust exemption, contracts with cable companies enjoying monopoly control over local markets, and no restraints from public regulations. Fan support has been enduring despite the game's commercial shenanigans, ethical miscues, and labor-management turmoil. If MLB or any of its parts has economic problems, it has nobody to blame but itself.

MLB's ownership ranks have never suffered from a lack of eccentricity or avarice. Despite management deficiencies, the game's sanctioned monopoly together with the reserve clause until 1976 and soaring media revenues from 1976 to the present have allowed the business of baseball to flourish. As economic imbalances and pressures increasingly have surfaced in recent years, MLB has stepped up its relentless commercialization of the game. Many players have responded in kind: concentrating on individual performance statistics, hiring overpaid agents, becoming entertainers on the field and product promoters off, and charging youngsters five to twenty-five dollars for their autographs. Owners have turned to the cities for yet more financial support and to pay television for more income.

With the prospective stagnation or diminution of national media revenues, the tendency toward siphoning baseball telecasting to cable and eventually to pay-per-view will be reinforced. The growing importance of local media revenues will aggravate the existing inequalities across teams, and, in an effort to avoid greater revenue sharing, the big-city owners will lead a new assault against the players' union, the cities, the minor leagues, and the fans.

Asked at a November 1991 business seminar in New York City what MLB would do to resolve its economic difficulties with the Players' Association, owner Eddie Einhorn responded emphatically with one word: "Strike!"[2] The disruption and debasement of our national pastime are avoidable, but *not* if matters are left solely to the owners to resolve. An active public policy is needed, encompassing the abrogation of MLB's antitrust exemption and the formation of a federal sports commission.

THE PROBLEM AREAS

There are five extant problem areas confronting MLB today: labor relations, revenue inequality among the teams, relations with the minor leagues, relations with the host cities, and the future of television and radio broadcasting.

Labor Relations

Baseball's labor relations have been unsettled, if not turbulent, for two decades. Since 1972, every time the Basic Agreement between MLB's Player Relations Committee and the Players' Association was renegotiated, there has been either a strike or a lockout. A new confrontation in 1993 seems inevitable.

The existing system, although it has led to the gradual disappearance of salary exploitation on average, still exploits players with less seniority and overall does a poor job in matching player performance and player salaries in particular years. The next five years or so are likely to be ones of only modest growth in MLB revenues, and there is little prospect that the post–1976 explosion of player salaries can continue. From 1976 to 1991 major league player salaries grew at an annual rate of 13.8 percent, and between 1990 and 1991 salaries grew by 42.5 percent. Baseball's small-city franchises will not be able both to absorb double-digit salary increases each year and still to remain profitable. If labor relations have been volatile with average salaries doubling every five years, what will happen when salary growth is in single digits or even if average salaries stagnate?

The 1990 Basic Agreement called for an economic study committee to be formed and to issue a report on reforming MLB's labor relations and economic policies by October 1, 1991. Not only was no report issued, but as of November 1991 the committee had scarcely developed sufficient consensus to hire its staff. Even with such a report, there is little likelihood that any meaningful internal reform would ensue. Similar efforts in the past have come to naught.

The present system, according to many baseball writers, has encouraged players to emphasize their quantitative, tangible contributions to their team and to avoid playing when mildly injured. Team play suffers. One method that has been used by manufacturing concerns, particularly in Japan, to encourage team play among the workers is profit sharing and participatory decision making. Walter Haas, owner of the Oakland A's and Levi-Strauss Co., ruminates quietly about the possible benefits of such a system but acknowledges that other owners would string him up if he tried to promote it seriously.

During the 1990 negotiations, the owners proposed, as a first offer, a team salary cap at 48 percent of average MLB team defined revenue (gate plus broadcasting revenues). Former Player's Association director Marvin Miller scoffs at the idea: "Why should labor accept a system that doesn't permit management to pay an individual as much as it wants?"[3] Perhaps, but if a reasonable cap level (see discussion in appendix A) can be identified, if the plan buys labor peace and reinforces competitive balance on the playing field, if it is accompanied by open books and profit sharing, and if the Players' Association is allowed to participate in MLB's major structural decisions, then it might be worth a try.[4]

Don Fehr, current director of the Players' Association, told the author that he would be willing to consider a salary cap/profit-sharing plan provided that the association was given veto power over important structural decisions.[5] Interestingly enough, Eddie Einhorn asked rhetorically during a recent public address: "What do we need owners for anymore?"[6] Don Fehr wonders why they were ever needed.

The results of our statistical exercises in chapter 4 suggested that players with less than six years' experience (pre–free agency) are systematically exploited. Some writers will dismiss this as insignificant on the grounds that what a player loses during his first years in the league will be made up during his later years. This indeed is true on average for players who are around for more than six years. But of those 10 percent of professional baseball players who are fortunate enough ever to play a game in the major leagues, only approximately one in eight plays more than six years in the majors. Back in 1980 the Players' Association put forward the demand that players be granted free agency rights after four years. That or a similar demand has not reappeared; instead, the

Players' Association has battled to preserve the players' salary arbitration prerogatives.

Although the final offer arbitration scheme employed by MLB is eminently sensible and has indeed encouraged prehearing settlement, salary arbitration is a financially and psychically costly process. It tends to fortify the premium on measurable individual records at the expense of team play, and several studies have questioned whether it saves the owners money relative to an earlier free agency rule.[7]

The varieties of possible new structures in MLB labor relations are too great to do justice to here. For our purposes, one point stands out. Whether or not player salaries come to better reflect player performance is entirely a matter for the Players' Association to work out with the owners; baseball fans, however, as participants in a primal cultural ritual and as taxpayers to a system that provides a panoply of subsidies to MLB, deserve the guarantee of a complete spring training and a complete 162-game schedule year in and year out.

The Minor Leagues

A second internal structural issue is the exploitative conditions for players in the minor leagues. Minor league players have no rights to bargain with different potential employers, receive very low to modest wages during their four to five and a half months of work, receive virtually no benefits, and have approximately only a one-in-ten chance of ever playing a single game in the major leagues. To some extent, the difficult conditions for minor leaguers can be justified by the similar situation of apprentices elsewhere in the arts and entertainment industry. The aspiring artist, performer, or athlete faces big odds, but the potential prodigious payoff of making it induces many to endure. One difference, of course, is that apprentices elsewhere in the arts and entertainment industry are not limited to selling their work at one gallery or to signing a contract with one studio. If they have marketable talent, they can sell it to any interested buyer. Minor leaguers are drafted by one team with which they must sign or stay out of professional baseball for at least one year. Once signed, they can be reserved by one club for up to seven years in the minors.

Baseball's problem is magnified by the small role currently played by intercollegiate competition. If baseball were as developed at the college level as basketball and football, the minor leagues as we know them would be obviated. The current issues of exploitation at the professional level, accordingly, would disappear. One problem is that there is little prospect for a significant expansion of college baseball, largely for climatic, calendar, and financial reasons. Another problem is that many people believe the current practices of college football and basketball exploit student athletes by making them sacrifice their studies while not paying them for their services.[8] An intermediate solution in baseball might be for colleges to allow their amateur athletes to contract to play professional baseball during a shortened summer season and still return to play college ball during the academic year.[9] This option would require a new conception of the amateur athlete, but the commercialization of college sports has left the existing distinction between professional and amateur athletes ambiguous at best. If a law student can work in a law office and be paid during the summer months, why cannot a prospective baseball player do the same in his profession?

A change along these lines would allow for a significant expansion of the semipro summer leagues, allow the baseball prospects to receive a college education and some modest compensation concurrently, and presumably improve the training of the players under MLB auspices. Further, the improved conditions of apprentice baseball would induce additional athletes to explore a baseball career, making it still more plausible for the major leagues to expand.

Ultimately, a policy of expansion offers the best prospect for minor leaguers. If MLB would expand by two additional teams in 1995 and then by four teams every three years beginning in 1998 until it reached forty-two teams, there would be 1,050 major leaguers by the year 2004, or 350 more than will exist in 1993.[10] Three hundred fifty additional athletes, who would have otherwise been stuck in the minor leagues, would play in the majors. With fourteen additional major league teams, each existing team would be able to eliminate one or two of its minor league franchises (presumably at the Single-A level), and minor league baseball would still be preserved in each of the cities currently hosting a team. The major league franchises would thus economize on their bloated and inefficient minor league systems. With lower player development expenses, the argument for requiring six years of major league experience before granting free agency to allow teams to recoup their development expenses would be weakened. Undoubtedly, the absolute quality of play would drop a bit for a few years, but it would still be considerably above where it was in the 1920s, 1940s, or 1960s, as argued in chapter 5. The ensuing greater dispersion of player talent would engender more challenges to individual records and contribute to the excitement of the game.

One possible drawback would be a stronger tendency for less competitive balance on the playing field, since greater talent dispersion would

some cases, for the city to buy tickets in order to bring attendance up to a guaranteed level. The cities, then, share amply in the downside risk; they should also share in the profits.

The Media

Electronic technology is advancing at a dizzying pace. By the year 2000 it is likely that a large share, if not a majority, of homes will be equipped with large-screen, high-definition televisions connected to a fiber optic wire or coaxial cable that carries digitally compressed sound and video information sufficient to display well over a hundred different shows at any one time. The technology would not only permit a household to pick up any baseball game being played, but also to control video angle shots, call for statistical information, and receive compact disc–quality audio. Who will own the fiber optic wire; whether there will be competitive distributors of television signals; who will own the programming and what their relation will be to the signal distributors; what the interlocks will be between the distributors, the programmers, and MLB—these are all questions that will determine the nature of baseball on television in the next century. At the end of 1991, the Federal Communications Commission (FCC) is just beginning to grapple with how to establish new rules of the game to manage the new technological capabilities efficiently.

It would be premature to speculate on what the telecommunications industry will look like and what specific policies need to be taken to safeguard the fans' interests. It is not premature, however, to identify principles that should be applied in defining the new policies.

One basic principle must be to assure fans a certain amount of free access to games, as long as over-the-air broadcast networks exist. The 1984 Cable Act permitted local distribution monopolies to be freed from any pricing regulations. The result has been monopoly pricing of different cable services. Through cost pass-alongs, monopoly pricing has facilitated the process of sports siphoning and tiering that has reduced baseball viewership in certain areas and in certain income brackets.

Vertical and horizontal integration in the industry helped to thwart the development of effective competition, and the Congress and the FCC have been complicitous in not checking the power of cable monopolies. Both Congress and the FCC have expressed a preference for competition over regulation, but the promised competition has not been forthcoming, with a few isolated exceptions.[17] Furthermore, it is not clear that competition between two or more distribution companies is preferable to a regulated monopoly. With coaxial cable, direct broadcast satellite, or digital compression/fiber optic technologies, there are significant economies of scale. If two or more companies share a given market, their average cost of supplying the service will be appreciably higher than if one company supplies the service. Thus a regulated monopoly charging average costs plus a modest markup may be a preferable policy outcome.

Collusive practices among cable programmers and distributors also need to be stopped. The Federal Trade Commission and the Justice Department should not stand idly by when two sports networks in a given region decide no longer to compete over sports contracting or when integrated telecommunications companies prevent competitive distributors from purchasing their programming.

MLB should not be allowed to define territorial restrictions on the broadcasting of its games. In exchange for the pooling rights conferred by the 1961 Sports Broadcasting Act, MLB should be compelled by application of antitrust statutes to allow fans in any area to purchase viewership of any desired game. Further, as sports siphoning becomes more comprehensive, it will be important for public policymakers to ensure that competitive prices are established for purchasing viewership of games.

Since the heresies of the American Association in 1882, allowing Sunday ball and beer to be consumed in the stands, baseball viewership has been part of U.S. mass culture. Relatively low basic admissions prices to the ballpark and access to free viewership on over-the-air television have preserved this attribute. As cable and pay-per-view television present ever richer commercial opportunities, a modicum of free viewership should be preserved.

It has been five years since a World Series game was played in the afternoon. The search for prime-time advertising dollars led baseball and the networks to schedule all World Series games at night. So shortsighted a measure is creating a generation of youngsters east of the Mississippi who will grow up without the possibility and the custom of watching baseball's premier contest.[18] Such habits are shaped largely during the formative childhood years, and their absence, whether or not salutary for the nation's well-being, cannot augur well for baseball's television ratings in the coming years. MLB, of course, is not alone among U.S. industries in pursuing a shortsighted commercial strategy.

ROADS TO REMEDY

Not all fans will be concerned with each of the foregoing issues in the abstract, but the fact is that they contribute to outcomes that do concern most fans: increasing cost of seeing games, greater burden for the taxpayers, periodic interruption of the playing season, vitiation of team play, possible team relocations, among others. There are three possible routes for remedy: MLB can be left to find its own solutions; Congress or the courts can sanction the full or selective application of antitrust laws; and/or public regulation can be introduced.

Internal Remedy

In chapter 2 we discussed the owners of MLB teams and their governing structure. This structure has been capable of periodic reform, but it has done little to redress its real problems when not forced to do so. Expansion came begrudgingly, but first only when the Continental League was about to become reality and later only when the courts or Congress made threatening noises. Until the Players' Association forced open the door of free agency, exploitation of players was the rule except for brief periods when competitive leagues bid up salaries. There is no prospect in the near future that the minor leaguers, the fans, or the cities will rise and organize to defend their interests against the baseball establishment. Further, baseball's owners and the Players' Association have established a poor track record of labor peace, and the owners have shown themselves prone to perpetual bickering over issues of revenue sharing.

As local revenue sources continue to grow and national sources stagnate, greater revenue sharing will become important for baseball's health. The prospects for finding an internal solution are not comforting. For obvious reasons, owners have widely divergent and deeply felt interests. At stake are both their income streams and franchise values. The typical attitude of big-city franchise owners was clearly expressed a few years back by Bill Giles, Philadelphia Phillies president and co-owner, in response to a proposal from then Baltimore Orioles' owner Edward Bennett Williams to increase revenue sharing: "Well, of course, if I were Edward Bennett Williams, I would feel that way, too. But I have a responsibility to the people who invested $30 million in this ball club and we would not have paid so much if we had to share our TV revenue to a greater degree."[19]

MLB uses three different vehicles to share revenues: gate, national media, and local pay TV. Not only is each governed by different voting rules, but, as explained in the last chapter, there is a lack of agreement about the interpretation of these rules. Before any substantial change is assayed, then, it will first be necessary to clarify the rules. Then it will be necessary to fashion a consensus. In the improbable event that the commissioner should invoke the "best interests of baseball" clause and attempt to impose a new revenue-sharing formula, it would be a good bet that the injured owners would defend their property rights in court. Here, as in the other issues, there is strong reason for pessimism if baseball is left to its own devices.

Antitrust Remedy

Views on the importance of baseball's antitrust exemption have varied widely. In their 1981 book *Baseball Economics and Public Policy*, economists Jesse Markham and Paul Teplitz argued that prior to the introduction of free agency, there was cause to remove baseball's antitrust exemption, but with free agency the exemption has little economic meaning. Their study was commissioned by MLB. Economist Gerald Scully agrees that not only do the players have free agency now but they have a powerful union to protect their interests, so lifting the antitrust exemption would accomplish little.[20]

On the other end of the spectrum is law professor Stephen Ross; he could scarcely paint a rosier picture of the benefits from applying antitrust statutes to baseball.

> Competing leagues would vie against each other for the right to play in public stadiums, driving rents up and tax subsidies down. Leagues would be more eager to add new expansion markets, lest those markets fall into the hands of a rival league. Because the competing leagues would bid on players, salaries would reflect more accurately the players' fair market value, and no one league would unduly restrict intraleague mobility of players. Teams thus could obtain more readily the right player for the right position. Leagues would hesitate to move prime games to cable for fear of losing their audience, as well as the loyalty of their fans, to a league whose games remained available on free television. The pressure of competition would force each league to maintain intelligent and efficient management.[21]

Reality lies somewhere in between these polar contentions that antitrust action would do away with all problems in MLB and that it would do nothing. Where does it lie? The first question to answer is what areas of MLB are still affected by its exemption.

Consider the players. Damages in the recent collusion cases against the owners were settled at $280 million (see chapter 1). If antitrust principles were applied to these cases, the Players' Association would have been entitled to triple damages, or $840 million. Realizing this, the Players' Association added a clause to the 1990 Basic Agreement stating that in the future owners' collusion over free agent salaries will be subject to triple damages. The owners accepted the change, so the players no longer need the Sherman Antitrust Act to enforce triple damages.

What about the players with less than six years' experience who do not have free agency rights? Since the Players' Association operates essentially as a union shop, including all major league players, the collective bargaining agreement legally binds all major leaguers to its provisions. Players without free agency cannot bring an antitrust suit against MLB because of the nonstatutory labor exemption that allows labor unions involved in bona fide, arm's-length bargaining to surrender possible protections under antitrust statutes. Removing the antitrust exemption, then, would have no direct effect on MLB's relation with the major league players.[22]

Minor leaguers are in a different category. They do not belong to the Players' Association or any other union, and MLB restrains them from entertaining competitive bids for their labor services. This is restraint of trade, and no labor exemption applies. Theoretically, a minor leaguer could sue MLB. Of course, such a suit would be time consuming and costly, and most minor leaguers have neither the money nor the interest to challenge their employers. Moreover, any lawyer would advise them that their chances in such a suit would be slim since the courts have repeatedly upheld MLB's antitrust exemption. Were the exemption lifted, this is an area that could well be affected.

The absence of a blanket antitrust exemption in the NFL and the NBA has not mattered in this regard because they do not have professional minor leagues; colleges serve in this capacity. Interestingly, however, both the NFL and the NBA have been challenged in court on a related issue where MLB is also vulnerable—the amateur draft. In all three sports, amateur players, out of either high school or college, are drafted by professional teams and prevented from seeking competitive bids for their services. The NBA and NFL have won their cases, basically on union shop grounds. That is, amateurs being signed in the basketball or football drafts are about to enter the "majors" and its players' union, so they are bound by the rules of the union's collective bargaining agreements. These rules accept the draft and, hence, by the labor exemption, the drafts are legal. Players drafted in baseball, however, are headed for the minor, not the major, leagues, where there is no union. Thus a challenge of baseball's June amateur draft would be quite compelling in the absence of baseball's antitrust exemption.

This matter has become even more relevant in 1992 with MLB owners' decision to alter the regulations on draftees in order to forestall the rapidly increasing bonuses. Brien Taylor's 1991 signing bonus was $1.55 million; just a few years earlier, in 1987, the first-round draft picks had signed initial contracts for between $80,000 and $175,000. Taylor's success in bargaining with the Yankees was linked to his threat to attend a junior college and then reenter the draft the next year; under previous rules, Taylor would have been allowed to try the market again after one year and hope for better results. The Yankees, unwilling to risk losing Taylor to another team, offered him this record bonus, but other teams in 1991 let their first-round draft picks go rather than pay the higher prices. MLB announced that these high prices for unproven amateur draft picks threatened the financial health of the game and in March 1992 changed the rules to attach high school draftees to the selecting team for five years. While some amateur may opt to test baseball's new rule in the courts, the existence of the antitrust exemption is certainly one factor that would lower the chances for success of such a challenge.[23]

The existence of the reserve system in baseball's minor leagues also makes it more difficult for competing leagues to establish themselves. When the Continental League was forming in the late 1950s, Branch Rickey appealed to MLB to allow the new league to draft and pay for players from its minors. MLB never responded to the request. The Continental League had the option of suing MLB for exploitative adhesion, but here again MLB was protected by the antitrust exemption. Not anxious to test its exemption over this issue and to otherwise alienate scores of politicians, MLB compromised on an expansion program that incorporated some of the prospective team owners from the Continental League. Another effort to form a third league was close to fruition in 1987 when the stock market crashed in October, financially decimating some of the monied individuals involved in the effort. The effort was revived with some new investors in 1990; one of the chief concerns was access to minor league talent. Without such access, the quality of play would be too low and the riskiness and expense of drafting players out of high school too great to make the new league viable. A third league in baseball does not have the option that the American Football League (AFL) or U.S. Football League (USFL) had in football to offer sweeter deals to college players. Unlike in college football and basketball, the overwhelming majority of baseball's college players are not ready for major league competition.[24]

Consider the media. Here antitrust has a straightforward role to play. MLB restrains trade when it imposes territorial restrictions on the broadcasting of its games. The right to negotiate a network package for over-the-air broadcasting conferred by the 1961 Sports Broadcasting Act (SBA) should be qualified to guarantee a certain level of fan access to free telecasting. Strictly speaking, the 175-game ESPN package is a violation of antitrust law since it is pay television and not protected by the SBA. If MLB's blanket exemption were lifted, the ESPN package would be subject to challenge. In exchange for the right to make such a package deal, MLB might be required to lift its local blackout provisions on Tuesday, Thursday, and Friday nights. Lifting these provisions would raise somewhat the value of the ESPN package and lower somewhat the value of local contracts, but on balance the gross revenues should not be affected. Revenues from local sources (of which only a small portion is shared) would simply be redistributed to national sources (all of which is shared).

Although not directed at baseball per se, the deregulation legislated in the 1984 Cable Broadcasting Act permits monopoly pricing of cable services by local cable companies. New technology may make this act obsolete by the year 2000, but if economic interests and political influence continue to conspire to hold back the deployment of new technology or if telcos and cable companies enter joint ventures to provide the new telecommunications services, then this act needs to be amended. Unregulated pricing and monopoly power in cable delivery have been allowed to coexist and undermine consumer welfare since December 1986. Unless or until competition is restored, cable prices need to be regulated.

Consider the cities. Stephen Ross and others claim that if baseball's exemption were removed, then the existing leagues would be broken up, opening the way for new teams to enter. Such expansion, indeed, might be an outcome of lifting baseball's antitrust exemption. First, however, a wealthy and patient plaintiff must be found.[25] The Players' Association has for years adopted a public posture against the exemption, and both Marvin Miller and Don Fehr have made noises about suing to break up the leagues if baseball ceases to be the only industry exempt from the nation's antitrust laws.[26] But since 1976 the Players' Association has done little to pursue available challenges to the exemption and has even given up attempting to lower eligibility for free agency. The Players' Association certainly stands to grow in membership if baseball expands, however, with expansion, it is possible that team average revenue would be lower than without expansion, and this would lead to lower average salaries (or slower salary growth). Not many unions in the United States have enthusiastically accepted the tradeoff of more jobs for lower wages.

Another possible plaintiff might be prospective owners of new teams. Whether or not such people would step forward is impossible to know, but it is a good bet that the process of divestiture would be a messy, multilayered, drawn-out, and expensive one—a veritable full-employment bill for lawyers.[27] What we get at the end may be rather different from what we bargained for.

It is conceivable, but hardly likely, that a city could sue baseball for restraint of trade in cases where cities have been prohibited from owning a baseball team.[28] San Diego could have sued MLB in 1990 when the owners rejected Joan Kroc's attempt to give the Padres to the city. Pittsburgh and Montreal also had recent opportunities to bring lawsuits over this issue. Either direct public ownership or a municipally organized restricted sale of stock to residents, as the Green Bay Packers used, is a feasible option that MLB's owners should not be allowed to veto.[29]

Applying antitrust has hardly been a godsend to the erstwhile NFL cities of Oakland and Baltimore. When Al Davis moved his Raiders to Los Angeles in 1982, the NFL was so embarrassed by his naked greed that it tried to stop him. Davis went to court and won on the grounds that the NFL was restraining trade and interfering with his property right.[30] Baltimore Colts' owner Robert Irsay, encouraged by the Davis precedent, packed up his bags in 1984 and was in Indianapolis in less time than it took Johnny Unitas to run out of the pocket. The NFL's St. Louis Cardinals followed suit in 1988 when they moved to Phoenix. From the metropolitan perspective, antitrust is not the preferred remedy. Antitrust may help ameliorate some of baseball's problems but by itself offers incomplete remedy.

Regulation

In the U.S. political atmosphere of the 1980s and early 1990s, advocating public regulation is sufficient cause to disqualify an entire book, if not a life's work. So the reader with opaque ideological blinders need read no further.

It is true that regulatory agencies in the United States have a checkered history.[31] More often than not these agencies have been staffed with people coming from or going to the industry they are regulating. This feature together with political pressures and personnel perquisites has resulted in many regulatory agencies being captured by the regulated industry. Other times regulations have been placed where they were not needed or they have been implemented ineffectively. But parts of the U.S. economy still require regulation and always will. The trick for public policy is to learn how to do it efficiently, not to bury it—not if we want to preserve our coastal waters, our ozone layer, our air, our forests, our farmland, our water supply, or restore stability to our financial system, among other things.

Regulation of baseball could take a minimalist form. Congress could legislate rules piecemeal that could be enforced by the watchful eye of a bureau in the Department of Commerce.[32] One such rule might be that the All-Star Game, the playoffs, and the World Series must be available on free television, and that a certain number be played in the afternoon (or begun prior to 6:30 P.M. East Coast time). A corollary might be that at least one-third of a team's regular-season games must be broadcast locally over the air. The 1989 Free Baseball Telecast Act went further than this by conditioning baseball's antitrust exemption on broadcasting at least 50 percent of televised games on over-the-air stations. The bill did not make it out of committee.[33]

A second rule might establish a franchise expansion timetable and the right of first refusal for cities before a team is allowed to relocate. A panel of franchise appraisers could set a fair market price.[34] In March 1984 the Sports Team Community Protection Act was introduced in the Senate, designed to control franchise relocation. In fact, this bill was the only one in the Congress that concerned either removing baseball's antitrust exemption or sports' regulation to ever make it out of committee. The version that made it out of committee, however, contained a number of exemptions for specific teams and was substantially watered down from the original. It was never voted on in the full Senate. A third rule might address revenue sharing among the teams. Senator William Proxmire of Wisconsin introduced such a bill in 1965, as did Senator Slade Gorton of Washington in 1991.[35] Again, neither bill made it out of committee.

A fourth rule might involve the maintenance of labor peace. A baseball (or sports) labor act might establish a mandatory cooling-off period with mediation support, followed by compulsory arbitration. Strikes or lockouts would be illegal and the schedule inviolable.

Alternatively, regulation could take on a maximalist form, creating an independent agency to set regulations and oversee their implementation. One advantage of this approach, compared to the minimalist approach, is that it would not require a separate act of Congress to amend, repeal, or add a new regulation as circumstances change. Were a federal commission to be created, it would make sense for it to be a general sports commission, with advisory groups for each sport. By the U.S. Constitu-

tion, the appointment of commissioners to such an agency is the preroga-
tive of the president, but the principle of bipartisanship can be applied to
limit the president to choosing no more than 50 percent plus one of the
commissioners from the same political party. Further, the term of the
commissioners could be staggered initially and then set not to coincide
with presidential terms in order to promote a greater independence from
the president.[36] The legislation may also contain the recommendation
that the president select the commissioners from lists provided by specified bodies (such as the players' unions, the owners, sportwriters and
broadcasters, amateur sports groups or the National Conference of Mayors). To reduce the likelihood of the commission being captured by the
industry, stipulating that the commissioners may neither come from nor
go to the industry after their service would be desirable. Unlike the
operation of electric utilities, for instance, the operation of a sports
league is not so technically complex to require that experts be drafted for
the regulatory commission from the industry itself. The advisory groups
similarly would be comprised of individuals recommended from interested parties in each sport.

The commission would take decisions concerning expansion timeta-
bles, relocation, broadcasting, revenue sharing, and labor relations.[37]
Franchise income statements would be supplied to the commission on a
regular basis. The operating costs of the commission and the advisory
boards would be financed by a special levy on the sports leagues' central
funds. Commission decisions would be appealable to a U.S. Circuit Court
of Appeals.

Legislation to create a similar Federal Sports Commission was introduced by Republican Senator Marlow Cook of Kentucky in 1972. In
introducing his bill, Senator Cook stated:

> The primary purpose of the Commission, therefore, is to provide the sports
> fan with a voice in the operation of that system—a voice that has hereto-
> fore been ignored. . . . It is inevitable that certain protests will be made
> during the course of these hearings that the area of sports is one that should
> remain free of governmental interference. I would hope that those wit-
> nesses . . . will consider the idea that it may be preferable to spare the world
> of sports the embarrassment and turmoil of constant litigation and conflict
> by establishing such a system of guidelines, rather than to subject sports
> to front page coverage which does nothing but harm the sports and the
> parties involved.[38]

Cook's bill did not explain convincingly how the fan's interests would
be represented on such a commission. Sport fans are an amorphous mass,

and it is far from clear how they could be represented directly. Certainly it is arguable that their interests will be represented indirectly because the president is elected and he or she appoints the commissioners. The sportswriters might or might not bring a fan's perspective to the advisory groups. In the case of baseball at least, a plausible channel exists for direct fan representation. The Society for American Baseball Research (SABR) is an organization of fans from business, academia, journalism, and baseball itself. SABR has regional branches and holds both regional and national meetings annually. While perhaps not the ideal solution, a representative from SABR would be one way to represent the interests of baseball fans. Similar organizations could be employed in other sports.

Senator Cook's 1972 bill met the fate of all such legislation; it did not make it out of committee. Congress has considered dozens of pieces of legislation concerning baseball's exemption and possible regulation. It has been urged to take action by Supreme Court justices, the Justice Department, and its own Select Committee on Professional Sports in January 1977. It has never come close. Why? The principal reason is that MLB has lobbied effectively to preserve its privileged position and there has been no countervailing lobby from the baseball players, the fans, or the cities. Most recently the Congressional Task Force on Baseball Expansion, which had set a goal of six new teams by the year 2000, has fallen quiet. The task force's most active members, Senators Tim Wirth of Colorado and Connie Mack of Florida, got what they wanted in the 1991 NL expansion decision and have not called a meeting of the group for well over a year.

The experience with congressional action and inaction regarding cable regulation both reflects this pattern and offers a grain of hope. Subject to a full barrage of campaign financing and lobbying by the National Cable Television Association (NCTA), Congress buckled and passed the Cable Broadcasting Act of 1984.[39] Repeated efforts by Congressman Edward Markey and Senator Howard Metzenbaum to undo the folly and injustice of this act were thwarted by the activities of the NCTA and their fifth column in Congress. Tim Wirth, "who has collected 19 percent of his campaign contributions over the last year and a half from cable executives and 33 percent of his PAC money from the cable industry itself— including $10,000 received in April [1990] from Malone's TCI," singlehandedly derailed the 1990 cable deregulation bill.[40]

But viewers from around the country have complained of poor service and high prices of local cable service. In some areas they have formed associations to represent their concerns. The National Conference of Mayors began to raise its voice in protest. At the end of 1991, a cable reregulation bill, having passed through the Senate's Telecommunications Subcommittee by a resounding 16-to-3 vote, seemed to be on its way to full Senate approval. House approval in the spring of 1992 appeared likely.[41] It is not easy, but Congress can be made accountable.

CONCLUSION

As the stakes get higher, relying on MLB ownership to resolve its internal problems and to deal equitably with its host cities and its fans is increasingly problematic. Some owners are competent, effective businesspeople who care about the game. Many others do not share these attributes. The disparate interests among them have rendered the owners as a group incapable of developing either stable and peaceful labor relations or a plan for revenue sharing among the teams. The resulting stresses and imbalances have led teams to turn to financially strapped cities for more subsidies, to pay television for more income, and to commercialization schemes that threaten to undermine the game's essence.

Testifying before the U.S. Congress in 1981, Howard Cosell argued:

> major league baseball must be made part of the United States of America and must be made subject to the anti-trust laws. It is not only what we call, Mr. Chairman, an anomaly at law . . . but it is totally repugnant . . . in a government of law . . . for one business to stand alone, to be subject neither to government regulation as the public utilities are nor to the applicability of the antitrust laws as all other businesses are.[42]

Baseball is only a game, but it is our national pastime and an integral part of our culture. The activity of rooting for baseball and other sports teams is one of the strongest expressions of community remaining in our society. How we treat baseball and how baseball treats us reflects our values, our needs, and our direction. Former baseball Commissioner Happy Chandler said in 1951: "I always regarded baseball as our National Game that belongs to 150 million men, women, and children, not to sixteen special people who happen to own big league teams."[43] This is as it should be, but we have to work to make it that way.

Appendix A to Chapter 4

The seminal empirical work on the relationship between pay and performance was Gerald Scully's 1974 article in the *American Economic Review*. A variation of Scully's methodology was used in the arbitration hearings before Thomas Roberts and George Nicolau in Collusion I, II, and III.[1] Most recently Scully presented an updated version of his 1974 two-equation model in his 1989 book *The Business of Major League Baseball*.

Scully's model posits, first, that team win percentage is determined by batting and pitching performance and, second, that overall team revenues are determined by team winning percentage, after controlling for the size of the team's geographic market. Thus the dollar value of a player's incremental contribution to team revenue (net marginal revenue product) can be estimated indirectly by identifying the effect of the player's performance on win percentage and then of win percentage on revenue.

Clearly, the model does not provide either a precise or a nuanced measure of a player's value. It does not include, for instance, the charisma contribution of certain star players such as Reggie Jackson and Dave Winfield, the contributions of base-stealing artists such as Rickey Henderson and Vince Coleman, the psychological or strategic contributions of players such as Tony Peña and Don Baylor, the fielding contributions of others such as Ozzie Smith and Don Mattingly; nor does it include the negative effects of poor fielding, bad baserunning, contentious or self-absorbed personalities, and so on. Yet if the model is properly specified, it can on balance capture the most important contributions of the great majority of ballplayers and provide a reasonable standard for gauging the equity of absolute and relative levels of pay.

Although Scully's two-equation model is not econometrically elegant, it is as reliable as any existing empirical or subjective procedure for estimating players' worth. We applied a modified Scully model to test the relationship between pay and performance from 1984 to 1989. What follows is an abbreviated discussion of the econometric testing behind the results presented in chapter 4. A more detailed presentation of the methodology is available.[2]

The most fundamental alteration made is rooted in a conceptual problem with the Scully model. His model purports to measure a player's marginal revenue product (MRP) while leaving ambiguous its notion of output. What is it that a player produces? Presumably, and consistent with the Scully model, a players produces walks, hits, and runs,[3] or intermediate outputs, that contribute to wins, or final output. But if wins is the final output, is it true that a ballplayer who bats below the league average or below the average for his position contributes to a team's winning? If a batter hits .230 or .150 without power, is he on balance increasing the team's win percentage or is he lowering it?

Scully's computations of player marginal revenue product assume a counterfactual for batters of no hits. That is, he assumes that if the player being evaluated did not play, then his replacement would have been up the same number of times and have had no hits, that is a zero batting or slugging average, or adjusted to the PROD (slugging average plus on-base average) concept, the replacement would have no hits and no walks. Since Scully's model excludes defensive performance (except for pitchers), it would be consistent to assume without a given player that there would be no replacement and the team's hitting performance would subtract both the number of at bats and bases of the player under evaluation. That is, a player's marginal product would be the difference between the team's PROD with him in the lineup and the team's PROD in his absence, or how much the player added to the team PROD.[4]

Although there is some theoretical ambiguity as to which is the correct concept of a player's marginal product, we prefer the latter. Consider an analogy to a goods-producing factory. In a manufacturing plant, if the marginal worker is not hired, the output of the factory does not decrease; rather it stays constant. In Scully's treatment, if a player is out of the lineup (not hired), the team's hitting performance falls (and markedly so). The limitation with our method is that it does not permit a direct, absolute measure of player marginal revenue product, as discussed later.

The second modification is in the specification of the win percentage equation. Scully uses batter slugging percentage and pitcher strikeout-to-walk ratio as regressors in this equation. They are not the best predictors of win percentage by a long shot. We use "production" (PROD), which is slugging average plus on-base average, and pitcher earned run average (ERA).[5]

The third modification is in the specification of the total revenue equation. Scully uses only current year win percentage (PCT) in his 1989 book; we add win percentage lagged one year, PCT (−1). We also add Standard Metropolitan Statistical Area (SMSA) income per capita and a dummy variable for the National League.[6]

The fourth change is that we consider *net* marginal revenue product. The concept of net marginal product adjusts for the presence of certain complementary inputs that allow the player to attain his productivity and that the franchise experiences as costs (auxiliary or collateral costs). A profit-maximizing employer will hire workers up to the point where the marginal factor cost (MFC) is equal to the gross MRP. The MFC, in turn, will equal the salary paid to the factor (the player) plus any necessary marginal auxiliary costs that accompany the factor.[7] Hence, the profit-maximizing condition can be written as:

(1) MFC = Gross MRP, *or*
(2) Salary + Marginal Auxiliary Cost = Gross MRP, *or*
(3) Salary = Gross MRP − Marginal Auxiliary Cost = Net MRP.

The difficulty, of course, lies in identifying and quantifying marginal auxiliary costs. Certainly, in the case of hitters the baseball bats a team purchases for a player are necessary auxiliary costs, as are the batting helmets, rosin, uniforms, and so on.[8] Similarly, it can be argued that the batting cages, mechanical or batting practice pitchers, the trainer and training room, and so on are all complementary factors that are not measured independently in the production function and should be considered as auxiliary costs. Only the cost increases in these items should be considered. It would also be appropriate to deduct marginal player development costs or the indirect cost of signing a free agent (the loss of a top-round draft pick in the June amateur draft). In our estimates, marginal auxiliary costs are assumed to equal 10 percent of gross marginal revenue product.[9]

The two equations used in our MRP estimates are:

(1) PCT = −0.024 + 1.380 PROD − 0.119 ERA
           (−0.48)   (17.8)   (−20.1)   adj. R^2 = .77

(2) TR = −492E+5 + 286E+5 PCT + 370E+5 PCT (−1) + 2.40 POP + 1740 YCAP
          (−7.71)   (3.38)   (4.34)   (10.2)   (5.42)
         + 321E+4 NL + 231E+4 TREND
           (3.01)   (5.49)   adj. R^2 = .77

where PCT is team winning percentage, TR is team total revenue, POP is SMSA population, YCAP is SMSA income per capita, NL is a dummy variable equal to 1 for a National League team and 0 for an American League team, and TREND goes from 1 in 1984 to 6 in 1989. Data are for teams, the t-statistics are below the coefficients, E + 5 denotes add five zeroes, and the equations are tested for six years, 1984 to 1989. Equations (1) and (2) are used to compute a player's marginal revenue product above that of the average player. That is, for batters the coefficients in equation (2) on PCT and PCT (− 1) (discounted by the average short-term Treasury Bill rate) are added together and multiplied by the coefficient on PROD in equation (1), and this product is multiplied by the player's impact on team PROD. The result is then added to the average team salary, yielding the player's gross MRP, which is then diminished by 10 percent to arrive at net MRP. The accuracy of the final estimate, thus, is sensitive to the extent to which the average player is paid his MRP.

The coefficient on POP in equation (2) signifies that team revenue grows by $2.40 for every additional person living in the city.[10] The combined coefficients on PCT and PCT(− 1) suggest that each .001 increase in a team's win percentage augments team revenues by $63,026. That is, a .001 increase in team win percentage adds as much to team revenue as does a population increase of 26,260 people. Alternatively, since each win contributes .00617 points to the win percentage, on the average each additional victory brings the same increment to total revenue as 162,000 people in a city's population. In appendix B we consider the interactive effect of PCT and POP.

The significant coefficient on YCAP in equation (2) shows a positive correlation between SMSA per capita income and team revenue. Higher income levels enhance an area's market and contribute to richer media contracts. The positive and significant coefficient on NL probably derives from the disproportionately favorable treatment of allocations from the major league central fund to National League clubs.[11] The positive coefficient on TREND simply reflects the strong upward trend in baseball revenues over the period.

Our MRP estimates do not have a particularly impressive correlation with player salaries. To predict actual salary, one would want to consider major league experience, lifetime performance, whether the player was a free agent or eligible for salary arbitration, whether the player was a record holder or All-Star team member along with other factors. Our intention here, however, is not to predict salaries but to see how well performance and pay are correlated in any given year.

Table A.1 summarizes our results comparing estimated MRPs and salaries for hitters from 1986 to 1989.[12] Our discussion of these results must begin with the caveat that 1986, 1987, and 1988 have been found to be years of ownership collusion over free agent salaries. The collusion cases further established that the adverse effects on player salaries went beyond 1988. Evidence presented before arbitrators Thomas Roberts and George Nicolau, as well as accounts elsewhere, make it clear that the most overt collusion took place prior to the 1986 season, following the September 1985 owners' meeting and the initiative of Lee MacPhail and Commissioner Peter Ueberroth.[13] Responding to the suit brought by the Players' Association, the owners' collusive practices became more indirect and diluted in 1987 and 1988.

In table A.1, the correlation between estimated MRPs and salaries for hitters is presented for each year between 1986 and 1989, controlling for years of major league service. For the regressions including all hitters, there is a significant correlation between salary and MRP for 1987 through 1989. The correlation for 1986, however, is insignificant. This is probably a function of the overt collusion among the owners following the 1985 season. There may as well have been some disincentive effects on performance for those players who previously looked forward to their free agent bargaining in future seasons.

If MRP was estimated exactly and labor markets functioned efficiently, then the expected results would be a zero constant term, a zero coefficient on service, and a coefficient of one on MRP. Many factors preclude such a result: imperfectly measured MRP, long-term contracts, minimum salaries, imperfect information, noncompetitive labor markets, and non-profit-maximizing behavior.

Nonetheless, service and MRP together explain between 42 and 54 percent of the variance in salary, depending on the year. Since the coefficient on MRP is so far below one (indeed, in the current year regressions it is always below 0.42, even for masters), it may be hypothesized that service is picking up some of the MRP. Specifically, our measure of MRP is based solely on on-field performance in the current year, but many players attract fans for their previous years' stellar performances. Players with more years of service, the argument might go, have a larger following of loyal fans and, hence, bring more people to the ballpark and viewers to the television. This perspective probably has some validity, but the extent to which service is picking up MRP must be modest. Fans, after all, hold their primary loyalty to teams, not players, and rising young stars can be every bit as exciting as declining old ones.

Generally, the significance level of the coefficients on MRP rises appreciably in the lagged specifications. Surely, it would rise even more were it not for long-term contracts. This result suggests the importance of imperfect information in the salary determination process. Where con-

TABLE A.1
Correlations between Salaries and MRPs

Year/Category	Number of Observations	Dependent Variable	Constant (000s)	Service[a] (000s)	MRP	Adjusted R^2
1986 All	211	1986 Salary	−32.4 (−0.83)	82.2 (14.6)	.0001 (0.35)	.50
	231	1987 Salary	−92.9 (−2.32)	75.1 (12.9)	.331[b] (9.04)	.57
< 2 years	42	1986 Salary	62.2 (3.81)	9.5 (0.91)	−.0000 (−.062)	.02
	58	1987 Salary	69.6 (3.22)	19.4 (1.39)	.017 (0.96)	.02
2 through 5 years	99	1986 Salary	−399.4 (−4.67)	133.0 (7.09)	.190 (6.44)	.52
	103	1987 Salary	−479.6 (−4.58)	159.3 (7.00)	.340 (9.23)	.60
> 5 years	70	1986 Salary	400.5 (2.14)	26.8 (1.51)	.251 (3.08)	.14
	70	1987 Salary	333.7 (1.50)	30.4 (1.44)	.404 (4.14)	.22
1987 All	246	1987 Salary	−156.2 (−3.61)	82.6 (14.7)	.201 (6.71)	.54
	257	1988 Salary	−100.2 (−2.39)	78.2 (13.7)	.318 (10.1)	.55
< 3 years	71	1987 Salary	43.0 (2.36)	23.7 (3.10)	.003 (0.31)	.09
	92	1988 Salary	−.2 (0.01)	62.4 (4.59)	.055 (2.81)	.23
3 through 5 years	81	1987 Salary	−740.4 (−4.30)	182.1 (5.39)	.271 (7.73)	.53
	85	1988 Salary	−532.0 (−3.00)	159.9 (4.57)	.375 (10.3)	.60
> 5 years	94	1987 Salary	319.5 (1.88)	38.7 (2.41)	.235 (3.76)	.17
	93	1988 Salary	428.2 (2.26)	26.1 (1.46)	.387 (5.59)	.26
1988 All	278	1988 Salary	−157.2 (−3.27)	78.6 (13.1)	.267 (7.17)	.49
	306	1989 Salary	−60.4 (−1.35)	71.9 (12.4)	.385 (10.2)	.51
< 3 years	70	1988 Salary	−56.4 (−1.65)	61.0 (4.57)	.055 (3.61)	.35
	94	1989 Salary	−120.5 (−2.39)	100.1 (4.80)	.164 (5.33)	.38
3 through 5 years	88	1988 Salary	−467.8 (−3.16)	139.5 (4.81)	.207 (5.81)	.39
	90	1989 Salary	−492.3 (−2.40)	160.6 (3.97)	.475 (9.45)	.54
> 5 years	120	1988 Salary	269.9 (1.66)	32.3 (2.14)	.417 (5.54)	.24
	122	1989 Salary	443.6 (2.76)	23.6 (1.57)	.422 (5.68)	.23

TABLE A.1 *(continued)*

Year/Category	Number of Observations	Dependent Variable	Constant (000s)	Service[a] (000s)	MRP	Adjusted R^2
1989 All	277	1989 Salary	−82.3 (−1.5)	78.7 (12.1)	.242 (5.88)	.42
	280	1990 Salary	31.9 (0.57)	65.5 (10.1)	.499 (12.3)	.52
< 3 years	51	1989 Salary	40.6 (2.17)	25.5 (3.46)	.003 (0.26)	.20
	53	1990 Salary	76.9 (2.03)	46.9 (3.10)	.036 (1.56)	.21
3 through 5 years	92	1989 Salary	−337.2 (−1.73)	124.0 (3.22)	.222 (5.07)	.28
	92	1990 Salary	−61.2 (−0.22)	96.9 (1.84)	.520 (8.64)	.45
> 5 years	134	1989 Salary	470.8 (2.93)	26.6 (1.83)	.325 (4.20)	.15
	135	1990 Salary	340.4 (2.39)	33.4 (2.61)	.562 (8.39)	.38

Note: T-statistics are in parentheses, below the coefficients.

[a]Service is the number of years a player appeared on the major league roster prior to the year in question. It differs from the official service calculation, which is based on days and is used to calculate eligibility for salary arbitration and free agency.

[b]MRP here is for 1986. The same pattern is followed in subsequent equations; that is, the second equation in each category tests the lagged relationship between salary and MRP.

tracts permit, next year's salary is more closely correlated with this year's performance than is this year's salary. This result also is testimony to the variability and unpredictability of player performance from one year to the next. It thus provides an insight into the perplexing question of why the era of free agency has not corresponded with dominance by big-city teams. That is, the unpredictability of player performance is one of the factors that makes it difficult to buy winning teams.

As expected, there is a strong, positive correlation between salary and service for all players. That is, independent of MRP, salaries rise systematically with years of experience. The coefficient on service in the all-players regression is very stable over the four years tested, ranging from 78.6 to 82.6. The interpretation of this coefficient is straightforward: In 1986, for instance, each additional year of service brought $82,200 in additional salary.

Within categories, it is not surprising that among apprentices, excepting 1988, there is no significant current-year correlation between salary and MRP. Even in the exceptional case, however, the coefficient on MRP suggests that salary rises only 5.5 cents for every $1 increase in MRP. Not only are apprentices under reserve, but their preprofessional or minor league records are not always reliable predictors of their proficiency at the major league level. Among journeymen, in contrast to the finding reported in Scully, Hirschberg, and Slottje,[14] there is a significant relationship between salary and MRP in each year (both current and lagged). Indeed, the t-statistics on MRP among journeymen are higher than among masters in every case.[15] It appears that salary arbitration does enforce a salary responsiveness to player performance, while long-term contracts among free agents attenuates the incentive linkage between salary and performance. Evidence from tables 4.7 and 4.8, however, clarifies that, although a systematic link is established between pay and output among journeymen, the reserve system for players with less than six years' service preserves the monopsony power of owners who are still able on average to pay journeymen below their MRPs.[16]

EVALUATION OF THE ESTIMATES

Our estimates hinge critically on the average salary per team. To the extent that the average player on a team is underpaid (overpaid), our MRP estimates will be too low (too high). What can be said about team average salaries from 1986 to 1989? Given collusion, it is likely that average team salaries were below the average player's marginal revenue product. That is, our MRP estimates are probably too low.

It is difficult to identify an independent standard to allow us to assess the proximity of average salary and average MRP, but perhaps some sense of it can be inferred from considering the player salary share in team revenues. At the beginning of the 1990 Basic Agreement negotiations, the owners proposed that a salary cap be introduced at 48 percent (including benefits) of "defined revenues." Defined revenues denoted all ticket and broadcast revenues; this excluded parking, concessions, and licensing income and amounted to roughly 82 percent of total revenue in 1989.[17] We can estimate, therefore, that 48 percent of defined revenues was equivalent to roughly 39.4 percent of total revenues including benefits, or 35.3 percent of total revenues excluding benefits. The actual average salary share in Major League Baseball excluding benefits was 35.3 percent from 1986 to 1989, exactly the same share offered by the owners in the first round. As in all negotiations, the owners would undoubtedly have been willing to go above their opening gambit. This fact together with the estimate that the salary share[18] rose to 42.9 percent in 1991 when MLB's profits were healthy suggest that the average salary was too low (below the average MRP) from 1986 to 1989.

Although the cost structure of the two sports is quite different, some have suggested a comparison between the player salary share in baseball with that in basketball. In basketball there is a salary cap set at 53 percent of gate and media revenues[19]; however, in the National Basketball Association there is no professional minor league system and the 53 percent includes all benefits, whereas the 48 percent in the MLB proposal included only pension and health contributions.[20] As shown in table 4.4, in baseball minor league player development costs approach 13 percent of total revenues. The baseball owners' proposed cap, then, would put the overall player compensation share considerably higher in baseball than in basketball. Further, the 48 percent cap was only the owners' first offer. It is also significant that a professional basketball team has but twelve players, while a baseball team has twenty-five. According to estimates from *Financial World*, actual 1990 salary shares in total revenue in professional sports were 30 percent in hockey, 33 percent in baseball, 41 percent in football, and 41 percent in basketball.[21]

Finally, it is appropriate here to recall that our estimates are based on official revenue figures provided by the teams to MLB. To the extent that teams engage in transfer pricing or other strategies that understate their real revenues, our MRP estimates will be too low.

Appendix B to Chapter 4

The most straightforward way to test the interactive effect of population and player performance on team revenues is to add a multiplicative term to the basic revenue equation presented in appendix A. In equation (1),

(1) $TR = f(POP, PCT, POP \times PCT, YCAP, NL, CITDUM, TREND)$

variables are the same as in appendix A, with the additions of POP × PCT (the multiplication of SMSA population by team win percentage) and CITDUM (a dummy variable equal to 1 when there are two teams in a city). This equation was tested for the years 1984 to 1989. The coefficient on POP × PCT tells us the nature of the interaction of team performance and city size. If stars are worth more to big cities, then this coefficient should be positive and significant.

In fact, the coefficient was negative but insignificant (the t-statistic was -1.02). The other variables were all positive and significant except CITDUM, which was negative and insignificant (t−statistic was -0.69).[1] The R^2 was .75.

A variety of alternative specifications were tested. Since total revenue figures are subject at least to accounting manipulation, we also used team attendance figures as the dependent variable. The results were not appreciably different, although the R^2 was considerably lower. We also used media population (the number of households with a television set within a set radius of the city) instead of SMSA population. Again, the results were not appreciably different except that the negative coefficient on the multiplicative term (media population times win percentage) was now significant at the .10 level. Finally, we also used team standing instead of win percentage. The results were little different.

Arguably, the weakness in these formulations is that we were testing only for current-year effects. Since we would expect that fans' response to a team (either by attending games or watching the team on television) is determined by the previous year's performance as well, the same equations were estimated using the sum of win percentage over the present and preceding year for both the PCT term and the multiplicative term. In these cases, the multiplicative term became positive but was still not statistically significant. The same was true when we added win percentage lagged for two as well as one year and when team standing was employed instead of win percentage.

One possible problem with these tests is that the high degree of multicollinearity among POP, PCT and POP × PCT makes it difficult to interpret the coefficient on the multiplicative term. For this reason and because the results were unexpected, we tested the basic total revenue

TABLE B.1
Split Sample Tests on POP and PCT

	Population: Top Half			Population: Bottom Half		
Dependent Variable	Coefficient on PCT	T-Statistic on PCT	Dep. Var.	Coef. on PCT	T-Stat. on PCT
TR	44,500,000	3.15	TR	47,400,000	6.23
ATT	4,490,000	5.61	ATT	5,960,000	8.33

Dep. Var.	Coef. on PCT2	T-Stat. on PCT2	Dep. Var.	Coef. on PCT2	T-Stat. on PCT2
TR	40,900,000	4.98	TR	34,600,000	8.00
ATT	3,280,000	7.01	ATT	3,990,000	9.49

	Population: Top Third			Population: Middle Third			Population: Bottom Third	
Dep. Var.	Coef. on PCT	T-Stat. on PCT	Dep. Var.	Coef. on PCT	T-Stat. on PCT	Dep. Var.	Coef. on PCT	T-Stat. on PCT
TR	23,400,000	1.26	TR	43,000,000	5.14	TR	57,200,000	6.47
ATT	4,680,000	4.54	ATT	6,200,000	7.42	ATT	6,000,000	7.96

Dep. Var.	Coef. on PCT2	T-Stat. on PCT2	Dep. Var.	Coef. on PCT2	T-Stat. on PCT2	Dep. Var.	Coef. on PCT2	T-Stat. on PCT2
TR	30,000,000	1.26	TR	32,000,000	5.14	TR	57,200,000	6.47
ATT	4,170,000	7.24	ATT	4,360,000	9.05	ATT	4,100,000	9.85

equation segmented by population size. First, equation (1) was tested for teams with above-average populations and then for teams with below-average populations. Second, the sample was divided into thirds, again by population size. If star players were worth more to big-city teams, then we would expect the coefficient on the PCT term to be significantly higher for teams in larger cities than teams in smaller cities. Alternatively, we would expect the product of PCT times its coefficient to be higher for large-city teams. Again, various specifications were tested, using attendance instead of total revenue and media population instead of SMSA population, and, again the econometric results did not support the hypothesis. In table B.1 we report on the results for the coefficients on PCT only, when the sample is divided in half and in thirds by population category, and when PCT2 is used (PCT in the present year plus PCT in the preceding year). ATT stands for attendance.

The results, if anything, suggest a tendency in the opposite direction to the hypothesis. That is, the coefficients on PCT and PCT2 do not get larger for teams in cities with larger populations. We attempt to explain this result in chapter 4 and conclude that agnosticism is the best posture regarding the differential productivity of ballplayers in big-city markets.

Notes

Preface

1. Angell 1990, p. 125.
2. Robichaux 1990.

Introduction

1. Vincent made these remarks at a press conference at Fairfield University in Connecticut on 21 February 1991; they were quoted in the *New York Times* (23 February 1991, p. 46).
2. Cited in *USA Today* (28 November 1990, p. 2c), giving Major League Baseball as the source.
3. Cited in Markham and Teplitz (1981, p. 1), emphasis added.
4. *Financial World,* 9 July 1991, pp. 42–43.
5. Prime Network is a regional sports programming network with over twenty-two subscribers operated and mostly owned by TeleCommunications Inc. (TCI). TCI is the nation's largest cable operator. In addition to Prime Network, it owns local cable delivery systems and has a substantial equity stake in Turner Broadcasting Systems, Discovery Channel, The Family Channel, QVC Network, Black Entertainment, Liberty Broadcasting, and American Movie Classics.

Chapter 1

Epigraph: Chandler is quoted in Lowenfish and Lupien (1980, p. 172).

1. On the ambiguity of baseball's origins as a game, see Gould (1990) and Zoss and Bowman (1989).
2. Goldstein 1989, p. 84.
3. Voigt 1976, p. 310. See also Voigt (1983, chap. 2).
4. See Levine (1985, pp. 6–8) for a discussion of these ingenious schemes.
5. Goldstein 1989, p. 85.
6. Dworkin 1981, p. 42.
7. For an excellent history of the Red Stockings, see Goldstein (1989, pp. 103–18).
8. U.S. Congress, House, 1952, p. 129.
9. Ibid.
10. Goldstein 1989, pp. 146, 149.
11. Alft 1952, p. 1432.
12. Seymour 1960, p. 78.
13. Levine 1985, p. 36.
14. Ibid., p. 38.
15. Ibid., p. 46.
16. Seymour 1960, p. 86.
17. Lowenfish and Lupien 1980, p. 18.
18. Canes 1974, p. 83.
19. U.S. Congress, House 1952, p. 132; Levine 1985, p. 53.
20. Berry, Gould, and Staudohar 1986, p. 52. Ward's top salary was $4,250 in 1889; Dunbar 1918, p. 291. Ward eventually earned a law degree at Columbia University and became the chief counsel for the National League. For a short period he owned the Boston Braves. See the excellent short biography of Ward in Allen (1990, pp. 42–45).
21. Quoted in Alft (1952, p. 1435).
22. Jennings, 1990, p. 5.
23. Of course, sometimes rich clubs sold players as well: "In 1886 Albert Spalding's [then owner of the Chicago NL team] sale of colorful outfielder Mike 'King' Kelly to Boston for $10,000 had caused much public notice. Spalding would later admit that he earned $750,000 from his Chicago club in the late 1880s. . . . The player sale was becoming common, but the player earned nothing" (Lowenfish and Lupien 1980, p. 31).
24. Alft 1952, p. 1441. To this day, the NL and the AL use different measures of attendance: the NL counts only those paid and present at the ballpark, and the AL counts all sold seats whether or not present at the game.
25. Alft 1952, p. 1441.
26. There was actually a previous court test of the reserve clause in 1882 when the Pittsburgh club of the NL sought an injunction to prevent its catcher, Charles Bennett, from moving to the AA's Detroit team. The Pennsylvania Federal

Court did not grant the injunction but gave no written opinion to explain its decision (Hailey 1989b, p. 642.)

27. Quoted in Berry and Wong (1986, vol. 1, p. 70).

28. Although 1890 was also the year of passage of the Sherman Antitrust Act, the act did not vest individuals with rights and remedies under its statutes. Hence, players could not sue the leagues on antitrust grounds. Not until the Clayton Act of 1914 were private individuals, as well as the government, vested with such rights.

29. See analysis of the PL's demise in Berry, Gould, and Staudohar (1986, p. 49).

30. Alft 1952, p. 1443.

31. By 1900 interlocking ownerships in the National League had progressed as follows: John Brush owned Cincinnati and held stock in New York; Arthur Soden owned one-third of Boston and was principal minority shareholder in New York; Ferdinand Abel owned 40 percent of Brooklyn, 40 percent of Baltimore, and was minority shareholder in New York; Frank Robison owned both St. Louis and Cleveland; Harry Vonderhorst owned 40 percent of stock in Brooklyn and 40 percent of Baltimore; Ned Hanlon owned 10 percent of Brooklyn and 10 percent of Baltimore; Charles Ebbets owned 10 percent of Brooklyn and 10 percent of Baltimore; A. G. Spalding owned a large block of stock in Chicago and some stock in New York. (From testimony of A. C. Allyn, Jr., former president of the Chicago White Sox, before the U.S. Senate 1965, p. 131.)

32. By the end of the 1890s team profits of $30,000 to $40,000 were not regarded as large (Alft 1952, p. 1440).

33. In another case Jack Harper, a pitcher for the St. Louis NL club, jumped to the St. Louis AL club in May 1902. The NL went to court to prevent the move. The courts upheld Harper issuing "a blistering condemnation of the entire baseball industry for its restrictive labor practices. Writing for the court, Judge John A. Talty cited the Fourteenth Amendment to the Constitution, which was passed after the Civil War to prohibit involuntary servitude" (Lowenfish and Lupien 1980, p. 69).

34. See discussion in Berry, Gould, and Staudohar (1986, pp. 24–29).

35. After this myth of creation was refuted decisively in 1937, other myths surfaced (Zoss and Bowman 1989, p. 43). It seems that every year a new letter or newspaper article is discovered identifying an earlier date when baseball was first played. The main problem is that baseball of the mid-1800s did not closely resemble today's game, and many features of today's game are similar to street games played in the United States and England in the eighteenth century as well as formal games played previously in England. A plethora of names accompany these various games; the appellation "base ball" surfaced in connection with street games both in the United States and England.

36. Lowenfish and Lupien 1980, p. 72; also see Gregory (1956, pp. 92–96).

37. Quoted in Lowenfish and Lupien (1980, p. 78).

38. Jennings 1990, p. 214.

39. Scully 1989, p. 33.

40. Cited in Berry, Gould, and Staudohar (1986, p. 28).

41. U.S. Congress, House, 1952, pp. 536, 1091. Cobb was still only one of five players whose salary exceeded $10,000 in 1918 when the modal salary was still below $5,000 (Lane 1918b).

42. Ellig 1987, p. 109; Voigt 1983, vol. 2, p. 117.

43. Although not decisive in the FL's early demise, the infant league was also weakened by restrictive practices between MLB and Western Union. Western Union, under pressure from MLB, did not carry line scores of FL games.

44. Lowenfish and Lupien 1980, p. 90.

45. Seymour 1971, p. 243.

46. Quoted in Lowenfish and Lupien (1980, p. 103).

47. Lowenfish and Lupien 1980, p. 106.

48. Seymour 1971, p. 334.

49. Lowenfish and Lupien 1980, p. 99, and Veeck 1965, p. 256.

50. Nash and Zullo 1985, p. 121.

51. Gregory 1956, p. 22; Will 1990a, p. 134; Quirk 1980, p. 127; U.S. Congress, House, 1952, p. 1050; Nash and Zullo 1986, pp. 94–95.

52. Seymour 1971, p. 344.

53. Quoted in Voigt (1989, p. 13).

54. Quoted in Gregory 1956, p. 22.

55. Seymour 1971, p. 428. Ruth's view of baseball compensation had evolved considerably from the time when he was offered his first professional contract. Then he gasped: "Do you mean that someone is gonna pay me for playing ball" (Gregory 1956, p. 165). Years later he had become a bit more critical and analytical: "It isn't right to call me or any ballplayer an ingrate because we ask for more money. Sure I want more, all I'm entitled to. Listen, a man who works for another man is not going to be paid any more than he's worth" (Jennings 1990, p. 219).

56. See Lasch (1978, p. 121).

57. Mean player salaries were $7,531 in 1929, $6,009 in 1933, and $7,306 in 1939 (U.S. Congress, House, 1952, p. 1611).

58. U.S. Congress, House, 1952, p. 1636.

59. Ibid., pp. 1603, 1606. One club, the NL Phillies, declared bankruptcy during World War II, was purchased by the league for $50,000 and then resold to DuPont heirs, led by Bob Carpenter.

60. U.S. Congress, House, 1952, p. 851.

61. The terms of the pension plan are described in detail in ibid., p. 269.

62. According to Lowenfish and Lupien (1980, p. 151), the minimum salary was lowered to $5,000 after Murphy's guild lost an organizing vote among the Pirates in 1946. Murphy commented: "The players have been offered an apple, but they could have had an orchard."

63. Apparently, the differential offered to Gardella was fairly typical. Chicago Cubs' second baseman Cy Block was being paid $5,000 by the Cubs and was offered $12,500 to play in the Mexican League (Interview, 5 January 1991).

64. Gardella's case was actually a bit different than the others because he was not playing under a major league contract at the time of his signing to play in the Mexican League; that is, he did not jump his contract. See Andreano (1965, p. 106).

65. Cited in Champion (1981, p. 2).

66. Quirk 1980, p. 110. Also see M. Miller (1991, pp. 178–97).

67. Lowenfish and Lupien 1980, p. 165.

68. Cited in Lowenfish and Lupien (p. 184); also in M. Miller (1991, p. 6).

69. Lionel Sobel, senior partner of Freedman and Sobel in Beverly Hills, California, makes this case in his testimony before the House Subcommittee on Monopolies in 1981, p. 116. Hailey offers a similar interpretation (1989b, p. 645).

70. Porter was baseball's chief counsel in the 1950s and '60s. He also happened to be a law partner of Abe Fortas, who was one of Lyndon Johnson's "closer friends and associates" (Veeck 1965, p. 85).

71. Porter 1961, p. 8.

72. Ibid.

73. The 1984 Sports Team Community Protection Act made it out of committee in the Senate in diluted form but was never voted on by the full Senate. See discussion of this bill in chapter 8.

74. Representative Emmanuel Celler (D-NY), in 1958 after deliberating on a sports exemption bill. Quoted in Ellig (1987, p. 41).

75. Veeck 1965, p. 78.

76. Cited in Hailey (1989b, p. 645).

77. Lowenfish and Lupien (1980, p. 187).

78. J. Miller 1990, p. 80.

79. *New York Times*, 2 July 1959, p. 28.

80. J. Miller 1990, p. 80.

81. The International League set the fee at $850,000 per team and the American Association at $800,000. The Continental League in compromise offered to pay each franchise 40 cents per admission to its park in 1960.

82. *New York Times*, 6 May 1960, p. 35.

83. Ibid.

84. J. Miller 1990, p. 83.

85. Quoted in ibid., p. 142. Also see the discussion of Cannon in Marvin Miller's autobiography (1991, pp. 6–8, 33–38, 65–66).

86. Drysdale 1990, chap. 10. For the owners' version of the holdout, see Bavasi 1987, chap. 9.

87. Cited in Lowenfish and Lupien (1980, p. 207).

88. Ellig 1987, p. 43.

89. Four of the justices had been Nixon appointees. Another, Lewis Powell, who owned stock in Anheuser-Busch, the parent company of the St. Louis Cardinals, abstained from voting (M. Miller 1991, p. 199).

90. Cited in M. Miller (1991, p. 142).

91. M. Miller 1991, p. 221.

92. Ibid., p. 222.

93. Quirk 1980, p. 114.

94. For an excellent, extended discussion of the Hunter case see M. Miller (1991, pp. 111–13 and 227–34). For a different view of the same proceedings, see Kuhn (1988, pp. 139–43).

95. Until 1973 the owners had a rule requiring a player to have signed a contract in order to play. The challenge made by McNally and Messersmith, therefore, would have been impossible prior to 1973 (Fehr 1980, p. 169).

96. Three types of free agents were actually delineated in the agreement. Reentry free agents were players with six years of service; they were also subject to a repeater rule—five years must pass before a player could repeat as a free agent. Nontender free agents were players whose club refused to offer them a new contract under the 20 percent rule. Nonrenewal free agents were players who were granted their outright release.

97. Of these, 111 players signed contracts for two years, 105 for three years, 21 for four years, 33 for five years, 10 for six years and 1 for ten years. Hill and Spellman 1983, p. 5.

98. *Official Baseball Guide* 1979, p. 314.

99. Berry, Gould, and Staudohar, 1986, p. 68.

100. The policy provided owners with $100,000 for each lost game.

101. M. Miller 1991, p. 318.

102. Ibid., p. 298.

103. Staudohar 1989, p. 56.

104. Jennings 1990, p. 62.

105. The share of national television revenue this represented fell from 33 percent to 17.4 percent but the actual dollar contributions more than doubled.

106. Pluto and Newman 1986, p. 304.

107. The order of the pick is in inverse order according to team standing. The compensation rules were altered again in the 1990 Basic Agreement and are described in chapter 4.

108. Helyar 1991, p. A12.

109. Quotes from Major League Baseball, Arbitration Panel, Decision on Grievance 87-3, 1990, pp. 10, 12.

110. Grievance 88-1, 1990, pp. 27, 9.

111. Option buyouts enable a team to buy itself out of the last option year of a contract; the share of new contracts containing such clauses fell by almost half. The number of new contracts containing performance bonuses fell from 272 in 1985 to 173 in 1986; the number with award and signing bonuses fell by over 50 percent; the number with no-trade clauses fell from 37 in 1985 to 17 in 1986.

112. According to *Newsweek*, 19 February 1990, p. 60, ticket sales and broadcast rights together came to 82 percent of total revenues in 1989. The 48 percent was to be applied to the salaries of all players on the active twenty-five-man major league roster plus the disabled list, not the forty-man roster (includes players reserved by the major league team but playing in the minors or on the

disabled list) as reported by Murray Chass (Chass 1990a). The salary cap proposal is discussed in more detail in appendix A.

113. The salary cap and other policies related to competitive balance are explored in
chapters 3, 4, and 8. The cap in basketball is set at 53 percent of defined
revenues (see discussion in appendix A to chapter 4).

114. Senator Mack is the grandson of the former and fabled owner and manager of
the Philadelphia Athletics. Grandfather Mack (né Cornelius McGilicuddy)
managed the A's from 1901 to 1950. Prior to that he played in the NL from
1886 to 1896 (with a year in the Players' League in 1890), compiling a lifetime
batting average of .245.

115. *Baseball America*, 25 June 1990, p. 6.

Chapter 2

Epigraphs: Veeck is quoted in Veeck (1965); Herzog is quoted in Herzog and Horrigan
(1987, p. 220); Berkow is quoted from the *New York Times* (13 October 1991, section
4, p. 2); Monaghan is quoted in Jim Fitzgerald, "Bo Protects the Taxpayers," *The
Detroit Free Press* (6 October 1991); Domino's is estimated to be worth $1 billion, as
cited in *Financial World* (9 July 1991, p. 40); Pagliarulo is quoted from an interview
with the author (11 November 1990).

1. Getting a fix on baseball's owners is no easy matter. They are basically inaccessi-
ble to the fan or researcher, and usually to the journalist as well. Most of them
feel they don't have to answer to anybody—or at least they behave as if they feel
that way. When information on the owners surfaces, it is often in connection to
some scandal. It is, however, possible to begin to piece together a picture of
ownership through their memoirs, biographies, rare interviews, congressional
testimonies, and other records.

2. Andreano 1965, p. 155.

3. Michener 1976, p. 441.

4. Ruppert's name is immortalized in Evers's (1990) uncannily amusing and provocative murder mystery concerning a fictional Yankees owner.

5. A prominent baseball commentator during the 1910s and 1920s reflected this
nonlinearity in providing widely divergent assessments of ownership patterns.
Writing in 1913, F. C. Lane commented: "The great development of baseball the
sport has been lost sight of in baseball the business. . . . The magnate has
assumed the attitude of the large business man" (1913, p. 26). Yet five years later
Lane was writing that the franchise owner "is usually in baseball primarily from
genuine interest in the sport" (1918b, p. 71).

6. Quoted in Hernon and Ganey 1991, p. 212. Most of the discussion of Gussie
Busch comes from this source.

7. Ibid.

8. Ibid., p. 389.

9. J. Miller 1990, pp. 101–13, 230–39.

10. Millson 1987 and interview with Pete Bavasi, 25 July 1990.

11. Noll 1988, p. 17.8.

12. In August 1991 Jacobs put his 87 percent share of the Orioles up for sale. Jacobs had bought the team from the widow of Edward Bennett Williams in 1988 for $70 million. *Financial World* (9 July 1991, p. 91) estimates the value of the team today at $200 million. *Business Week* (18 November 1991 p. 116,) puts the value at $255 million. Although these estimates appear too high, they are indicative of the recent explosion in franchise prices, especially when a team cuts a lucrative deal with its host city for a new ballpark with cheap rent, guaranteed ticket sales, and numerous luxury boxes. As of November 1991 Jacobs reportedly had a change of heart, deciding not to sell after all.

13. Abramson and Cohen 1991, p. 1. Also see Bianco et al. (1991).

14. Abramson and Cohen 1991, p. 1.

15. Quoted in *New York Times*, 31 July 1990, p. B9. Steinbrenner remains the principal partner of the Yankees with somewhere between 49 and 55 percent ownership. His role as managing partner, however, was terminated by Commissioner Vincent in 1990.

16. *Media Sports Business*, 31 December 1990, p. 1; *1991 Radio, TV, Cable Directory* (Durham, N.C.: Baseball America, 1991).

17. C. Smith 1991d, p. B13.

18. Hernon and Ganey 1991, p. 211.

19. Veeck 1965, p. 330.

20. Okner reports that the IRS subsequently lowered the share of the franchise value ascribed to the players' contracts of the Braves from 99 to 90 percent (1974, p. 166). Nowadays, it is more common to depreciate players over five years.

21. More precisely, since there was a loss carryforward for five years and carryback for three years at the time, the group needed a total net income of $3.06 million over an eight-year period, and it did not matter if it had losses or low profits in a particular year. Today, loss carryforwards are for fifteen years and carrybacks are for three years.

22. If organized as a partnership or Subchapter S corporation, baseball losses can offset individual income. If organized as a corporation and 80 percent or more of the team is owned by the parent company, the parent company can use baseball losses to offset profits of other corporate activities.

23. This fact also implies that the typical baseball owner would have strong outside business interests and that the full-time owners, such as Bill Veeck, Calvin Griffith, and George Halas, would become an extinct breed. While this is certainly the case, now it is more a consequence of the explosion in franchise values rather than because of the tax loophole. In 1991 the value of that loophole was greatly diminished by the low top marginal tax rates—31 percent for individuals and 34 percent for corporations.

24. The tax system offers an interesting counterincentive for team owners whose franchise value has multiplied since purchase. Consider George Steinbrenner, for example. He bought the Yankees in 1973 for $10 million. His player contracts were fully depreciated at least eight years ago. In 1991 the Yankees were worth

approximately $250 million. Were he to sell the team so that the next owner could begin to depreciate players again, he would have to pay capital gains tax on $240 million (assuming no additional investments on improving the team). If he passes on the team to his son Hank in his will, however, Hank would pay the estate tax (which he pays on any inherited asset), but he would pay capital gains only on any appreciation beyond $250 million. Thus the Steinbrenner family saves roughly $36.5 million (.31 × $240 million × .49) in capital gains taxes by not selling the team until after George Steinbrenner's death. According to the Vincent verdict in the Spira case, Steinbrenner was to reduce his ownership of the Yankees down to 49 percent by August 21, 1991. Several news reports in January 1992, however, indicated that Steinbrenner still owned 55 percent of the Yankees at that time.

25. Jim Quirk estimates that the existence of the tax shelter roughly doubled franchise values from 1959 to 1975 when the top income tax bracket was 72 percent and teams could assign 90 percent of their value to player contracts. After the 50 percent limit on the share of player contracts and the reduction of the top bracket to 50 percent in 1976, the existence of the shelter raised franchise values by approximately 25 percent. With the further reduction of the top marginal rate to 28 percent in 1986 and the elimination of the differential treatment for long-term capital gains, Quirk estimates that the shelter increased franchise values by only 10 percent in 1990. Of course, the top corporate rate has also come down to 34 percent and the top individual rate was raised slightly to 31 percent in 1990.

26. For a normal tangible asset, the amount of its depreciation must be deducted from the company's purchase price when calculating capital gains from an eventual sale of the company. This results in higher ("recaptured") capital gains and, hence, higher taxes. Noll (1988) mistakenly reports that in the case of baseball players, there is usually no recapturing because the character of the players changes so dramatically over the course of an ownership period. Noll misses the 1976 tax code change that obligates teams to shift recapture from a player-by-player basis to a team basis. Prior to 1976, the owner was not subject to recapture to the extent that players who were on a team when it was purchased by a particular owner were not on the team when it was sold. Since 1976 this loophole has been closed. Even with full recapture, however, the right to depreciate player contracts has an economic value equal to the additional interest income earned from deferred tax payments.

27. Veeck 1965, p. 328.

28. As we shall discuss below, the Florida Marlins and Colorado Rockies will not receive any money from the national television contracts with CBS and ESPN during their first year in the major leagues (worth roughly $15 million per team in 1993) and will incur an estimated additional start-up cost of some $25 million. The actual franchise value then might be put as high as $135 million.

29. Bill Giles, owner of the Phillies, bought into the club in 1981 (at an implied price of $30 million for the entire franchise) during the early stages of the takeoff in franchise values.

30. A fuller accounting of his escapades with the Yankees can be found in Madden and Klein's *Damned Yankees* (1990).

31. According to one account related to the author, Steinbrenner actually invested up front less than $100,000 of his money. More recently, it has been claimed that Steinbrenner and his minority partners pocketed $100 million (presumably coming as a signing bonus) of the roughly $500 million provided in the twelve-year cable contract between the team and MSG network, rather than reinvesting it in baseball operations. See, for example, *USA Today*, 16 January 1992, p. C3. Another story reaffirms that Steinbrenner and his partners walked off with $100 million of the cable contract and claims that Steinbrenner was motivated to do this in order to bail out his troubled American Ship Building company (Sloan, 1992; also see Nocera, 1990).

32. These quotes, including Steinbrenner's in the previous paragraph, are taken from *USA Today*, 20 August, 1990, p. 7C, after Steinbrenner's partial banishment from baseball.

33. David Kaplan et al. 1990 in *Newsweek*, p. 53.

34. Quoted in Jennings 1990, p. 77.

35. Cited in Dodd (*USA Today*, 21 February 1991, p. 1C).

36. Ringolsby 1990a, p. 5.

37. *Plaintiffs' Memorandum in Opposition to Defendants' Motion for Summary Judgment*, Court of Common Pleas, Hamilton County, Ohio, 30 August 1990, p. 8; Also see Louis Nippert et al., Plaintiffs, *Complaint for Declaratory Judgment and Partnership Accounting*, Court of Common Pleas, Hamilton County, Ohio, September 1989.

38. Ibid., pp. 20–22.

39. These are the words of *Baseball America* columnist Jerry Crasnick (10 December 1991, p. 11).

40. Ibid.

41. See Veeck 1965, pp. 305–7.

42. See the *Wall Street Journal* (9 July 1990, p. B7); and Belsie (1987, p. 7).

43. Sargeant 1989, p. 16.

44. Mayor's press release, 4 October 1991, p. 3. See discussion in chapter 6.

45. Hernon and Ganey 1991, p. 228.

46. Ibid., p. 290.

47. Bavasi 1987, p. 147. Bavasi tells a variety of interesting and critical anecdotes about his other baseball bosses as well. At one time, for instance, subsequent Padres' owner Ray Kroc fitfully instructed him to "get rid of that son of a bitch" after left fielder Nate Colbert allowed a ball to bounce over his head (p. 156).

48. Greenberg 1989, p. 245.

49. Ibid., p. 246.

50. Ibid., p. 223.

51. J. Miller 1990, p. 100. Also see Veeck (1965, pp. 74–95), who claims that three-quarters of the AL owners held stock in CBS.

52. Veeck 1965, p. 95.

53. Jennings 1990, p. 74.

54. He further pointed out that if Ted Turner did not own both the Braves and WTBS, MLB might never have been able to convince teams covered by a superstation to make special payments to the central fund. See chapters 3 and 7.

55. Cited in U.S. Congress, House, 1952, p. 474.

56. Bill Veeck was particularly critical of his fellow owners. Here's a typical comment on Senators' owner Calvin Griffith: "It is difficult to forget the pleasant days, not too far gone, when the Griffith family was prepared to sell you anybody on the club if you waved enough money in front of them. Besides, you think of that silly operation of theirs, with all the relatives on the payroll for performing duties just barely visible to the naked eye, and it is hard to take Calvin seriously. And if we are going to be honest about these guys, Calvin always seemed so stupid that you almost felt sorry for him" (Veeck 1965, p. 144).

57. Jennings 1990, p. 30.

58. Comments like these or one owner denouncing another for greed are heard commonly in off-the-record statements. Eisenhardt's interview appeared in *Sport*, May 1983. The quote is from page 23.

59. Helyar 1991, pp. A1, A12.

60. Quoted in Rushin (1991, p. 40).

61. See the fascinating history of the Blue Jays by Millson (1987).

62. It is probably too soon to judge the direction of August Busch III, Gussie's son. The major new thrust in policy seems to be a greater reluctance to spend big dollars on free agents. The Cards let Jack Clark go after the 1987 season and Terry Pendleton after 1990.

63. Like subsequent commissioners, Landis found it a relatively simple matter to sanction individual owners. In 1941 Landis ordered Charles Adams of the Boston Braves to divest himself either of his baseball stock or his racing stable. He disposed of the stable. In 1943 Landis suspended William Cox of the Phillies for life for betting on games.

64. Harold Seymour portrays Landis as an egocentric, eccentric goofball (1971, pp. 367–80). George Will seems to concur: "Landis was a grandstanding judge—in baseball lingo, a hot dog. . . . He tried to extradite the Kaiser because a Chicagoan died when a German submarine sank the *Lusitania*. Landis enjoyed stiff drinks of whiskey but handed out stiff sentences to people who violated Prohibition" (Seymour 1971, p. 368).

65. Quoted in the *New York Times*, 6 November 1964, p. 43.

66. Voigt 1983, vol. 3, p. 309.

67. Ibid.

68. See his autobiography *Hard Ball* (1988). Also see Marvin Miller's *A Whole Different Ball Game* (1991).

69. Chass 1991a, p. s3.

70. The commissioner's term was lowered from seven to five years beginning with Ueberroth. Kuhn's first year in 1969 was as a temporary fill-in.

71. Nightengale, Bob (1990, p. 14); also see M. Miller on Vincent (1991, pp. 393–98).

72. To be sure, the commissioner's position used to be even more vulnerable. When Bowie Kuhn was commissioner, reappointment as well as initial election re-

quired a three-quarters vote. (See Kuhn's revealing discussion of his own undo-
ing, 1988, pp. 366–403.) The rule was changed during Ueberroth's reign.

73. In the end, Jim Bouton's summary characterization of the commissioner's job
seems as apt as any: "the person in charge of protecting the financial interests
of the twenty-six business groups which make profits from baseball" (Bouton
1990, p. 408).

Chapter 3

Epigraphs: Spalding is quoted in Lee Allen (1990, p. 67); Fehr is quoted in Hoffer
(p. 47).

1. Quoted in *USA Today Baseball Weekly*, 28 June–4 July 1991, p. 6.
2. U.S. Congress, House, 1952, p. 1610; Horowitz 1974, p. 290; Noll 1988, pp.
17.34–35; Markham and Teplitz 1981, pp. 89, 159; *Sport*, June 1990, p. 70;
Paul Kagan Associates, *Media Sports Business*, 30 June 1991, pp. 1–3.
3. Horowitz 1974, p. 291; Berry and Wong, 1986, vol. 1, p. 62; Paul Kagan Associates, *Media Sports Business*, 30 June 1991, p. 2. These estimates do not include
an additional $10 million or more from MLB's foreign television and radio
contracts with some 71 countries (C. Smith 1991a, p. 24). Every day during the
season an MLB game is broadcast in Japan.
4. Between 1977 and 1988, the national revenues were not split exactly evenly.
The NL and the AL each received half, and then the NL share was divided twelve
ways and the AL share fourteen ways. In 1993 the two expansion franchises will
receive nothing from national broadcasting revenues, while the other twenty-six
franchises will receive approximately $15 million each.
5. Paul Kagan Associates' publication *Pay TV Sports*, 31 December 1984, reported
that revenue sharing of pay television receipts began on an experimental basis
in 1984 and was continued systematically thereafter. Sources inside MLB suggest this practice began in 1982.
6. The Yankees are involved in a dispute over unpaid taxes with the City of New
York that also involves, among other things, how to interpret their cable revenues. See Holtzman 1991.
7. The old formula applied in the AL was more precise, but resulted in fewer shared
revenues (apparently on the order of 10 to 15 percent of gross receipts). The
former formula set an amount paid into a league pool, later divided equally
among all the teams. The amount paid into the pool was based on the number
of subscribers to the team's pay television channel, with varying contributions
per subscriber depending on whether the service was carried on basic, premium,
or pay-per-view cable.
8. The channels of the Angels (KTLA), Rangers (KTTV), and Red Sox (WSBK) have
also been broadcast to a sufficiently broad area to be considered superstations at
times. These teams have reportedly also made modest payments to MLB. WSBK
is the only "superstation" that does not use satellite uplinks. It transmits via
MMDS (microwave).
9. Superstations are over-the-air stations that are uplinked to satellites and rebroad-

cast across the country. Federal Communication Commission (FCC) regulations do not allow the rebroadcasting of such signals to be limited, but transmitters (for example, local cable companies) are required to make per-subscriber payments to the originating station via the U.S. Copyright Tribunal. The baseball teams, not the stations, then pay a small share of their revenues to the MLB Central Fund.

10. 1989 *10-K Report* of Turner Broadcasting, p. 11.

11. U.S. Congress, House, 1952, p. 1521.

12. Markham and Teplitz 1981, pp. 85, 159; *Sport*, June 1990, p. 70. According to *Sports Illustrated*, 16 April 1990, p. 43, ticket sales in 1990 were projected to fall to 38.5 percent of total revenues.

13. U.S. House of Representatives, Committee on the Judiciary, Subcommittee on Monopolies and Commercial Law, *Antitrust Policy and Professional Sports, Oversight Hearings*, 1982, p. 434.

14. Scully (1989, p. 113) estimates that the ticket price is only one-third the cost of attending a ball game for a family of four. But, according to data from MLB, the actual share is closer to one-half (Staudohar 1989, p. 18). In 1988 the average costs for a family of four attending a major league game were as follows:

Tickets	$28.32
Food and beverage	$18.08
Souvenirs	$2.48
Parking	$3.60
TOTAL	$52.48

If we add $10 for gasoline and tolls, tickets would be approximately 45 percent of the total cost of attending a game.

15. In this case, they would have to spend enough on concessions and parking to generate an additional $1.1 million in net income.

16. Scully (1989, pp. 111–13) presents a basic econometric estimation of the elasticity of demand. He finds a somewhat inelastic demand at the average ticket price, but given the error in estimation he cannot reject the hypothesis of unitary elasticity (profit-maximizing price). The problem with Scully's estimate and the limitation of all similar estimates is the inadequacy of the measurements available. Scully regresses 1984 attendance on average ticket price, 1983 and 1984 win percentage, and 1984 population; he leaves out income per capita, income distribution, position of team's finish, number of star players on the team, area weather, whether the stadium is indoors, age and seating capacity of the stadium, tradition of baseball in a city, and the like. An earlier study by Noll (1974) using 1970–71 data included many of these additional variables but, like Scully's estimate, used average ticket prices. Unfortunately, fans do not buy average tickets, they buy box seats, grandstand seats, or general admission. Different income groups buy different types of tickets; the markets for each are largely separate. It might well be, for instance, that a team is charging below a profit-maximizing price for box seats but above a profit-maximizing price for general

admission. Further, different stadiums have different proportions of box, grandstand, and general admission seats. These proportions would have to be controlled if average ticket price were to be used with any precision.

I was able to obtain data for average seat prices as well as general admission
prices by team for 1984 to 1989. Using a variety of linear and nonlinear specifications as well as a variety of independent variables, I found a price elasticity of
between −0.18 and −0.37 for average ticket prices and of between −0.41 and
−0.57 for general admission (on the assumption that general admission attendance was one-third of the total). The coefficients, however, were not significant,
which is likely due to the measurement difficulties already mentioned. Adjusting for the fact that ticket costs are around one-half of the total cost of attending
a game, these estimates again do not contradict the proposition that pricing
policies are consistent with profit maximization. They are, however, also consistent with the previous suggestion that revenues may be augmented by charging higher prices for box seats. This, of course, is precisely what the teams are
doing with the expansion of luxury box seating. Also see Coffin (1990) and Baade
and Tiehen (1990).

17. Lawes 1991, p. 3.
18. Levine 1985, p. 46; and Chandler (1985, p. 35) writes that these boxes were still
    in use in the 1920s.
19. Michener 1976, p. 428.
20. Interview with the Blue Jays' ticket office, 10 August 1990.
21. The luxury boxes of the basketball Detroit Pistons' new arena reportedly bring
    in some $13 million annually.
22. These prices are from the "Luxury Suite Menu" and are for single orders.
    Although it is not specified in the menu, it appears that each order can serve
    several people.
23. Voigt 1983, vol. 1, p. 230, 1890s.
24. Scully 1989, p. 17; Markham and Teplitz 1981, p. 91.
25. Davis 1974, p. 357.
26. See *Sport Magazine,* June 1990, pp. 74–75. MLB also followed the initiative of
    the NBA in pursuing its international marketing strategy.
27. The Players' Association separately leases rights to card companies to use photo-
    graphs of its membership. This is discussed in the next chapter.
28. Madden 1991, p. 37.
29. Net sales are equal to wholesale sales minus quantity discounts and returns.
30. According to Markham and Teplitz (1981, p. 85), total MLB income from licens-
    ing amounted to $600,000 in 1977. The 8.5 percent royalty is cited in Lubove
    (1991, p. 180) and in the *Annual Report* of Scoreboard Inc. (1990). Another
    source in MLB says that in 1990, only $32 million in licensing income was
    distributed to teams. If this is accurate the difference may be accounted for in
    large part by a higher retention of revenues for the central fund and by greater
    (excessive) administrative costs within MLB properties.
31. See Lubove 1991, p. 182.
32. Ibid.

33. This is the figure that Seattle Mariners' owner Jeff Smulyan gave to the media. *Seattle Times*, 8 September 1991, p. A1.

34. Markham and Teplitz 1981, pp. 91–92. For the AL, 13.4 percent of revenues came from gate sharing and 5.4 percent came from the central fund; for the NL, 6.3 percent came from gate sharing and 5.7 percent from the central fund.

35. Ringolsby 1991, p. 5, McDermott 1991d, p. A17.

36. Data on 1991 player salaries is from *USA Today*, 5 November 1991, pp. 4c and 6c. The range of player development expenses is estimated in *Baseball America*, 10 March 1992. Also see, Peter Gammons (25 December 1991, *Baseball America*, p. 5), says the average club expenditures on player development are between $3.5 and $4 million. John Scher (*Baseball America*, 8 August 1990, p. 4) puts the average closer to $6 million. Scher's figure is more representative of the other estimates seen by the author.

37. A typical policy would cover player salaries for games missed due to injury (prorated by the player's salary) with a deductible of $250,000.

38. *Memorandum of Understanding*, MLB and MLBPA, 18 March 1990, p. 2.

39. The major league umpire salary range in 1950 was $5,000 to $12,000; in 1990 it was $41,000 to $105,000 excluding bonuses.

40. M. Miller 1991, p. 288.

41. Chass 1991d, p. 3.

42. Millson 1987, p. 137. Beeston made these comments in reference to the Blue Jays' 1978 profit of $4 million.

43. Andreano 1965, p. 156.

44. Actually, since December 1982 MLB has had a "60/40" rule that requires no more than 40 percent of any team's capitalization be in debt. The Players' Association filed a grievance when the rule was instituted, claiming that it would serve to limit salary growth. The grievance was lost and clubs were given three years to bring their liabilities into line.

45. Scully 1989, p. 138. Also, in 1982, Oakland paid its owners $1.4 million in interest.

46. Noll 1985.

47. This is above and beyond the $300,000 of obligatory contributions to the foundation designated in Dave Winfield's contract.

48. For instance, the 1991 audit report on the Yankees for the years 1987 to 1989 by the New York City Office of the Comptroller suggests a consistent pattern of underreporting (see Holtzman 1991). Another possible example is suggested by Mike Pagliarulo, former Yankee third baseman, who stated that the Yankees received $1 million per sign for advertising in the stadium in the mid-1980s. Although his figure seems excessive, even a third to a half of this amount would amount to an appreciable additional source of revenue.

49. When the player is assigned to another team, the compensation received is far less than the initial book value of the player's contract estimated when the team was purchased.

50. Although the Tribune Company is publicly held, neither the Annual Report nor the 10-K Report contain any financial details on the Cubs or on WGN. All

corporations owning a MLB team follow a standard practice of listing only a joint summary of all the subsidiaries in the entertainment field.

51. Personal communication; also see Quirk's forthcoming text on the economics of sports with Roger Noll and Rodney Fort.

52. This is a nominal rate. The consumer price index increased at 3.4 percent annually over this period, so the real rate of growth in franchise values is 2.9 percent per year.

53. Gammons 1989, p. 61. At the end of 1991, Smulyan put the Mariners up for sale at $100 million.

54. The Orioles sold at the end of 1988 for $70 million. Their previous sale was for $12.3 million in August 1979.

55. In order, they are the Yankees, the Mets, the Dodgers, the Orioles, the Red Sox, and the Blue Jays. Other appraisers would put the Phillies, the White Sox, the Cubs, and the Angels close to the $175-million mark. *Financial World*, 9 July 1991, p. 42.

56. See, for instance, *Sport*, June 1990, p. 70, and Sandomir 1990, p. 43.

57. *Media Sports Business*, 28 August 1991.

58. *Financial World*, 9 July 1991, p. 42; *Business Week*, 23 April 1990, p. 122, estimated Yankee profits at near $50 million. They did not provide a methodology. The figure seems excessive, but everything is relative. *New York Times* sports columnist Ira Berkow (1990) estimated the Yankees' profits at $80 million a year before taxes. He also estimated the least profitable teams were Milwaukee and Cincinnati, with about $30 million each in profits.

59. The estimated profit figure is from *Financial World*. The Vincent claim is from M. Miller (1991, p. 406).

60. Berry, Gould, and Shaudohar 1986, p. 257.

61. Quoted in Attner (1991c, p. 17).

62. Gammons 1989, p. 61.

63. *Media Sports Business*, 30 June 1991, p. 2.

64. *Business Week*, 16 April 1990, p. 78; *Sport*, June 1990, p. 71.

65. *Sport*, June 1990, p. 71.

66. The actual amount of the grant is in dispute. The city has apparently already contributed $20 million and argues that is all it ever committed. The Pirates' ownership, on the other hand, contends that the commitment was for $25 million and is seeking the balance of $5 million.

67. Each AL team will receive $3 million.

68. Hoffer 1991, p. 47.

69. After a trip to Seattle in late August 1991, Vincent was quoted in the *New York Times* (21 August 1991, p. B13) as saying: "It is not my problem, frankly. People say Fay Vincent should keep baseball in Seattle. It's Seattle that has to keep baseball in Seattle."

70. *Media Sports Business*, 30 June 1991, p. 2.

71. At the end of the 1991 season, Herzog reentered MLB, this time as general manager for the California Angels.

72. Herzog and Horrigan 1987, p. 213. Other interviewees, who once worked for

Kauffman and requested anonymity, shared Herzog's appraisal and were confident that Kauffman was in baseball for the money.

73. This is not to say that there have not been clubs in financial distress at other times. MLB loaned money at interest to the St. Louis Browns to keep them afloat, arranged for the sale of the Philadelphia Athletics, and more recently advanced funds to both the San Francisco Giants and San Diego Padres (Berry, Gould, and Staudohar 1986, p. 78).

Chapter 4

Epigraphs: Friend is quoted in Andreano (1965, p. 143); Miller is cited in Fainaru (1991, p. 23); Molitor is quoted in *Baseball America* (25 March 1991); Bronfman is cited in Chase (1990e); and Berra is quoted in Ellig (1987, p. 1).

1. *New York Times*, 10 April 1991, p. B5, and 21 November 1991, p. B18. The yearly average salaries are based on all players on the active twenty-five-man major league rosters or the disabled lists on August 31 each year. The increase, in fact, is overstated because contracts signed prior to the 1990 season were structured to minimize the impact of an anticipated work stoppage during the season on player salaries (that is, with lower salaries in 1990 and higher salaries in subsequent years).

    Pete Bavasi, president of Sportsticker and former executive of the Padres, Indians, and Blue Jays, argues that the salary explosion has less to do with a rational owner response to institutional change and more to do with the departure of Commissioner Peter Ueberroth. Bavasi credits Ueberroth with having maintained "salary discipline" among the owners. Letter to author, 22 March 1991. Also see Helyar (1991).

2. Canseco was quoted in *USA Today*, (28 February 1991, p. 3C).

3. Quoted in *Baseball America* (25 April–9 May 1991, p. 2).

4. In an interesting twist, the higher one's income, the more likely was the response that baseball players are overpaid. *New York Times*, 10 April 1991, p. B5.

5. Estimate from Ringolsby (25 December 1990, p. 5).

6. This share is based on an estimated $110 million for Yankees' team revenue in 1991. This estimate is from a quote of Brewers' owner Bud Selig in Ringolsby (1991, p. 5). Another take on the comparison between Ruth and today's players is offered by Hadley et al. (1991, p. 3) who apply Ruth's performance statistics to 1991 salary parameters and find that Ruth today would be worth $6.77 million. Of course, were Ruth playing today, he would not have the same statistics. This point is discussed in chapter 6.

7. According to one estimate, CEOs at the largest companies in the United States are paid 150 times more than the average U.S. worker, while in Japan this ratio is only 17. See Crystal (1991).

8. Drucker is quoted in Lublin (1991, p. B1); Silk 1991, p. D2.

9. *New York Times*, 4 May 1990, p. A28. Also see Hoffman and Greenberg (1989, chap. 5).

10. This information comes from the MLB Basic Agreement of 1990, pp. 24–25.

11. In his autobiography, Hank Greenberg (1989) states that the 1950 winner's share was $8,000 per player. Don Drysdale (1990, p. 61) states that the 1956 full losers' share for the Dodgers was $6,934. Zimmerman (1960) states that the winners' share in 1959 was $11,231 and the losers' share $7,275. These figures suggest that the numbers presented in Jennings for 1950 and 1960 may be too low.

12. M. Miller 1991, p. 144.

13. Berry and Wong 1986, vol. 1, p. 329.

14. Markham and Teplitz 1981, p. 40. At the time, union dues were $3 per day for each day on the twenty-five-man major league roster.

15. M. Miller 1991, p. 148.

16. One recent estimate puts the figure as high as $70,000 per player. See Schwarz 1992, p. 13. Shares are prorated according to days on the active roster. The Players' Association retained one-third of net licensing income in 1990 and one-half in 1991 to build a war chest for a possible labor dispute after the 1992 or 1993 season.

17. See discussion in Fainaru (1991). Apparently most players leave healthy tips for the clubhouse manager who is responsible for ordering the food. According to one source, the biggest tipper is George Brett, who has been known to leave the clubhouse manager $300 for a three-game series.

18. A far cry from the 1870s and 1880s when, according to Baseball's 1876 Constitution, "each player must pay $30 for the uniform furnished him by the club for the season of 1877, and must, at his own expense, keep the same clean, and in good repair." Quoted in Jennings (1990, p. 3).

19. Interview on 25 June 1990; also see M. Miller (1991, pp. 277–78).

20. Sobel 1988, p. 1–10, and documents provided to the author by the Players' Association.

21. M. Miller 1991, p. 277.

22. This critical view of agent ethics is echoed by Berry, Gould, and Staudohar (1986, p. 11).

23. Even masters are limited by so-called repeater rules. Once a player becomes a free agent, except in special cases, he must wait at least five years before he can become one again.

24. See Dworkin (1986) and Jennings (1990, pp. 200–9).

25. Schultz 1991, p. 30. Although it seems Schuerholz did not have much difficulty in this regard in 1991.

26. Chass 1990b.

27. Chass 1990d.

28. For an interesting discussion of management's perspective on arbitration, see the interview with Roy Eisenhardt, former vice president of the Oakland A's, in *Sport Magazine* (May 1983).

29. Econometric evidence on the independent effects of salary arbitration can be found in Hadley and Gustafson (1991).

30. The compensation procedure is as follows. For "Type A" free agents (players ranked in the top 30 percent at their position), the signing team loses a first-

round amateur pick if it is among the second half of selecting teams. If the signing team is among the first half of selecting teams, then it loses a second-round pick. A team's selection position is determined in inverse order to its win percentage. The team that loses a Type A free agent receives this pick plus an additional "sandwich" pick between the first and second rounds of the draft; however, the sandwich pick does not come from the signing team. For "Type B" free agents (players ranked between the 30th and 50th percentiles at their position) the compensation procedure is the same but without the sandwich pick. For "Type C" free agents (players ranked between the 50th and 60th percentiles at their position) the team that loses such a player is awarded a sandwich pick between the second and third rounds, but the signing team does not lose a pick. See MLB, Basic Agreement (1990, pp. 52–53).

31. *USA Today*, 29 June 1990, p. 6c.
32. The top average annual salaries for 1992 are as follows: Bobby Bonilla, $5.8 million; Jack Morris, $5.43 million; Roger Clemens, $5.38 million; Dwight Gooden, $5.15 million; and Danny Tartabull and Barry Larkin, around $5.1 million each. Sandberg's salary for 1992 is $2.1 million but will average $7.1 million per year during 1993–96.
33. Scully 1989, p. 32.
34. Jennings 1990, p. 16.
35. Ibid.
36. This is how the Players' Association computes team salaries. Benefits are excluded. The 1991 estimated share is based on $58 million average team revenues from Mariners' owner Jeff Smulyan. If this figure excludes undistributed central fund revenues, then the salary share in 1991 would be lower than 42.9 percent. It does not include damage payments from collusion. *Media Sports Business*, 30 June 1991, p. 1; *USA Today*, 5 November 1991, pp. 4c, 6c; *Seattle Times*, 12 September 1991, p. A1; data from Players' Association.
37. NBA teams also carry extra players on a practice squad and NFL teams carry players on their developmental team. See also discussion in appendix A.
38. *Media Sports Business*, 30 June 1991, p. 1.
39. Berry, Gould, and Staudohar 1986, p. 53.
40. Ibid.
41. Cited in Helyar (1991). Also see Lehn (1990a, b).
42. Jennings 1990, p. 232.
43. Lehn 1990a, p. 46.
44. Lehn (1990a) also disaggregates the data and concludes that neither artificial turf nor additional innings pitched in the AL resulting from the designated hitter explained the increased disability.
45. Fainaru 1991, p. 30.
46. B. Nightengale 1990, p. 9. As noted in chapter 3, as of September 1991 Herzog was back in the game, but this time in the front office.
47. Fainaru 1991, p. 23.
48. That is, the estimating equations covered all four years, 1986 to 1989, so the resulting coefficients reflected the higher revenues in later years. Hence the

estimates for MRP in 1986 and 1987 are biased upward slightly and those for 1988 and 1989 are biased downward slightly.

49. This effect will also be influenced by the degree of revenue sharing among teams and the competitive desire of each league to have a superstar in its league if not on a particular team.

50. Scully 1989, p. 47.

51. "Satisfice" means that instead of maximizing profits, the owner simply tries to meet a satisfactory level of profits.

52. Rottenberg 1956.

53. Microeconomists will recognize this as an application of the Coase theorem, named after Ronald Coase, the 1991 Nobel laureate in economics.

54. According to Quirk and El Hodiri (1974, p. 53), between 1920 and 1950 four of the sixteen teams depended on player sales for financial survival (their net income from player sales exceeded their overall net income). Between 1969 and 1976, of 975 transactions, 593 players were traded from one team to another and 382 were sold from one to another. Between 1976 and 1981, there were 719 transactions, 376 trades (52 percent), 230 sales (32 percent), and 113 (16 percent) free agent signings. That is, the number of player sales per year declined by 16 percent between the immediate pre–free agency and free agency periods.

55. See G. Daly (1992).

56. The historical evidence is presented by Scully (1989, pp. 90–91).

57. Quirk and El Hodiri 1974, p. 48.

58. Data on signing bonuses is from Schwarz (10 October 1991, p. 3).

59. Quirk and El Hodiri (1974) found from 1929 to 1950 a simple correlation of 0.81 between amount spent acquiring players and team standing in the American League. In the National League the correlation for all eight teams was -0.13; excluding St. Louis and Brooklyn, two teams that relied almost exclusively on their farm systems, the correlation was 0.89 (Quirk and El Hodiri 1974, p. 54).

60. Lehn (1990b) has postulated information asymmetries in the free agent market. Observing a higher disability rate among those eligible for free agency who actually move to new teams, Lehn argues that the players' original club lets him go only when it knows something other teams do not about his physical soundness. Were this hypothesis true, it would be an additional factor making it more difficult to buy a winning team, but it would do little to help explain why it is more difficult to buy a winning team today than in the era when player trades and sales predominated. Given the prevalence of medical and physical testing, it does not seem that this factor could play a major role today.

61. Will 1990a, pp. 310–11.

62. Little League, for instance, was first introduced just before World War II. See Zoss and Bowman (1989).

63. This point is further elaborated in chapter 6.

64. Although team average salaries are leveling, individual player salaries have become more unequally distributed since free agency. The gini coefficient of player salaries was .756 in 1965, .757 in 1974, .785 in 1986, and .788 in 1990

(Fort 1991, p. 43.) The trend can be understood to be largely a function of the explosion of salaries at the top end since 1976.

65. Quoted in the *Seattle Times* (28 July 1991, p. A1).

66. J. Miller 1990, p. 59.

67. Greenberg 1989, p. 215.

68. Of Van Poppel's $1.2 million, $500,000 was a signing bonus. Taylor's $1.55 million was a signing bonus and more than tripled Van Poppel's. Prior to Taylor, the highest signing bonus was $575,000. A first-round pick cost 32 percent more in 1990 than in 1989. About one-third of first-round picks do not reach the majors. See Schwarz (10 October 1991, p. 3). Also see *Baseball America* (10 November 1991, p. 10).

69. Quotes are from *USA Today* (28 August 1991, p. 7c).

70. This will be elaborated on in chapter 7.

71. Sommers and Quinton (1982), using data from 1976 and 1977, do find empirical support for his hypothesis. Perhaps the rapid revenue growth from national media contracts since 1977, along with equal revenue sharing from this source, has vitiated the interactive effect. If so, this effect may present itself in the 1990s.

72. Strictly speaking, in economics jargon it would require that both teams are covering their average variable costs. Even with negative cash flows, it would be in the small-city team's interest to borrow in order to hire a player for a salary up to his MRP, because this would help the team to minimize its losses.

73. It will be recalled that this rule requires a team's capital to be no less than 60 percent equity or no more than 40 percent debt.

Chapter 5

Epigraphs: Herzog is quoted in Herzog and Horrigan (1987, p. 226); and Murray is quoted in *Baseball America* (25 June 1990).

1. The bondage holds for the remainder of the first summer, June through early September, and then three full minor league seasons, unless the player is traded or released. Of course, any breach of contract by the team also liberates the player from his obligations to that team.

2. There are also Triple-A and Double-A drafts that operate under different rules and prices (compensation to original club in Triple-A draft is $12,000 and in Double-A is $4,000). They allow a small amount of player movement from club to club at the minor league level—probably fewer than thirty players a year on average. The 1991 Rule V draft was larger than usual at the minor league level, involving 44 players, while only eleven were involved at the major league level.

3. According to a study by *Baseball America* (11 November 1991, p. 10), of 3,809 players who signed their first professional contracts during 1982 to 1984, 405 played at least one game in the major leagues. Peter Gammons, based on a different survey, reported that only one in nineteen professional players made it to the majors (Gammons 1990, p. 42). Of those who play one game, less than half are still in the majors after two years.

4. Markham and Teplitz 1981, p. 51. Markham and Teplitz report on a random sample of 812 players done between 1968 and 1977 (pp. 48–51). The average time it took in the minors before making it to majors was 4.6 years, and 30 percent of first-time major leaguers were back in the minors or out of baseball the next season. Of the 812, only 650 remained in baseball after one year, only 400 after two years, one-third remained after three years, one-fourth after four years and one-tenth after seven years. About one in six recruits entering professional ball made it to the forty-man major league roster. Of those who did make it, 45 percent played for one year or less and 25 percent played for more than two years. Only one in fifty major league recruits played in the majors more than six years.

5. The median salary is that salary for which half the players earn less and half the players earn more. All first-year minor leaguers begin with an $850 monthly salary.

6. The average salary in Triple-A in 1950 was $876 per month, or $3,942 over the four-and-a-half-month season.

7. The National Association Agreement, Section 23.02a, reads: "The relationship between a club and a player created by contract may be terminated by the club before the expiration of the specified term by notice in writing of unconditional release tendered the player by the club. Liability for salary to such player shall not extend beyond the date on which such notice is given." Major League Baseball, *Professional Baseball Rules Book*, Part III, p. 65.

8. Fainaru 1991, p. 13.

9. Seymour 1971, p. 415. Also see Sullivan (1990) and Hoie (1989a, b).

10. Gregory 1956, p. 154.

11. U.S. Congress, House, 1952, p. 873.

12. Ibid., p. 1611.

13. Ibid., p. 197.

14. J. Miller 1990, p. 53. See Ellig (1987, pp. 55–56) for a more detailed breakdown of the shift in ownership and working agreement ties during the 1950s.

15. See Davis (1974).

16. U.S. Congress, House, 1952, pp. 159–161.

17. Reichardt's bonus in 1990 dollars is $870,259. Data on nominal bonuses is from Schwarz (1991b, p. 3).

18. Will 1990c, p. 59.

19. Community ownership in minor league ball also exists at other levels and varies in form from thousands of local individual stockholders to public ownership (municipality or county, or both). In addition to promoting a larger and more solid fan base, community ownership also seems to increase linkages to the local economy; that is, purchasing from local merchants appears to be enhanced. One study estimated that the community-owned, IL team in Scranton/Wilkes-Barre, Pennsylvania, generated $7 of business for the local economy for every $1 spent at the ballpark. Although a multiplier of seven seems a bit high, it is perhaps indicative of this possible effect (C. Smith 1990b). We return to discuss community ownership in chapter 6.

20. Lamb 1991, p. 5.

21. *Baseball America*, 10 September 1990, p. 11.

22. Team operations costs at the minor league level include uniforms, equipment, lodging and board on road trips, and travel. The share of these and other costs covered by the major league club is set by the Professional Baseball Agreement (PBA). See discussion in text of the 1990 PBA.

23. Conklin 1959, p. 21; Bowie Kuhn in U.S. Congress, House, 1984; Moore 1985, p. 20; *Sports Illustrated*, 16 April 1990.

24. The Professional Baseball Agreement (PBA) sets the overall terms of the relationship between the major and minor leagues. Each major league franchise signs the Player Development Contract with its minor league affiliates and is governed by the PBA.

25. C. Smith 1990a, p. 52.

26. Jon Scher in *Baseball America* (1991, p. 13).

27. Interview with Charlie Eshbach, president of the Double-A Eastern League, 1 January 1991.

28. Quoted in *Baseball America* (25 January 1991, p. 16).

29. Gyorgy 1991, p. 11.

30. Moorad 1987, p. 5.13. During 1965 to 1968 the average draft signing was for $7,500 (Okner 1974, p. 171).

31. Junior colleges have a different status in MLB from four-year colleges. Once a player enrolls in a four-year college, he cannot be signed until after his junior year or he turns twenty-one, whichever is sooner. A junior college player can be signed after the first school year. In both cases draft rights last for only one year, although MLB is now thinking about increasing the rights to two years or more.

32. More precisely, Taylor's signing bonus was $1.55 million. On top of that, he will receive the fixed first-year salary of $850 a month. Van Poppel's package included a signing bonus of $500,000 and three years' average salary of $400,000. Van Poppel was able to receive more than the fixed first-year salary because he was placed on the forty-man major league roster.

33. See, for one, Schwarz (1991).

34. According to estimates by *Financial World* (9 June 1991), the ten teams with the lowest total revenues in 1990 were in descending order: San Diego Padres with $47.2 million in revenues; Pittsburgh Pirates with $41.1 million; Houston Astros with $40.0 million; Minnesota Twins with $38.6 million; Milwaukee Brewers with $38.4 million; Detroit Tigers with $38.0 million; Atlanta Braves with $35.4 million; Montreal Expos with $35.3 million; Cleveland Indians with $34.8 million; and Seattle Mariners with $34.0 million.

35. Haudricourt 1991, p. 2.

36. See the detailing of these expenses in the case of the Chicago White Sox's Donn Pall in D. Nightingale (1990).

37. See discussion below and in chapter 8.

38. A complementary reason may be the prior development of MLB's minor league system. When professional baseball, unlike football and basketball, first developed, only a small portion of the population attended college; hence, reliance on colleges to develop players was not a viable option.

39. The amateur summer leagues are organized primarily for college players who are bound for professional baseball. Those leagues using wood bats receive modest support from MLB. The Great Lakes League, for instance, received a $58,000 subsidy from MLB in 1991. (Interview with Tom Francis, co-owner of Lima Locos in that league.) The eight leagues are: Cape Cod League, Atlantic Collegiate League, Central Illinois Collegiate League, Great Lakes League, Jayhawk League, Northeastern Collegiate League, San Diego Collegiate League, and Shenandoah Valley League.

40. For an interesting critique of college sports, see Sperber (1990).

41. See Sperber (1990). According to Staudohar (1989, p. 91), 40 percent of NFL players in 1986 had college degrees. The NCAA, the NBA, and the NFL all claim that the share of players with college degrees is unavailable information.

42. At their option, clubs can offer draftees participation in MLB's college scholarship program. As of 1990, this program provided a maximum assistance of $1,500 a semester (MLB, III, p. 41).

Chapter 6

Epigraphs: Cosell and Turner are cited in the U.S. House of Representatives, 1984, pp. 139 and 97.

1. *USA Today*, 5 September 1990, p. 7C.

2. Helyar 1990b, p. A8.

3. *Business Week*, 7 May 1991, p. 145.

4. U.S. Congress, House, 1952, p. 959.

5. See, for instance, Bowie Kuhn's testimony before the U.S. Senate's Professional Sports Antitrust Immunity Hearings in 1982, U.S. Congress, Senate, 1983.

6. The Packers are a nonprofit community organization, with some 2,000 local stockholders. No individual can hold more than 200 shares, and shares cannot be traded. The Packers also play some of their "home" games in Milwaukee. In the past MLB discussed having the Orioles play some home games in Washington, D.C., and some commentators have suggested that the Seattle Mariners play some home games in Portland and Vancouver. (See Morris 1987.) Five of the nine teams in the Canadian Football League in the late 1970s were community owned; according to one study, the teams thrived on the playing field and in the balance sheet. They also contributed more to the local economy. (See Goodman 1979, p. 197.)

7. The moves were: Boston Braves to Milwaukee (NL) in 1953; St. Louis Browns to Baltimore (AL) in 1954; Philadelphia Athletics to Kansas City (AL) in 1955; Brooklyn Dodgers to Los Angeles (NL) in 1958; New York Giants to San Francisco (NL) in 1958; Washington Senators to Minnesota (AL) in 1961; Milwaukee Braves to Atlanta (NL) in 1966; Kansas City Athletics to Oakland (AL) in 1968; Seattle Pilots to Milwaukee (AL) in 1970; and the Washington Senators to Texas (AL) in 1972. (See Quirk 1973, pp. 48–49.)

8. The three-fourths was later changed to two-thirds.

9. Burk 1989, p. 19.

10. Henschen et al. 1989, p. 14.
11. Sullivan 1987, p. 95. For an interesting and detailed discussion of the political machinations surrounding the ceding of Chevas Ravine to the Dodgers, see Burk (1989).
12. Zimmerman 1960, p. 55.
13. Drysdale 1990, p. 83.
14. Quirk 1973, p. 48.
15. Veeck 1965, p. 305.
16. Drysdale 1990, pp. 11, 81.
17. Ibid., p. 92.
18. The St. Louis Browns, for instance, proposed a move to Los Angeles, which was to be voted on at MLB meetings on December 8, 1941. The plan was scrapped following the attack on Pearl Harbor. See Ellig (1987 p. 132).
19. U.S. Congress, House, 1952, pp. 732–33.
20. Bavasi 1987, p. 82.
21. Veeck 1965, p. 301.
22. Ibid., p. 303.
23. The Braves' local television revenues increased from $500,000 in 1965 to $1.5 million in 1966. The migratory motive of higher TV revenues has been common: When the Senators moved to Minnesota in 1961 their TV revenues tripled, and when the A's moved to Oakland in 1968 their TV revenues increased more than sevenfold. J. Miller 1990, p. 298.
24. U.S. Congress, House, 1984, p. 145.
25. Veeck 1965, p. 301.
26. Henschen et al. 1989, p. 21.
27. Ibid., p. 26.
28. Markiewicz 1991, p. 6A.
29. Wayne County also plans to introduce a hotel tax to cover interest expenses. The county has the authority to levy the tax but must seek voter approval for the bond.
30. The city plan included 10,000 lighted parking spaces, but Schembechler wants 12,000 to 15,000. The county/city plan would have given the new stadium more parking than three-quarters of MLB ballparks. The plan also included an annual rent of $4 million.
31. See Pepper (1991).
32. Gillmor 1991.
33. According to the same press release, Mayor Young had been involved in discussions with Monaghan about a new stadium since March of 1984. Young made four trips to Lakeland, Florida, to talk with Monaghan and, in March 1989, he made a fifth trip with Governor James Blanchard. This trip followed a study commissioned by the city on new stadium possibilities.
34. Gavrilovich 1991, p. 3.
35. Ellig 1987, p. 221.
36. Interview with Connie Prater, *Detroit Free Press* (7 October 1991).
37. U.S. Congress, Senate, 1973, p. 175.

38. Ibid.

39. *Official Baseball Guide* 1976, p. 284.

40. Baade and Dye 1990, p. 4.

41. McDermott 1991b, p. A1.

42. McDermott 1991c.

43. Quoted in Chass (1991c, p. B9).

44. The financial problems of Emmis are discussed in McDermott 1990 and 1991a. The Emmis network included eleven radio stations, built up by Smulyan from one five-watt Indianapolis station in 1980. In November 1991 Smulyan announced a deal to sell Emmis's most profitable station, WFAN in New York, to Infinity Broadcasting for $70 million. WFAN is a sports talk station that carries the Mets. Four other stations in the Emmis chain were also sold during 1991. *Media Sports Business*, 31 December 1991, p. 8.

45. Curiously, this sum is larger than Smulyan's cumulative loss (including extraordinary expenses) while owning the team. Therefore, this would appear to give him a cash surplus, even if his numbers are to be believed. Possibly this has already been shifted toward Emmis.

46. From interviews with *Seattle Times* reporters Terry McDermott and Joni Batter. Smulyan has, however, begun to sell off several of the radio stations in his Emmis chain in an apparent effort to gain maneuvering room with the Mariners. See *Media Sports Business* (31 December 1991, p. 8) and note 44 above.

47. As explained in chapter 3, the team's operating profitability would be the same whether Smulyan used his own funds to buy the team and had no interest expense or he borrowed the money to buy the team. The interest expense is properly understood as a return to capital. Naturally, it is also an opportunity cost and would be considered by any rational investor choosing between investment options.

48. It is noteworthy that Smulyan does not include a separate item for player depreciation expense. It is possible that he thought such an item would be subject to public ridicule and instead subsumed it under general administrative expenses.

49. Noll 1985; Scully 1989.

50. McDermott 1991d.

51. *New York Times*, 11 September 1991, p. B18. At season's end, the Mariners finished at 93.9 percent of the AL's average team attendance. The Twins have a similar escape clause in their thirty-year lease of the $62 million Metrodome, built by Minneapolis in 1982. The Twins can break their lease if ticket sales fall below the league average over a three-year period. In 1984, when Calvin Griffith began to threaten to exercise this escape clause, the community raised almost $5 million to purchase 1 million tickets. See Wong (1985, p. 41); Morris (1987, p. 18).

52. Interview with *Seattle Times* reporter Joni Batter, 21 January 1992.

53. Anderson 1992, p. B11. Also see Gammons 1992, p. 52.

54. J. Miller 1990, p. 71.

55. Some, of course, raised their voices in protest: "A November 1957 article in

American City entitled 'Is Big League Baseball Good Municipal Business?' noted that all municipal stadiums were losing money and bluntly asked if the big cities with their declining tax bases and growing urban ills could afford to invest scarce public dollars in sports facilities." Cited in J. Miller (1990, p. 71).

56. A provision in the 1986 Tax Reform limits the exemption on interest income from municipal bonds floated for the purpose of stadium construction intended for private use. The limitation did not come into play until 1990. Other things being equal, this will raise the cities' financing cost for stadium construction in the future. It does not seem, however, to have curtailed new building; another testimony to the bargaining power of baseball franchises.

57. Okner 1974.

58. The most expensive stadium built to date is the Toronto SkyDome, completed in 1989, at a cost of US $514 million. The rental deal, however, was so unfavorable to the Ontario Provincial Government that in November 1991 the Skydome was sold for $110 million to private investors. The discrepancy is not quite as great as it appears, because the government had already recouped some of its costs from the sale of luxury boxes and still carried a debt of over $200 million from construction costs. *USA Today Baseball Weekly*, 22 November 1991, p. 3.

59. Okner 1974, p. 342.

60. Seattle is the one exception and it also had a football team. Baade and Dye 1990, p. 14.

61. Ross 1989, p. 644.

62. Gregory 1956, p. 15.

63. Berry and Wong 1986, vol. 1, p. 39. This includes the $12 million the city spent to purchase the stadium.

64. Ibid., p. 39. See also Wong (1985, p. 44).

65. After paying the Yankees $10,000 in 1976, in 1977 the city netted a measly $171,000 in rental income from the stadium. See R. Goodman 1979, p. 17.

66. Holtzman, 1991, Part I, p. 2, exhibit A.

67. Ibid., p. 6.

68. Holtzman 1991 Part II, p. 7. Of this sum, the Yankees paid $734,340 in delinquent electricity charges but are contesting the balance. Even if the Yankees pay annual rent in the range of $1.0 to $2.0 million in a typical year for conducting their $100 million-plus business (the stadium also includes a deluxe complex of suites on the mezzanine level behind home plate that houses the Yankees' central offices), this is a lease arrangement that would leave most CEOs salivating. Still, Steinbrenner has complained publicly that the city stiffed the Yankees for several dozen parking spaces. (Interview on WOR radio, New York City, 25 June 1990.) Laughable perhaps, but these could be the makings of a legal pretext for the Yankees to one day threaten relocation across the Hudson before their lease expires in 2002.

69. Some do better than this: Robert Short, the last owner of the Washington Senators, was described by one business historian as utterly incompetent. After driving attendance to new lows in Washington, D.C., he was rewarded by being allowed to move after the 1971 season to Arlington, Texas, which offered him

a $7 million loan and a rent-free stadium. (J. Miller 1990, p. 177.) According to Noll (1988, p. 17.34), in 1985 the average rent paid by major league teams was $1.4 million, with a high of $2.5 million and a low of $0.6 million.

70. The $15 million was essentially a gift to the private investors to finance the initial purchase. The city also pledged to kick in another $5 million to $10 million to help out with operating expenses. The subsequent amount is still in dispute. Interviews with Bernie Mullens, former chief business officer of the Pirates, 1 July 1991, and with Mark Driscoll, Pirates' director of media relations, 6 November 1991.

71. Hoffer 1991, p. 47.

72. Hernon and Ganey 1991, p. 391.

73. The new Florida Marlins will play in a privately owned ballpark, Joe Robbie Stadium, which is also used by the football Dolphins. Huizenga somehow persuaded Robbie's children to sell him 50 percent of the stadium, which cost $102 million to build, for only $5 million. Hoffman and Greenberg 1989, p. 159; DeGeorge 1991, p. 101.

74. Baim 1990.

75. Hewes and Cohen 1990, p. 54.

76. Morris 1987, p. 18.

77. Hewes and Cohen 1990, p. 57.

78. Ibid., p. 58.

79. Ibid.

80. Stevenson 1990, p. F5.

81. Interview with Brian Riley, staffer on domestic commerce for Senator Connie Mack, 8 October 1991.

82. Angell 1990, p. 61.

83. *World Almanac* 1991, p. 917.

84. The actual average number of assigned players per team in the 1903 Agreement was 19.3. It is likely, however, that several teams, especially those with fewer than 16 assigned players, added players to their rosters by the beginning of the next season. Indeed, the Agreement anticipated as much in its provision for the purchase of minor league players between September 1 and October 15. The assumed average of 20 per team in 1903 appears conservative when one considers the number of assigned players on the following teams: Cleveland: 22 players; St. Louis NL: 24; Brooklyn: 27 (U.S. Congress, House, 1952, pp. 520–21). To be sure, the 1903 Agreement stipulated no player limit per club, and by 1910 three major league clubs were reported to be carrying over 50 active players on their rosters (Ibid., p. 525). The limit of 25 active players was not imposed until 1912.

85. Topp 1989, p. 410.

86. James 1988, p. 21.

87. Danny Ainge chose basketball but his future in baseball was not promising. Deion Sanders, Bo Jackson, and D. J. Dozier chose both, but they at least seem to increasingly prefer baseball over football as favoring the preservation of their physical attributes. According to his doctors, Jackson has little choice at this

point. To be sure, some players have left baseball for another sport, but there is little evidence that the numbers are great.

88. Kahn 1991, p. 395. The increase in minority players is also evident over the last twenty-five years. In 1966, Latin and black players together accounted for 21.5 percent of all major leaguers, while in 1991 they accounted for 31.8 percent. See Schwarz 1991c, p. 12.

89. This is also true of subsequent youth baseball leagues. See, for one, Zoss and Bowman (1989, chap. 7).

90. One baseball record that has been broken repeatedly in recent years is stolen bases. But this record is clearly more a product of one individual's prowess than of competing forces.

91. U.S. Congress, House, 1952, p. 1078. George Will makes the same point (1990a, p. 308).

92. On Reds' profitability, see Nippert (1989 and 1990). Also relevant but not systematically captured in the media market as defined by Arbitron is a city's outer market—that is, roughly the viewing public outside a radius of thirty-five miles. Including the outer market would shuffle somewhat the order of cities, but it would not alter the underlying pattern.

93. The ranges are similar for National League teams. Calculated from data in U.S. Congress, House, 1952, pp. 94–95.

Chapter 7

Epigraphs: Metzenbaum is cited in U.S. Congress, Senate, 1991, p. 3; the fan's letter appears in the 12–18 July 1991 issue, p. 15; Vecsey's column appeared October 1991, p. B19; and Kohl's quote appeared in U.S. Congress, Senate, 1991, p. 16.

1. U.S. Congress, Senate, 1965, p. 195; various issues of *Media Sports Business*.
2. In 1897 each team received $300 worth of free telegrams in compensation for telegraph rights. Adomites 1989, p. 671.
3. Seymour 1971, p. 345.
4. Ibid., p. 346.
5. U.S. Congress, House, 1952, p. 742.
6. Adomites 1989, p. 672.
7. Garrett and Hochberg 1988, p. 18.18.
8. Horowitz 1974, p. 290; U.S. Congress, House, 1952, p. 1610.
9. J. Miller 1990, p. 298.
10. U.S. Congress, House, 1952, p. 1610; Horowitz 1974, p. 290; Noll 1988, pp. 17.34–35; Markham and Teplitz 1981 pp. 89, 159; *Sport*, June 1990, p. 70; Paul Kagan Associates, *Media Sports Business*, 30 June 1991, pp. 1–3.
11. The word "substantial" is from MLB's director of broadcasting, Dave Allworth (interview, 1 March 1991). MLB has had a contract with the NHK network in Japan since 1987 at least. NHK broadcasted 165 MLB games a year during 1990 and 1991, and paid an estimated $10 million or more for these rights. Mexico received 135 MLB games in 1991. According to Claire Smith (1991a, p. 24), MLB has signed broadcasting contracts with 71 countries. MLB also signed a contract

with the Voice of America's TV Martí to broadcast World Series games to Cuba. The total value of these contracts is a closely guarded secret.

12. Horowitz 1974, p. 291; Berry and Wong 1986, vol. 1, p. 62; Paul Kagan Associates, *Media Sports Business*, 30 June 1991, p. 2. These estimates do not include revenue from MLB's foreign TV and radio contracts.

13. The revenues have been shared equally among all clubs since 1989. Between 1977 and 1988, however, the national revenues were not split exactly evenly. Over this period, the national contract revenues were divided into two parts: those coming from the telecasts of regular season games and those coming from the telecasting of the All-Star Game, the playoffs, and the World Series. The former sum was divided into twenty-six equal parts, the latter sum was divided first into two equal amounts going to each league and then divided among fourteen teams in the AL and twelve teams in the NL. Thus NL clubs received a larger amount until 1989. In 1993 the two expansion franchises will receive nothing from national broadcasting revenues, while the other twenty-six franchises will receive over $15 million each.

14. *Financial World*, 9 July 1991, pp. 42–43. Increasing local media revenue inequality should not be confused with the distribution of team total revenues, which, as detailed in chapter 4, has undergone a gradual leveling trend since 1950. The latter is due primarily to the more rapid growth of national media revenues.

15. The NL shares 25 percent of "net receipts" from local pay TV and, as of 1991, the AL shares 20 percent of "net receipts." The problem, as explained in the text, is that the actual payments are significantly diminished by creative interpretations of what constitutes "net receipts."

16. Superstations are over-the-air stations that are uplinked to satellites and rebroadcast across the country. FCC regulations do not allow the rebroadcasting of such signals to be limited, but transmitters (for example, local cable companies) are required to make per-subscriber payments to the originating station via the U.S. Copyright Royalty Tribunal. The baseball teams, not the stations, then pay a small share of their revenues to the Major League Baseball central fund. There are five significant superstations (WTBS, WGN, WOR, WPIX, and KTLA) and two minor ones (KTTV and WSBK). WSBK uses microwave transmission, not satellite uplink, but reaches a large enough area outside of greater Boston to qualify as a superstation by MLB's standards.

17. 1989 *10-K Report* of Turner Broadcasting, p. 11.

18. The passage of the SBA is usually interpreted primarily as a response to the 1954 U.S. District Court decision that found the National Football League's exclusive contract with CBS violated a 1953 consent order prohibiting the league or its teams from restricting the area of telecasts of its games.

19. This policy has not treated all fans equally. The Los Angeles Raiders, for instance, play in the LA Coliseum, where seating capacity approaches 92,000. The Coliseum is rarely sold out, so Raiders' home games are virtually never televised. Of course, the same principle applies for the Rams who play in Anaheim where the football seating capacity exceeds 69,000.

20. Naturally, the Packers are also aided by playing a number of their home games in Milwaukee and by the community ownership of the club.

21. Paul Kagan Associates, *Media Sports Business*, 30 June 1991, p. 2.

22. Noll 1988, p. 17.8.

23. The NBA attempted to further diminish superstation coverage by five games per year until reaching zero games in 1995. In January 1991 the Chicago Bulls challenged the superstation restriction in Federal District Court and won. The court ruled that the SBA does not protect this restrictive practice, but the NBA is appealing the case. Neither the Bulls nor the superstation WGN pay the NBA for superstation coverage. The 1976 FCC Compulsory License ruling gives stations the right to uplink their signals and cable companies the right to downlink and distribute the signal to their subscribers by paying a modest fee to the government's Copyright Royalty Tribunal. The desirability of the compulsory license is being debated actively currently in the Congress and the FCC.

24. The superstations and the FCC's compulsory license ruling limit this restrictive practice for over-the-air broadcasting, but MLB adheres to the practice regarding pay television.

25. One possible standard to evaluate this question comes from the 1984 *NCAA* v. *The Regents of Oklahoma* case before the Supreme Court. In that decision the Supreme Court suggested that a reasonable criterion would be whether or not the package deal increased the number of viewers or, as a proxy for the number of viewers (since that cannot be measured precisely), whether or not it increased the number of telecasts. With this criterion, most present or future deals would probably be found to involve an unlawful restraint of trade.

26. Some writers have suggested that there is a basis for challenging such an application of the Holmes decision, but this basis seems to rest on a rather esoteric and unpersuasive reading of the Blackmun decision in the 1972 Flood case. See chapter 1.

27. Rates rose at over 12 percent per year between 1986 and 1990, well above the rate of inflation. Cable industry executives claim that this large increase was making up for the previous period of controlled rates. The problem with this rationale is that the cable industry is a decreasing-cost industry and is very capital intensive. If the industry's costs were constant or falling and its return was reasonable, there is no reason for a catch-up in rates. Since rate deregulation, the value of cable franchises has more than tripled, from less than $700 per subscriber on average to over $2,400 per subscriber. U.S. Congress, House, 1990, Part II, p. 22.

28. DBS involves satellite transmissions to a napkin-size dish that can be installed on a windowsill and is capable of carrying over 100 channels by analog signal transmission. With digital compression, DBS would eventually be able to carry several hundred channels. DBS is used by millions of households in Japan, but only experimentally at this time in the United States.

29. Actually, less than 3 percent of cable systems continued to be subject to regulation, and even then only on basic service. Basic service is defined as the level of service that includes only local over-the-air channels.

30. The FCC modified the definition of effective competition in mid-1991 from three to six channels. This included another 30 percent of cable systems in the provisions for rate regulation of basic service. To avoid significant regulation, these cable systems simply reduced the number of channels on basic service to the minimum and created new categories, such as expanded basic, with additional programming that are not subject to regulation. Moreover, the reduced basic service can only be regulated in the event of future price increases above 5 percent. The assertion holds that as of late 1991, the cable industry is not subject to significant rate regulation.

31. U.S. Congress, Senate, 1991, p. 115.

32. *Business Week* (13 May 1991, p. 44) reported on a survey of these sixty-five cities where MMDS (aka wireless) competed with cable. Lehigh Valley, Pennsylvania, is one such area. In 1990 one company there offered a service of forty channels for $12.99 a month; the other offered thirty-eight channels for $12.50 a month. U.S. Congress, House, 1990, vol. 1, p. 16.

33. Ibid.

34. Fiber optic and/or coaxial cable together with digital cable compression are surpassing DBS at the technological cutting edge. Applied together, they can be cheaper, more secure, and provide higher quality than DBS.

35. Horizontal integration is when companies producing the same good or service merge. Vertical integration is when companies producing different stages (for example, textile and garments, or drilling equipment and oil prospecting) of a particular good or service merge, or when a company extends its operations into another stage of a product's elaboration.

36. U.S. Congress, House, 1990, Part II, p. 137.

37. U.S. Congress, Senate, 1991, p. 3.

38. U.S. Congress, House, 1990, p. 22. That is precisely what happened as a result of the agreement between two New York cable monopolies, Paramount's MSG and NBC/Cablevision's SportsChannel. New York's baseball, hockey and basketball fans will recall that particular agreement well. It was preceded by over ten months during which sports fans in those areas of greater New York serviced by Cablevision did not have access to Yankees', Knicks', or Rangers' games over cable, and cable in each case was contracted to broadcast more games than over-the-air television. The barren period followed MSG's outbidding of Cablevision's SportsChannel for coverage of the Yankees. Cablevision would not come to an agreement with MSG about broadcasting the latter's signals, and Cablevision's vertical integration enabled it to engage in a restrictive practice.

39. The last effort, in 1985, by MLB to establish its own channel was undermined by big-city owners who saw the project as reducing their local media income advantage. The idea is being kicked around again but suffers from the same problem.

40. Jeff Smulyan, owner of the Seattle Mariners, owns the Emmis Corporation, which owns WFAN, which radio broadcasts the New York Mets. The Phillies broadcast over-the-air with WTXF, which is now owned by Paramount; Para-

mount also owns the flagship station for the Houston Astros, KTXH, and MSG, which carries the Yankees on cable. Until 1986 WTXF (formerly WTAF) was owned by the Taft Broadcasting Company, which also had a 50 percent interest in the Phillies. MSG, of course, also owns Madison Square Garden, the New York Knicks, and the New York Rangers. These manifold linkages notwithstanding, Noll's estimate that roughly half of MLB's teams are owned either by a broadcaster or by the team's principal broadcast sponsor seems too high (Noll 1988, p. 17.8.)

41. This guideline was recommended by an owners' television committee and adopted by the owners over the objections of then-commissioner Peter Ueberroth. The owners were concerned with the proliferation of superstations. Ueberroth, with reason, argued that this guideline would not curtail superstation coverage of MLB, it would only make it more difficult for MLB to arrange to be compensated for its rights.

42. Although approximately 60 percent of the nation's households have cable, cable services are estimated to be available to more than 85 percent of households. Nevertheless, the extension of cable services in particular areas has lagged woefully behind the signing of cable contracts. For instance, back in 1989, when Yankee owner George Steinbrenner was signing his contract for exclusive cable rights with Madison Square Garden Network, only 5.8 percent of the residents of the Bronx had cable television in their homes and only 2.9 percent of the residents of Brooklyn had cable (U.S. Congress, Senate, 1991, p. 22.)

43. U.S. Congress, Senate, 1991, p. 100. Einhorn is quoted in the testimony of Preston Paddler, the president of the Association of Independent TV Stations.

44. See the discussion in chapter 1 of the beginnings of the American Association in 1882.

45. Ratings are taken from a compilation by *Media Sports Business* (31 January 1991, p. 2). One ratings point is equal to 1 percent of the number of television households in a given market.

46. Goldman 1991a, p. B1.

47. Rubin 1991, p. 18.

48. By some estimates, there are over 12 million inveterate gamblers in the United States, and almost 80 percent of them bet on sports contests. There is at least one legal market for betting on daily baseball games in Las Vegas and there are several well-organized underground markets.

49. Hoffer 1991, p. 48. Queenan at *Barron's* estimated that ESPN lost $53 million (1991, p. 10), while Attner at *The Sporting News* estimated its losses at $50 million (1991c, p. 11.) John Mansell of Paul Kagan Associates estimates that ESPN losses from the MLB contract in 1990 were $37 million.

50. Despite its ratings drop in 1991 of 4.7 percent, ESPN actually had 23,000 more viewers for an average game than in 1990. The apparent discrepancy is explained by the growth in the number of television and cable households. WTBS's ratings for the third quarter 1991 were up 17.6 percent over 1990. *Sports Media Business*, 31 October 1991, p. 2.

51. Bierbaum 1991.

52. *Wall Street Journal*, 29 October 1991, p. B6. Also see *The Hollywood Reporter*, 29 October 1991, p. 1.

53. See Goldman 1991b, p. B6.

54. Indeed, it is appropriate to recall that the Toronto Blue Jays' market is not even counted in the U.S. ratings; all the same, Toronto residents still buy U.S. products. Thus, published ratings exclude hundreds of thousands of Canadian viewers.

55. *Forbes*, 1 April 1971, p. 24.

56. *Fortune*, 15 April 1985, p. 19.

57. The number of television households nationally has been increasing at approximately 1 to 1.5 percent per year.

58. Erardic 1991; also see Rushin (1991), and W. O. Johnson (1991).

59. Quoted in the *Springfield Republican* (24 February 1991, p. C3).

60. Cited in Attner (1991c, p. 11).

61. The inner market includes all households in the New York City area of dominant influence (ADI) as defined by Arbitron, or roughly households within a thirty-five-mile radius of the city. Needless to say, the outer market to New York City is very substantial as well. Also excluded from the figure are all those viewers throughout the United States who were watching the Mets on WOR's superstation distribution.

62. The Mets renegotiated their cable contract with Sportschannel after the 1991 season. The new contract reportedly will bring the Mets between $22 and $24 million a year—from cable television alone. Just in time for Bobby Bonilla!

63. For instance, the Major League Agreement, Article V, Section 2.b.4., states that a three-quarters vote of all member clubs is needed to amend any provision bearing on revenue sharing that affects both leagues, excepting provisions for amending the Central Fund Agreement which needs three-quarters vote in each league. But the Central Fund Agreement clause has another qualifier that excepts provisions governing radio and television. Article V, Section 2.b.1.iv., states that any action relating to radio or television requires only a simple majority vote of the clubs; however, this provision is ambiguous because it seems to apply only to the signing of contracts with outside companies, not internal revenue sharing. Further, internal revenue sharing appears to be governed by the three-quarters rule just mentioned. Each league has its own agreement and its own television and radio rules.

64. The previous procedure set at an AL meeting on 8 December 1982, required a three-fourths vote to change the television rules. Prior to the 1982 meeting a unanimous vote was required.

65. See Holtzman 1991, Part 2.

66. Quoted in Gyorgy (1991b, p. 9).

67. For an interesting discussion of the degradation of sport by commercialism, see Lasch (1978, chap. 5).

Chapter 8

Epigraphs: Burger is cited in Michener (1976, p. 482); Michener's quote is from Michener (1976, p. 503); Lipsky's quote is from U.S. Congress, House (1984, p. 67); and Reinsdorf is quoted in Hoffer (1991, p. 47).

1. It warrants cautioning that at least one source in MLB says that the teams received considerably less than $3 million in 1991 from licensing. My figure is based on conversations with personnel in MLB Properties and with estimates reported in journalistic sources discussed in chapter 3.

2. Paul Kagan Inc. seminar on Media Sports Business at the Park Lane Hotel on 6 November 1991. Einhorn was the luncheon speaker.

3. Interview, 25 June 1990.

4. Profit sharing would make more sense on a league-wide basis, perhaps proportionate to team standing, rather than on a team-by-team basis. If the latter were attempted, it would work powerfully against the interests of ballplayers on small-city teams.

5. Interview on 1 November 1991.

6. Paul Kagan seminar, 6 November 1991.

7. See, for one, Hadley and Gustafson 1991.

8. One study finds that only 40 percent of college football players graduate college, and most of those who do finish their college education do so only because they are spoon-fed a special diet of "gut" courses. Staudohar 1989, p. 91.

9. Existing summer leagues for college players offer no remuneration. The suggestion here is for players to be paid and for the existing leagues to be expanded.

10. In chapter 6, using population/player ratios, we concluded that were this ratio the same in 1990 as in 1903, the beginning of the modern baseball era, then MLB would be able to support forty teams. If the U.S. population were to grow at 0.9 percent annually until 2004, the 1903 ratio would support forty-five teams in 2004.

11. See chapter 3 for a discussion of these estimates. These estimates, of course, are only averages. Low-income teams received considerably more of their income from shared sources (for example, the Seattle Mariners receive approximately 55.5 percent of their $36 million total revenues from shared sources) and high-income teams considerably less (for example, the New York Yankees received around 17.2 percent on total revenues of close to $110 million). Team total revenue estimates are from Ringolsby (1991, p. 5) and McDermott (1991a, p. 417).

12. Team revenue estimates from McDermott (1991a, p. A17) and Ringolsby (1991, p. 5).

13. The bill applies to teams not in Florida prior to 1 July 1990. *Financial World*, 9 July 1991, p. 41.

14. In a 1974 study Roger Noll found that New York City could support three teams in the early 1970s. If the New York metropolitan area can support three profes-

sional hockey teams, there is a strong prima facie case that it can also support three baseball teams.

15. Erardic 1991 and Nippert et al. 1989 and 1990.

16. The possible franchise expansion cities are (in order of the size of their media markets): Washington, D.C.; Tampa–St. Petersburg; Phoenix; Sacramento; Hartford–New Haven; Orlando; Indianapolis; Portland; Charlotte; Nashville; Raleigh–Durham; Columbus; New Orleans. Buffalo, New York, frequently mentioned as a 1993 NL expansion site, ranks thirty-eighth in U.S. media market size.

17. The October 1991 FCC recommendation that the telephone companies (telcos) be allowed to supply video services to the home has left many expecting cutthroat competition between the existing cable companies and the telcos. The greater likelihood is that the two groups will cooperate. Once a permissive legal framework is in place, laying the fiber optic infrastructure across the country will cost over $200 billion and take up to a dozen years. The telcos could benefit from developing a mixed system, using the coaxial cable already laid by the cable companies. Though not as flexible and with somewhat lower capacity, coaxial cable does carry digitally compressed signals. The telcos continue to own the poles needed by the cable companies, and it is in neither's interests to engage in open competition.

18. Indeed, when several games of the 1991 Series went past midnight into extra innings, many adults went to bed not knowing the games' outcomes.

19. Quoted in J. Miller (1990 p. 257).

20. Scully 1989, pp. 192–93.

21. Ross 1989, p. 646. Also see Ross (1991).

22. It may, however, have an indirect effect if it were to lead to league restructuring and expansion.

23. The courts also could determine that baseball's draft is legal on a "rule-of-reason" basis, arguing that the current procedures are necessary for the survival of the game.

24. It is also possible that, with MLB's various media interlocks, negotiating a sufficiently lucrative radio and television contract would be more difficult for a new league.

25. Ross's scheme does not actually depend on finding a plaintiff. He proposes that Congress pass legislation to force sports leagues to divide up into at least three separate business entities. Ross argues that the leagues could cooperate in postseason championships and establishing common playing rules but on little else. The legislation would preclude interleague agreements on the number and location of franchises, rules for allocating players, and the sale of broadcast rights. Ross's plan is interesting, but the ensuing disarray, if not chaos, in the sports leagues would be unnecessarily debilitating and disruptive to the spirit and the finances of professional sports.

26. Don Fehr, current director of the Players' Association, stated at U.S. Senate hearings in 1982 (1983, p. 381): "It [MLB] divides the geographic market to

prevent competition there. It divides the broadcast market to prevent competition there, and . . . by virtue of interlocking agreement with all major and minor league teams, it effectively controls access to the industry, because it controls the stadiums, and substantially all cities in the country."

27. Lacking a blanket exemption, the NFL has been hit with over sixty lawsuits since 1966. Roberts 1991, p. 135.

28. In response to such a suit, MLB could argue that it is a single legal entity and, thereby, has the right to choose its business partners. The single-entity defense has been argued forcefully by Gary Roberts (1991). Sports leagues in a sense are a single entity, but for business purposes they are clearly separate companies, each with its own owners and out for its own profit. Reality is more complex than Roberts's argument allows.

29. State ownership, as Governor Mario Cuomo has proposed for New York State and the Yankees, is another possible variant.

30. Oakland was unsuccessful in the California courts when it tried to invoke eminent domain to prevent the Raiders' relocation.

31. Both regarding the antitrust exemption and any future regulatory action, there are issues of policy synchronization with Canada. It is assumed that Canada will continue to follow the U.S. lead in MLB.

32. One existing bureau, the National Telecommunications and Information Administration, might be appropriate, or a new bureau on entertainment or sports might be established. It is ironic that the Commerce Department is the closest independent government agency this country has to a department of culture. The United States is one of the few countries in the world without a government department or ministry of culture and/or sports.

33. The bill also had several qualifications and exemptions that made it difficult to treat as a serious piece of legislation.

34. The most standard formula today sets baseball franchise values at fifteen times cash flow or at two times total revenues. This formula, however, seems to underestimate substantially the market value of many franchises, especially those benefitting from a new stadium.

35. Hoffman 1981, p. 843.

36. Such a scheme has the potential drawback that accountability could be diminished.

37. Labor relations should include the overseeing of equal employment opportunity practices. City governments can also become involved here. Just as businesses that contract with the federal government are required to follow affirmative action hiring policies, city governments could require sports teams that benefit from city contracts and subsidies to adhere to affirmative action guidelines. The occasional exhortations out of Commissioner Vincent's office and National League president Bill White's office have been insufficient to promote the incorporation of minorities into baseball's management ranks. Just how ineffective MLB's efforts have been was poignantly revealed when the new expansion franchise in Denver failed to interview even one minority person for any of its

six top management positions (C. Smith 1991e, p. 28). Furthermore, excellent black managerial candidates Don Baylor, Chris Chambliss, and Bill Robinson were not only passed over but apparently were not even seriously considered by any of the major league clubs hiring new managers after the 1991 season. On the resulting progressive alienation of black fans from MLB, see Schwarz 1991c.
38. 5.3445, 92nd Congress, 2nd Session, introduced 30 March 1972.
39. The NCTA pays its chief Washington lobbyist a $800,000 salary, according to *New York Post* columnist Phil Mushnik (interview, 24 June 1990.) And in 1990 the NCTA lavished $565,000 on congressional campaigns (Lewyn 1991, p. 67).
40. L. J. Davis 1990, p. 38.
41. See Pasdeloup (1991).
42. U.S. Congress, House, 1984, p. 141.
43. Lowenfish and Lupien 1980, p. 172.

Appendix A

1. Roberts actually employed a modified Scully-type model as one of three empirical estimates in computing damages. Nicolau heard testimony based on a Scully-type model, but he did not use it in calculating damages.
2. A. Zimbalist, "Pay and Performance in Major League Baseball: Beyond the Scully Model," in P. Sommers 1992.
3. According to several studies, measures of defensive performance are not significantly correlated with pay.
4. This would be the same as assuming that the player was replaced and his replacement batted the team average, in terms either of slugging or slugging plus on-base average (PROD).
5. The measures of performance used in this exercise, of course, are imperfect. Home runs enter slugging percentage as four times more valuable than singles. A single and a walk enter equally. Stolen bases and caught stealing do not figure in our measurement at all. Kevin Ryan (1991) has suggested a purer measurement based on Thorn and Palmer (1989). They ran computer simulations of over 100,000 baseball games and estimated the run values of every type of play. For instance, a single is estimated to be worth .47 runs, a walk .33 runs, a double .78 runs, a triple 1.09 runs, a homer 1.40 runs. We used the "run value" performance measure and came up with very similar estimates. The fit of our regressions was not improved.
6. A dummy variable for two-team cities was also added but was not significant in any of a variety of specifications and even had a positive sign in some equations. Naturally, the addition of independent variables will not affect the coefficients on PCT and population (POP) unless the new variables are themselves correlated with PCT and POP.
7. Of course, insofar as the owner's labor market circumstance emulates that of a monopsonist, the marginal factor cost will also include extra payments that the owner will make to other players. This would result in lower salaries. It seems reasonable to expect that in some instances paying more to one player will raise

the salary demands (and, ultimately, the salary) of other players. If nothing else, baseball's salary arbitration procedure will ensure that this happens to some degree, but here there is an interesting twist. Namely, one owner raising the salary of a player may not only raise his or her labor costs but may raise the labor costs of his or her fellow owners. This fact raises once again the whole question of the appropriate unit for and the modeling of the analysis of profit-maximizing behavior in sports leagues.

8. The player is responsible for his own glove and spikes, although in many cases their cost is covered as a minor part of an endorsement contract.

9. The basis for this percentage is discussed in Zimbalist (1992).

10. City media population (number of households with television sets within a certain radius) was also used in addition to SMSA data. The results were very similar. Efforts to pick up a revenue-diminishing effect from having two teams in the same city came to naught. Perhaps the synergy of two teams on a city's baseball culture negates the sharing of a particular market by two teams. See detailed discussion in Zimbalist (1992).

11. Through the 1988 season, revenues from the national media packages, after deductions for administrative expenses, were divided roughly 50/50 between the two leagues. However, since the National League had twelve teams and the American League had fourteen, the per-team share for NL clubs was approximately 16.6 percent higher than for AL clubs. The formula was changed after the 1988 season to provide equal revenue to all clubs. The previous inequality is one of the reasons why the AL claimed it was entitled to share in the NL expansion sale of two franchises for $95 million each.

12. Our sample includes all hitters, according to 1990 team rosters. Since some of these players did not play in previous years, the sample size decreases for each preceding year. Only players for whom complete data was available in a particular year were included.

13. Kuhn 1988, 170–72; Helyar 1991; MLB, Arbitration Panels, various years.

14. Scully, Hirschberg, and Slottje 1990.

15. The closer correlation between salary and MRP among journeymen than among masters suggests the testing of curvilinear forms in the regressions for all players. Semilog and quadratic forms were tested but were inconclusive.

16. This finding also appears in Scully, Hirschberg, and Slottje (1990).

17. *Newsweek*, 19 February 1990, p. 60.

18. Again, based on the twenty-five-man roster plus disabled list on August 31 and excluding benefits.

19. The actual procedure is to use total gate and media revenues for all teams and then apply the 53 percent as a share of this figure divided by the number of teams. This way each team has the same dollar cap, although the cap can be exceeded by a team seeking to re-sign a free agent from its own team. Teams in the NBA have the right to match other teams' offers on their own free agents.

20. MLB pension and health contributions came to an additional $55 million, or roughly 4 percent of MLB total revenues in 1990.

21. These shares include only salary paid to players at the major league level.

Appendix B

1. Some authors have assumed that the proper way to treat population in two-team cities was to divide it by two; that is, that having two teams diminshed the effective population by 50 percent. This practice implicitly assumes that fans in a city are either for one team or the other but not both and that interest in one team does not enhance overall interest in baseball. It overlooks the possibility that having two or more teams in one city might deepen the baseball culture in the area and thereby increase the number of fans. Finally, teams' output is not homogeneous—for example, Yankee fans cannot watch Dwight Gooden pitch at Yankee Stadium or on MSG network. Equations predicting either total revenue or attendance were tested using three population variables: POP, no adjustment for two-team cities; POP2 (0.5 × POP) for two-team cities; and POP3 (0.7 × POP) for two-team cities. POP3 was introduced to represent an intermediate state between mutual exclusivity of fan support and no symbiosis, on the one hand, and no exclusivity and complete symbiosis, on the other. In every case, the t-statistics on POP were higher than those on POP3, which, in turn, were higher than those on POP2.

References

ABRAMSON, JILL, AND LAURIE COHEN. "Eli Jacobs, Financier and Orioles Owner, Covers All the Bases." *Wall Street Journal*, 15 May 1991.

ADOMITES, PAUL. "Baseball on the Air." In *Total Baseball*, ed. John Thorn and Pete Palmer. New York: Warner Books, 1989.

ALFT, E. C., JR. "The Development of Baseball as a Business: 1876–1900." In U.S. Congress, House of Representatives, Committee of the Judiciary, Subcommittee on Monopolies and Commercial Law, *Organized Baseball*, Hearings (1951), 82d Congress, 1st Session, Washington, D.C.: USGPO, 1952.

ALLEN, LEE. *Cooperstown Corner: Columns from The Sporting News*. Cleveland: Society for American Baseball Research, 1990.

ANDERSON, DAVE. "Just Give Me $10 Million, Baby." *New York Times*, 16 September 1990.

———. "Approve the Seattle Nintendos." *New York Times*, 29 January 1992.

ANDREANO, RALPH. *No Joy in Mudville*. Cambridge, MA: Schenkman, 1965.

ANGELL, ROGER. "The Sporting Scene." *The New Yorker*, 3 December 1990.

ANHEUSER-BUSCH CORPORATION. *10-K Report* and *Annual Report*, St. Louis, MO: Author, various years.

ASINOF, ELIOT. *Eight Men Out: The Black Sox and the 1919 World Series*. New York: Holt, Rinehart & Winston, 1963.

ATTNER, PAUL. "How Professional Sports Governs Expansion Will Mean Success or Failure for 21st Century." *The Sporting News*, 18 March 1991a.

———. "Playing the Markets." *The Sporting News*, 25 March 1991b.

——. "Big Bang: The Vision, The Future." *The Sporting News*, 1 April 1991c.

BAADE, ROBERT, AND RICHARD DYE. "Sports Stadiums and Area Development: A Critical Review." *Economic Development Quarterly*, 2, no. 3 (August 1988).

——. "The Impact of Stadiums and Professional Sport on Metropolitan Area Development." Working Paper, Lake Forest College, February 1990.

BAADE, ROBERT, AND LAURA TIEHEN. "An Analysis of Major League Baseball Attendance, 1969–1987." Working Paper, Lake Forest College, May 1990.

BAIM, DEAN. *Sports Stadiums as "Wise Investments": An Evaluation*. Detroit: Heartland Institute Policy Study, No. 32, November 1990.

——. *The Sports Stadium as a Municipal Investment*. Westport, CT: Greenwood Press, 1992.

BARROW, EDWARD. "What's the Matter with the Minors?" *Baseball Magazine* (May 1917).

BASEBALL BLUE BOOK. St. Petersburg, FL: Baseball Bluebook Inc., various years.

BASEBALL ENCYCLOPEDIA, 8th ed. New York: Macmillan, 1990.

BAUGHMAN, JAMES. *Television's Guardians: The FCC and the Politics of Programming, 1958–1967*. Knoxville: University of Tennessee Press, 1985.

BAVASI, BUZZIE. *Off the Record*. Chicago: Contemporary Books, 1987.

BELSIE, LAURA. "Domino's Fatalities Raise Safety Issue in Fast Food Industry." *Christian Science Monitor*, 26 July 1989.

BERKOW, IRA. "Yes, Virginia, There Will Be Baseball." *New York Times*, 17 February 1990.

BERRY, ROBERT, AND GLENN WONG. *Law and Business of the Sports Industries*, vols. 1 and 2. Dover, MA: Auburn House, 1986.

BERRY, ROBERT, WILLIAM GOULD, AND PAUL STAUDOHAR. *Labor Relations in Professional Sports*. Dover, MA: Auburn House, 1986.

BIANCO, ANTHONY, ET AL. "Inside the Shadowy Empire of Eli Jacobs." *Business Week*, 18 November 1991.

BIERBAUM, TOM. "Series Helps CBS Slide Into 1st." *Variety*, 30 October 1991.

BOUTON, JIM. *Ball Four*. New York: Macmillan, 1990.

BURK, GREG. "Dodger Blood: Hating and Loving the Team of Clean." *LA Weekly* 11, no. 25 (1 June 1989).

CANES, MICHAEL. "The Social Benefits of Team Quality." In *Government and the Sports Business*, ed. Roger Noll. Washington, D.C.: Brookings Institution, 1974.

CHAMPION, WALTER, JR. "Baseball's Third Strike: Labor Law and the National Pastime." *Pennsylvania Law Journal & Reporter* 4, no. 20 (25 May 1981).

CHANDLER, JOAN. *Television and National Sport: The U.S. and Britain*. Urbana: University of Illinois Press, 1988.

CHASS, MURRAY. "Owners Offer Revenue-Sharing Deal." *New York Times*, 11 January 1990a.

——. "Players Big Winners as Arbitration Ends." *New York Times*, 22 February 1990b.

——. "Owners Might Have Avoided Trouble by Listening to Finley." *New York Times*, 4 March 1990c.

————. "Pay Cut Is Now Seldom-Used Tool." *New York Times,* 11 March 1990d.

————. "Bronfman Proposes Revenue Sharing." *New York Times,* 5 December 1990e.

————. "Kuhn's Descent from Commissioner to Legal Outcast." *New York Times,* 12 May 1991a.

————. "Vincent Splits Expansion Booty." *New York Times,* 7 June 1991b.

————. "Expansion Losers Turn to a Decidedly Unreliable Plan 2." *New York Times,* 12 June 1991c.

————. "Money, Money and More Money." *New York Times,* 21 November 1991d.

CHELIUS, JAMES, AND JAMES DWORKIN. "An Economic Analysis of Final-Offer Arbitration as a Conflict Resolution Device." *Journal of Conflict Resolution* 24, no. 2 (June 1980).

COFFIN, DONALD. "The Business of Major League Baseball: A Review." *SABR's By the Numbers* 2, no. 1 (January 1990).

COLE, BARRY, AND MAL OETTINGER. *Reluctant Regulators: The FCC and the Broadcast Audience.* Reading, MA: Addison-Wesley, 1978.

CONKLIN, WILLIAM. "Shear Criticizes Circuit Head for Comments on Third League." *New York Times,* 29 July 1959.

CRASNICK, JERRY. "Reds' Schott Stirs Up Trouble Again." *Baseball America,* 10 December 1991.

CRYSTAL, GRAEF. *In Search of Excess: The Overcompensation of American Executives.* New York: Norton, 1991.

DALY, GEORGE. "Counterintuition, Contracting Costs and the Baseball Player's Labor Market." In *Diamonds Are Forever: The Business of Baseball,* ed. Paul Sommers. Washington, D.C.: Brookings Institution, 1992.

DALY, JOHN, ED. *Pro Sports: Should the Government Intervene?* Washington, D.C.: American Enterprise Institute, 1977.

DAVIS, LANCE. "Self-Regulation in Baseball." In *Government and the Sports Business,* ed. Roger Noll. Washington, D.C.: Brookings Institution, 1974.

DAVIS, LANCE, AND JAMES QUIRK. "The Ownership and Valuation of Professional Sports Franchises." Social Science Working Paper No. 79, California Institute of Technology, Pasadena, CA, April 1975.

DAVIS, L. J. "Television's Real-Life Cable Baron." *New York Times Magazine,* 2 December 1990.

DeGEORGE, GAIL. "The Dolphins Never Played This Rough." *Business Week,* 28 October 1991.

DELLINGER, HAROLD. "Rival Leagues." In *Total Baseball,* ed. John Thorn and Pete Palmer. New York: Warner Books, 1989.

DEMMERT, HENRY. *The Economics of Professional Team Sports.* Lexington, MA: D. C. Heath, 1973.

DODD, MIKE. "Cincinnati Fans Still Her No. 1 Priority." *USA Today,* 21 February 1991.

DRYSDALE, DON. *Once a Bum, Always a Dodger.* New York: St. Martin's, 1990.

DUNBAR, WILLIAM. "Baseball Salaries Thirty Years Ago." *Baseball Magazine* (July 1918).

DWORKIN, JAMES. *Owners versus Players: Baseball and Collective Bargaining.* Boston: Auburn House, 1981.

———. "Salary Arbitration in Baseball: An Impartial Assessment after Ten Years." *Arbitration Journal* 41 (March 1986).

ECONOMIC REPORT OF THE PRESIDENT. Washington, D.C.: USGPO, 1990.

EISENHARDT, ROY. Interview in *Sport Magazine* (May 1983).

EINSTEIN, CHARLES, ED. *The Fireside Book of Baseball,* 4th ed. New York: Simon & Schuster, 1987.

ELLIG, JEROME. "Law, Economics, and Organized Baseball: Analysis of a Cooperative Venture." Ph.D. diss., Department of Economics, George Mason University, 1987.

ERARDIC, JOHN. "Sports Spotlight." *Cincinnati Enquirer,* 13 May 1991.

EVERS, CRABBE. *Murderer's Row.* New York: Bantam, 1990.

FAINARU, STEVE. "A Whole New Ball Game: The High-Stakes Business of Baseball." *Boston Globe Magazine,* 25 August 1991.

FEHR, DONALD. "The Relationship of the Baseball Players' Association, Team Management and the League." In *Current Issues in Professional Sports,* ed. Michael Jones. Durham, NH: Whittmore School of Business and Economics, 1980.

FIMRITE, RON. "What If They Held a Sporting Event and Nobody Came?" *Sports Illustrated,* 22 July 1991.

FINS, ANTONIO. "Stee-rike! Steinbrenner Just Can't Get a Hit." *Business Week,* 23 April 1990.

FORT, RODNEY. "A Pay and Performance Omnibus: Is the Field of Dreams Barren?" Paper prepared for the Middlebury Conference on the Economics of Baseball, 5–6 April 1991.

GAMMONS, PETER. "Rich Man's Game." *Sports Illustrated,* 11 December 1989.

———. "The Trail through the Minors Is Tortuous." *Sports Illustrated,* 23 July 1990.

———. "Misplaced Hysteria." *Boston Sunday Globe,* 26 January 1992.

GARRETT, R. A., AND P. R. HOCHBERG. "Sports Broadcasting." In *Law of Professional and Amateur Sports,* ed. Gary Uberstine. New York: Clark Boardman Co., 1988.

GAVRILOVICH, PETER. "Tigers Want Mayor to Pitch Relief." *Detroit Free Press,* 7 October 1991.

GILDER, GEORGE. "Now or Never." *Forbes,* 14 October 1991.

GILLMOR, DAN. "Major Leagues Palm on Taxpayers." *Detroit Free Press,* 7 October 1991.

GOFF, BRIAN, AND ROBERT TOLLISON, EDS. *Sportometrics.* College Station: Texas A & M University Press, 1990.

GOLDMAN, KEVIN. "CBS May Strike Out Again with Baseball." *Wall Street Journal,* 11 September 1991a.

———. "CBS Takes $322 Million Pretax Charge on Sports Contracts." *Wall Street Journal,* 4 November 1991b.

GOLDSTEIN, WARREN. *Playing for Keeps: A History of Early Baseball.* Ithaca, NY: Cornell University Press, 1989.

GOODMAN, ROBERT. *The Last Entrepeneurs: America's Regional Wars for Jobs and Dollars*. New York: Simon & Schuster, 1979.

GOULD, STEPHEN JAY. "Can Baseball Save America?" *New York Review of Books* 37, no. 15 (11 October 1990).

GREENBERG, HANK (WITH IRA BERKOW). *Hank Greenberg. The Story of My Life*. New York: Times Books, 1989.

GREGORY, PAUL. *The Baseball Player: An Economic Study*. Washington, D.C.: Public Affairs Press, 1956.

GYORGY, DEAN. "Majors, Minors Adjust to New Deal." *Baseball America*, 25 September 1991a.

———. "Baseball Braces for TV Negotiations." *Baseball America*, 10 December 1991b.

HADLEY, LAWRENCE, AND ELIZABETH GUSTAFSON. "Major League Baseball Salaries: The Impacts of Arbitration and Free Agency." *Journal of Sport Management* 5, no. 2 (July 1991).

HADLEY, LAWRENCE, ET AL. "Who Would Be the Highest Paid Baseball Player?" University of Dayton, School of Business Administration, Working Paper 91-08, July 1991.

HAILEY, GARY. "The Business of Baseball." *SABR Review of Books* 9 (1989a).

———. "Baseball and the Law." In *Total Baseball*, ed. John Thorn and Pete Palmer. New York: Warner Books, 1989b.

HAUDRICOURT, TOM. "Teams Soon May Retain Rights to Drafted Players." *Baseball America*, 25 October 1991.

HELYAR, JOHN. "It's the Minor League Entrepeneurs vs. Majors' Moguls." *Wall Street Journal*, 3 December 1990a.

———. "Big League Battle: Baseball's Expansion Is a High-Stakes Game of Money and Politics." *Wall Street Journal*, 21 December 1990b.

———. "Playing Ball." *Wall Street Journal*, 20 May 1991.

HENSCHEN, BETH, ET AL. "Professional Sports Franchises, Economic Development and Municipal Government: A Contemporary Policy Dilemma." Paper presented at the annual meeting of the Midwest Political Science Association, 13–15 April 1989, Chicago, IL.

HERNON, PETER, AND TERRY GANEY. *Under the Influence: The Unauthorized Story of the Anheuser-Busch Dynasty*. New York: Simon & Schuster, 1991.

HERZOG, WHITEY, AND KEVIN HORRIGAN. *White Rat*. New York: Harper & Row, 1987.

HEWES, HAVELOCK, AND NEIL COHEN. "Whose Teams Are They, Anyway?" *Sport* (July 1990).

HILL, JAMES, AND W. SPELLMAN. "Professional Baseball: The Reserve Clause and Salary Structure." *Industrial Relations* 22, no. 1 (Winter 1983).

———. "Pay Discrimination in Baseball: Data from the Seventies." *Industrial Relations* 23, no. 1 (Winter 1984).

HOFFER, RICHARD. "The Buck Stops Here." *Sports Illustrated*, 29 July 1991.

HOFFMAN, DALE, AND MARTIN GREENBERG. *Sport$Biz: An Irreverent Look at Big Business in Pro Sports*. Champaign, IL: Leisure Press, 1989.

HOFFMAN, GREGG. "Brewer's Await County Decision on New Stadium." *USA Today Baseball Weekly*, 8–14 November 1991.

HOFFMAN, SCOTT LEE. "Pooling of Local Broadcasting Income in the American Baseball League: Antitrust and Constitutional Issues." *Syracuse Law Review* 32 (1981).

HOIE, BOB. "The Minor Leagues." In *Total Baseball*, ed. John Thorn and Pete Palmer. New York: Warner Books, 1989a.

———. "The Farm System." *Total Baseball*, ed. John Thorn and Pete Palmer. New York: Warner Books, 1989b.

HOLTZMAN, ELIZABETH. "Audit Report on Rent and Reimbursements Due from the New York Yankees Partnership." Bureau of Audit, Office of the Comptroller, City of New York, Parts 1 and 2, July 1991 and September 1991.

HOROWITZ, IRA. "Sports Broadcasting." In *Government and the Sports Business*, ed. Roger Noll. Washington, D.C.: Brookings Institution, 1974.

JAMES, BILL. *The Baseball Book.* New York: Random House, various years.

JENNINGS, KENNETH. *Balls and Strikes: The Money Game in Professional Baseball.* New York: Praeger, 1990.

JOHNSON, ARTHUR. "Public Sports Policy." *American Behavioral Scientist* 23, no. 3 (January–February 1978).

JOHNSON, WILLIAM OSCAR. "Sports in the Year 2001." *Sports Illustrated*, 22 July 1991.

JONES, MICHAEL, ED. *Current Issues in Professional Sports.* Durham, NH: Whittmore School of Business and Economics, 1980.

KAHN, LAWRENCE. "Discrimination in Professional Sports." *Industrial and Labor Relations Review* 44, no. 3 (April 1991).

KAPLAN, DAVID, ET AL. "The Most Hated Man in Baseball." *Newsweek*, 6 August 1990.

KLATELL, DAVID, AND NORMAN MARCUS. *Sports for Sale: Television, Money and the Fans.* New York: Oxford University Press, 1989.

KLEIN, FREDERICK. "On Sports: Houston Astrodome at 25." *Wall Street Journal*, 25 May 1990.

KOPPETT, LEONARD. "A Strange Business, Baseball." *New York Times Magazine*, 2 September 1973.

KUHN, BOWIE. *Hardball: The Education of a Baseball Commissioner.* New York: McGraw-Hill, 1988.

LABATT. *Annual Report.* Toronto: Author, 1990.

LAMB, DAVID. "Don't Let Big Business Destroy Magic of the Minors." *The Sporting News*, 17 June 1991.

LANE, F. C. "Shall Certain Magnates Defy the Public?" *Baseball Magazine* (May 1913).

———. "A Rising Menace to the National Game." *Baseball Magazine* (July 1918a).

———. "The Truth about Commercialism in Baseball." *Baseball Magazine* (December 1918b).

LASCH, CHRISTOPHER. *The Culture of Narcissism.* New York: Norton, 1978.

LAWES, RICK. "Astrodome Cuts Prices." *USA Today Baseball Weekly*, 11 July 1991.

LEHN, KENNETH. "Property Rights, Risk Sharing, and Player Disability in Major League Baseball." In *Sportometrics*, ed. Brian Goff and Robert Tollison. College Station: Texas A & M University Press, 1990a.

———. "Information Asymmetries in Baseball's Free Agent Market." In *Sportometrics*, ed. Brian Goff and Robert Tollison. College Station: Texas A & M University Press, 1990b.

LEWYN, MARK. "Why Cable Companies Are Playing So Rough." *Business Week*, 12 August 1991.

LEVINE, PETER. *A. G. Spalding and the Rise of Baseball*. New York: Oxford University Press, 1985.

LIEB, FREDERICK G. *The Pittsburgh Pirates*. New York: G. P. Putnam's Sons, 1948.

LOWENFISH, LEE, AND TONY LUPIEN. *The Imperfect Diamond: The Story of Baseball's Reserve System and the Men Who Fought to Change It*. New York: Stein and Day, 1980.

LUBLIN, JOANN. "Highly Paid Chiefs Earn Criticism, Too." *Wall Street Journal*, 4 June 1991.

LUBOVE, SETH. "Going, Going, Sold!" *Forbes*, 14 October 1991.

McCARTHY, MICHAEL. "Atlanta's Braves Try Some Weird Pitches, But Some Fans Still Balk." *Wall Street Journal*, 8 June 1990.

McDERMOTT, TERRY. "He's on First." *Seattle Times*, 8 April 1990.

———. *Seattle Times*, 8 January 1991a.

———. "Smulyan's Growing Financial Problems." *Seattle Times*, 23 June 1991b.

———. "Can Major League Baseball Survive in Seattle?" *Seattle Times*, 28 July 1991c.

———. "Winning, Success Don't Always Mix." *Seattle Times*, 29 July 1991d.

———. "Saving the Mariners: Easier Than It Seems." *Seattle Times*, 8 September 1991e.

———. "Smulyan Told Bankers He'd Sell M's." *Seattle Times*, 27 August 1991f.

———. "Smulyan May Cede Control of Radio Firm." *Seattle Times*, 11 September 1991g.

———. "M's Salaries Biggest Gap in Forecasts." *Seattle Times*, 12 September 1991h.

McDERMOTT, TERRY, RON JUDD, AND JONI BALTER. "A Lot Less Than $16 Million." *Seattle Times*, 8 September 1991.

MADDEN, BILL. "The Collector." *The Sporting News*, 25 February 1991.

MADDEN, BILL, AND MOSS KLEIN. *Damned Yankees*. New York: Warner Books, 1990.

MAJOR LEAGUE BASEBALL. Basic Agreement. New York: 1980, 1985, 1990.

———. Memorandum of Agreement. New York: 1981.

———. Memorandum of Agreement. New York: 1985.

———. Memorandum of Agreement. New York: 1990.

———. Arbitration Panel. Panel Decision No. 66. Grievance 83-1. New York: 1985.

———. Arbitration Panel. Decision on Grievance 87-3. New York: 1988a.

———. *Professional Baseball Rules Book*. New York: 1988b.

———. Arbitration Panel. Present Status of the Disposition on Grievance No. 86-2. New York: 1989.

———. Arbitration Panel. Remedial Reward on Grievance 87-3. New York: 1990a.

————. Arbitration Panel. Decision on Grievance 88-1. New York: 1990b.

MAJOR LEAGUE BASEBALL PLAYERS' ASSOCIATION. "MLBPA Regulations Governing Player Agents." New York: 1988.

————. "Benefit Plan." New York: n.d.

MANN, STEVE. "The Business of Baseball." In *Total Baseball*, ed. John Thorn and Pete Palmer. New York: Warner Books, 1989.

MARKHAM, JESSE, AND PAUL TEPLITZ. *Baseball Economics and Public Policy.* Lexington, MA: D. C. Heath, 1981.

MARKIEWICZ, DAVID. "Sweetheart Deal Kept White Sox from Moving to Florida." *Detroit News*, 3 October 1991.

MEDIA SPORTS BUSINESS. Carmel, CA: Paul Kagan Associates, various issues.

MICHENER, JAMES A. *Sports in America.* Greenwich, CT: Fawcett, 1976.

MILLER, JAMES E. *The Baseball Business: Pursuing Pennants and Profits in Baltimore.* Chapel Hill: University of North Carolina Press, 1990.

MILLER, MARVIN. *A Whole Different Ball Game: The Sport and Business of Baseball.* New York: Birch Lane Press, 1991.

MILLSON, LARRY. *Ballpark Figures: The Blue Jays and the Business of Baseball.* Toronto: McClelland & Stewart, 1987.

MOORAD, JEFFREY. "Negotiating for the Professional Baseball Player." In *Law of Professional and Amateur Sports*, ed. Gary Uberstine. New York: Clark Boardman Co., 1988.

MOORE, THOMAS. "Baseball's New Game Plan." *Fortune*, 15 April 1991.

MORRIS, DAVID. "Public Ownership of Sports Teams." *TWA Ambassador* (January 1987).

NAGATA, YOICHI, AND JOHN HOLWAY. "Japanese Baseball." In *Total Baseball*, ed. John Thorn and Pete Palmer. New York: Warner Books, 1989.

NASH, BRUCE, AND ALLAN ZULLO. *The Baseball Hall of Shame*, vols. 1 and 2. New York: Pocket Books, 1985 and 1986.

NIGHTENGALE, BOB. "Herzog Turned Off by Baseball's Greed." *Baseball America*, 10 August 1990.

NIGHTINGALE, DAVE. "The $1.8 Million Odyssey." *The Sporting News*, 18 June 1990.

————. "N. L. Has Some Doubts about Miami." *The Sporting News*, 17 June 1991.

NIPPERT, LOUIS, ET AL. *Complaint for Declaratory Judgment and Partnership Accounting,* Case no. A8988180. Court of Common Pleas, Hamilton County, Ohio, 13 September 1989.

————. *Plaintiffs' Memorandum in Opposition to Defendants' Motion for Summary Judgment,* Case no. A-8908180. Court of Common Pleas, Hamilton County, Ohio, 30 August 1990.

NOCERA, JOSEPH. "George Steinbrenner, Welfare Case." *Esquire*, July 1990.

NOLL, ROGER. *The Economic Viability of Professional Baseball.* Report to the Major League Baseball Players' Association, July 1985.

————. "The Economics of Sports Leagues." In *Law of Professional and Amateur Sports*, ed. Gary Uberstine. New York: Clark Boardman Co., 1988.

NOLL, ROGER, ED. *Government and the Sports Business.* Washington, D.C.: Brookings Institution, 1974.

OFFICIAL BASEBALL GUIDE. St. Louis: The Sporting News, various years.

OFFICIAL BASEBALL REGISTER. St. Louis: The Sporting News, various years.

OKNER, BENJAMIN. "Taxation and Sports Enterprises." In *Government and the Sports Business,* ed. Roger Noll. Washington, D.C.: The Brookings Institution, 1974a.

———. "Subsidies of Stadiums and Arenas." In *Government and the Sports Business,* ed. Roger Noll. Washington, D.C.: The Brookings Institution, 1974b.

PARAMOUNT COMMUNICATIONS INC. *Annual Report 1990* and *10-K Report, 1990.* New York.

PASDELOUP, VINCENTE. "Debate Grows Louder on Compulsory License." *Cable World,* 4 November 1991.

PEPPER, JON. "Downtown Ballpark Is Food for Thought, But Idea Gives Bo an Upset Stomach." *Detroit News,* 6 October 1991.

PLUTO, TERRY, AND JEFFREY NEWMAN, EDS. *A Baseball Winter: The Off-Season Life of the Summer Game.* New York: Macmillan, 1986.

PORTER, PAUL. *Organized Baseball and the Congress.* New York: Major League Baseball, 1961.

"PRO SPORTS: A BUSINESS BOOM IN TROUBLE." *U.S. News & World Report,* 5 July 1971.

QUEENAN, JOE. "Squeeze Play: Plutocrat Players, Balky Payers May End Baseball's Big Boom." *Barron's,* 29 April 1991.

QUIRK, JAMES. "An Economic Analysis of Team Movements in Professional Sports." *Law and Contemporary Problems* 38, no. 1 (Winter–Spring 1973).

———. "The Reserve Clause: Recent Developments." In *Current Issues in Professional Sports,* ed. Michael Jones. Durham, NH: Whittmore School of Business and Economics, 1980.

QUIRK, JAMES, AND MOHAMED EL HODIRI. "The Economic Theory of Professional Sports Leagues." In *Government and the Sports Business,* ed. Roger Noll. Washington, D.C.: Brookings Institution, 1974.

RIESS, STEVEN. *City Games: The Evolution of American Urban Society and the Rise of Sports.* Urbana: University of Illinois Press, 1989.

———. "The New Sport History." *Reviews in American History* 18, no. 3 (September 1990).

RINGOLSBY, TRACY. "Reds Organization Schott to Hell." *Baseball America,* 25 November 1990a.

———. "GMs Become Endangered Species." *Baseball America,* 25 December 1990b.

———. "Debt Affects Franchise Operation." *Baseball America,* 10 January 1991.

ROBERTS, GARY R. "Professional Sports and the Antitrust Laws." In *The Business of Professional Sports,* ed. P. Staudohar and J. Mangan. Urbana: University of Illinois Press, 1991.

ROBICHAUX, MARK. "Major League Baseball Players, Owners Reach Accord, But the Damage Remains." *Wall Street Journal,* 20 March 1990.

ROSENTRAUB, MARK, AND SAMUEL NUNN. "Suburban City Investment in Professional Sports." *American Behavioral Scientist* 21, no. 3 (January–February 1978).

Ross, Stephen F. "Monopoly Sports Leagues." *Minnesota Law Review* 71, no. 3 (February 1989).

——. "An Antitrust Analysis of Sports League Contracts with Cable Networks." *Emory Law Journal* 39, no. 2 (Spring 1990).

——. "Break Up the Sports League Monopolies." In *The Business of Professional Sports*, ed. P. Staudohar and J. Mangan. Urbana: University of Illinois Press, 1991.

Rottenberg, Simon. "The Baseball Players' Labor Market." *Journal of Political Economy* 64 (June 1956).

Rubin, Bob. "The 'Big Event' Strategy Backfired for CBS." *Inside Sports* April 1991.

Rushin, Steve. "Baseball 1991: Going, Going, Gone." *Sports Illustrated*, 15 April 1991.

Ryan, Kevin. "Pay and Performance Research in Major League Baseball." Ms., Middlebury College, April 1991.

Sandomir, Richard. "A Whole New Ball Game." *Sports Illustrated*, 16 April 1990.

Sargeant, Georgia. "Domino's Quick Delivery: Public Safety vs. Profits." *Trial* 25 (November 1989).

Scher, Jon. "Majors, Minors Relationship Has Long, Stormy History." *Baseball America*, 10 November 1990.

——. "Majors, Minors Set to Sign Long-Term Deal." *Baseball America*, 10 January 1991.

Schroeder, Michael. "Pittsburgh's Pirates May Have to Sail Away." *Business Week*, 16 April 1990.

Schultz, Jeff. "Salary Arbitration Is Big League Business." *The Sporting News*, 11 February 1991.

Schwarz, Alan. "Acrimony Surrounds Taylor Deal." *Baseball America*, 25 September 1991a.

——. "Boras' Clients Break the Bank," *Baseball America*, 10 October 1991b.

——. "Game's Black Interest Wanes." *Baseball America*, 25 December 1991c.

——. "Card Business Expands Limits." *Baseball America*, 25 January 1992.

Scoreboard Inc. *10-K Report* and *Annual Report*. Cherry Hill, NJ: 1990.

Scully, Gerald. "Pay and Performance in Major League Baseball." *American Economic Review* 64 (December 1974).

——. *The Business of Baseball*. Chicago: University of Chicago Press, 1989.

Scully, Gerald, J. Hirschberg, and D. Slottje. "A Test of the Efficient Labor Market Hypothesis: The Case of Major League Baseball." Ms., 1990.

Seymour, Harold. *Baseball: The Early Years*. New York: Oxford University Press, 1960.

——. *Baseball: The Golden Age*. New York: Oxford University Press, 1971.

Silk, Leonard. "Predicting the Pay of Ballplayers," *New York Times*, 21 June 1991.

Siwoff, Seymour, et al. *The 1990 Elias Baseball Analyst*. New York: Macmillan, 1990.

Sloan, Allan. "Yankees' Profits Bail Out Boss." *Newsday*, 19 January 1992.

Smith, Claire. "Minors and Majors Ready to Split." *New York Times*, 25 November 1990a.

————. "Scranton Franchise Packs a Big Clout." *New York Times*, 9 December 1990b.

————. "Baseball: Land of Rising Opportunities." *The Sporting News*, 4 March 1991a.

————. "Root of Pirates' Evils Is Hardly Surprising." *New York Times*, 10 March 1991b.

————. "The State of the Game." *Inside Sports*, 1 April 1991c.

————. "McMullen Giving Up Best Seat in the House." *New York Times*, 4 September 1991d.

————. "Baseball's Angry Man." *New York Times Magazine*, 13 October 1991e.

SMITH, MYRON, JR. *Baseball: A Comprehensive Bibliography*. Jefferson, NC: McFarland & Co., 1986.

SOBEL, LIONEL. "The Regulation of Player Agents and Lawyers." In *Law of Professional and Amateur Sports*, ed. Gary Uberstine. New York: Clark Boardman Co., 1988.

SOKOLOVE, MICHAEL. *Hustle: The Myth, Life and Lies of Pete Rose*. New York: Simon & Schuster, 1990.

SOMMERS, PAUL, ED. *Diamonds Are Forever: The Business of Baseball*. Washington, D.C.: Brookings Institution, 1992.

SOMMERS, PAUL, AND NOEL QUINTON. "Pay and Performance in Major League Baseball: The Case of First Family Free-Agents." *Journal of Human Resources* 17 (1982).

SPERBER, MURRAY. *College Sports, Inc.: The Athletic Department vs. The University*. New York: Henry Holt & Co., 1990.

STARK, JAYSON. "McCarver Evaluates Winter Transactions." *Baseball America*, 10 January 1991.

STATISTICAL ABSTRACT OF THE UNITED STATES. Washington, D.C.: USGPO, various years.

STAUDOHAR, PAUL. *The Sports Industry and Collective Bargaining*, 2d ed. Ithaca, NY: ILR Press, 1989.

STEVENSON, RICHARD. "Pony Up $95 Million? Sure, for a Baseball Team." *New York Times*, 23 September 1990.

SULLIVAN, NEIL. *The Dodgers Move West*. New York: Oxford University Press, 1987.

————. *The Minors: The Struggles and the Triumph of Baseball's Poor Relation from 1876 to the Present*. New York: St. Martin's, 1990.

SYMONDS, WILLIAM. "Have Team, May Travel." *Business Week*, 1 July 1991.

THORN, JOHN, AND PETE PALMER, EDS. *Total Baseball*. New York: Warner Books, 1989.

TIME WARNER INC. *10-K Report*. New York: 1990.

TOPP, RICHARD. "Demographics." In *Total Baseball*, ed. John Thorn and Pete Palmer. New York: Warner Books, 1989.

TRIBUNE COMPANY. *10-K Report* and *Annual Report*. Chicago: 1990.

TURNER BROADCASTING SYSTEMS CORPORATION. *10-K Report* and *Annual Report*. Atlanta, GA: 1989 and 1990.

UBERSTINE, GARY, ED. *Law of Professional and Amateur Sports.* New York: Clark Boardman Co., 1988.

U.S. CONGRESS. HOUSE OF REPRESENTATIVES. COMMITTEE OF THE JUDICIARY. SUCBOMMITTEE ON MONOPOLIES AND COMMERCIAL LAW. *Organized Baseball, Hearings (1951).* 82d Congress, 1st Session. Washington, D.C.: USGPO, 1952.

———. *Oversight Hearings (1981–82).* 97th Congress, 1st and 2nd Sessions. Washington, D.C.: USGPO, 1984.

U.S. CONGRESS. HOUSE SELECT COMMITTEE ON PROFESSIONAL SPORTS. *Final Report.* Washington, D.C.: USGPO, 1976.

U.S. CONGRESS. HOUSE OF REPRESENTATIVES. COMMITTEE ON ENERGY AND COMMERCE. SUBCOMMITTEE ON TELECOMMUNICATIONS AND FINANCE. *Cable Television Regulation* (April–May 1990). Parts 1 and 2. 101st Congress, 2d Session. Washington, D.C.: USGPO, 1990.

U.S. CONGRESS. SENATE. *Federal Sports Act of 1972, Hearings.* 92nd Congress, 2d Session. Washington, D.C.: USGPO, 1973.

U.S. CONGRESS. SENATE. COMMITTEE ON THE JUDICIARY. SUBCOMMITTEE ON ANTITRUST, MONOPOLIES AND BUSINESS RIGHTS. *Professional Sports Antitrust, Hearings.* Washington, D.C.: USGPO, 1965.

———. *Professional Sports Antitrust Immunity: Hearings.* 97th Congress, 2d Session, 1982. Washington, D.C.: USGPO, 1983.

———. *Professional Sports Antitrust Immunity: Hearings.* 99th Congress, 1st Session, 1985. Washington, D.C.: USGPO, 1985.

———. *Competitive Problems in the Cable Television Industry.* 100th Congress, 2d Session, 1988. Washington, D.C.: USGPO, 1988.

———. *Competitive Problems in the Cable Television Industry.* 101th Congress, 1st Session, 1989. Washington, D.C.: USGPO, 1990.

———. *Sports Programming and Cable Television.* 101th Congress, 1st Session, 1989. Washington, D.C.: USGPO, 1991.

VECSEY, GEORGE. "Baseball Weather: Sterile." *New York Times,* 10 October 1991.

VEECK, BILL (WITH ED LINN). *Veeck—As in Wreck.* New York: G. P. Putnam's Sons, 1962.

———. *The Hustler's Handbook.* New York: G. P. Putnam's Sons, 1965.

VOIGT, DAVID. *America through Baseball.* Chicago: Nelson-Hall, 1976.

———. "A Century of Baseball Strife," *Baseball Historical Review* 1 (1981).

———. *American Baseball,* 3 vols. University Park, PA: Pennsylvania State University Press, 1983.

———. "Getting Right with Baseball." ms., 1989.

———. "The History of Major League Baseball." In *Total Baseball,* ed. John Thorn and Pete Palmer. New York: Warner Books, 1989.

WHITE, JOSEPH B. "Detroit Facing Suicide Squeeze at Grand Old Tiger Stadium." *Wall Street Journal,* 24 April 1991.

"WHO SAYS BASEBALL IS LIKE BALLET?" *Forbes,* 1 April 1971.

WILL, GEORGE. *Men at Work: The Craft of Baseball.* New York: Macmillan, 1990a.

———. "No Hits, Many Errors." *Newsweek,* 26 March 1990b.

———. "A One-Man Error Machine." *Newsweek,* 6 August 1990c.

Wong, Glenn. "On Franchise Relocation, Expansion and Competition in Professional Team Sports: The Ultimate Political Football?" *Seton Hall Legislative Journal* 9, no. 1 (1985).

World Almanac and Book of Facts. New York: Pharos Books, 1991.

Wulf, Steve. "Minor League Baseball." *Sports Illustrated*, 23 July 1990.

Young, Coleman. "Mayor's Press Release." Detroit. 4 October 1991.

Zimbalist, Andrew. "Salaries and Performance in Major League Baseball: Beyond the Scully Model." In *Diamonds Are Forever: The Business of Baseball*, ed. Paul Sommers. Washington, D.C.: Brookings Institution, 1992.

Zimmerman, Paul. *The Los Angeles Dodgers.* New York: Coward-McCann, 1960.

Zoss, Joel, and John Bowman. *Diamonds in the Rough: The Untold History of Baseball.* New York: Macmillan, 1989.

Index

Texas Rangers, 68
Ticket sales, *see* Gate revenue
Tigers, Detroit, 8, 55, 68, 129
Tiger Stadium, 130
Time-Warner, 154, 155
Toledo Mud Hens, 139
Toolson, George, 15, 19, 152
Topps, 79, 80
Toronto, 16
Toronto Blue Jays, 33, 42
Toronto SkyDome, 51, 55, 227n58
Trades, 10-and-5 Rule covering, 20–21
Transfer pricing techniques, 65, 67
Travel expenses, 80
Travellers, Arkansas, 116
Tribune Company, 33, 43, 66, 156, 215n50
Triple-A players, 106, 107, 112
Trump, Donald, 140
Turner, Ted, 31, 33, 39, 65, 123, 128–29
Turner Broadcasting Systems (TBS), 43, 50, 150, 154, 155
Twins, 99, 160
Type A free agents, 23, 24
Type B free agents, 24

Ueberroth, Peter, 23–24, 41, 42, 44, 64, 191, 217n1
Ulmer, Dan, 114
Umpires, 89; early teams and, 4; unionization of, 43
Union Association, 4
United States Football League (USFL), 144, 180
USA Today, 64

Valentine, Bill, 116
Vancouver Canadians, 112

Van Poppel, Todd, 100, 117–18, 221n68, 223n32
Vecsey, George, 147
Veeck, Bill, 29, 40, 211n56; franchise movements and, 126–27, 128, 129; reserve clause and, 13–14; revenue sharing from gate income and, 57; tax factors in team ownership and, 32, 34, 35
Veterans Act, 12
Viacom, 154
Vincent, Fay, xiii, 69, 167, 216n69, 237n37; as commissioner, 44–45; expansion teams and, xvi, 72, 125, 131; minor leagues and, 114, 117; ownership of teams and, 135; salary of, 60
Vogel, Edward, 40
Voigt, David, 30–31, 32, 44, 57
Von der Ahe, Chris, 31, 32
Vonderhorst, Harry, 203n31

Wagner, Robert, 16
Walsh, Christy, 11
Ward, John Montgomery (Monte), 5, 6, 30, 202n23
Washington Senators, 11, 125
Webb, Del, 99–100, 126
Western League, 7, 107, 126
Western Union, 148, 204n43
WFAN, 226n44, 232n40
WGN, 66, 156
White, Bill, 237n37
White Sox, *see* Chicago White Sox
White Stockings, Chicago, 3
Will, George, 97, 211n64
Williams, Edward Bennett, 177, 208n12
Winfield, Dave, 187
Wirth, Tim, 26, 142, 185
Wood, Bill, 100
WOR-TV, 162, 230n16
Work stoppages, *see* Strikes
World Football League, 144